Regulating Unfair Trade

PIETRO S. NIVOLA

Regulating Unfair Trade

THE BROOKINGS INSTITUTION
Washington, D.C.

Library of Congress Cataloging-in-Publication data

Nivola, Pietro S.
    Regulating unfair trade / Pietro S. Nivola.
        p.   cm.
    Includes bibliographical references and index.
    ISBN 0-8157-6090-6 : —ISBN 0-8157-6089-2 (pbk.) :
    1. United States—Commercial policy.   2. Foreign trade
regulation—United States.   3. Competition, Unfair.   I. Title
HF1455.N58   1992
382'.3'0973—dc20   92-36232
                                                           CIP

9 8 7 6 5 4 3 2 1

THE BROOKINGS INSTITUTION

The Brookings Institution is an independent organization devoted to nonpartisan research, education, and publication in economics, government, foreign policy, and the social sciences generally. Its principal purposes are to aid in the development of sound public policies and to promote public understanding of issues of national importance.

The Institution was founded on December 8, 1927, to merge the activities of the Institute for Government Research, founded in 1916, the Institute of Economics, founded in 1922, and the Robert Brookings Graduate School of Economics and Government, founded in 1924.

The Board of Trustees is responsible for the general administration of the Institution, while the immediate direction of the policies, program, and staff is vested in the President, assisted by an advisory committee of the officers and staff. The by-laws of the Institution state: "It is the function of the Trustees to make possible the conduct of scientific research, and publication, under the most favorable conditions, and to safeguard the independence of the research staff in the pursuit of their studies and in the publication of the results of such studies. It is not a part of their function to determine, control, or influence the conduct of particular investigations or the conclusions reached."

The President bears final responsibility for the decision to publish a manuscript as a Brookings book. In reaching his judgment on the competence, accuracy, and objectivity of each study, the President is advised by the director of the appropriate research program and weighs the views of a panel of expert outside readers who report to him in confidence on the quality of the work. Publication of a work signifies that it is deemed a competent treatment worthy of public consideration but does not imply endorsement of conclusions or recommendations.

The Institution maintains its position of neutrality on issues of public policy in order to safeguard the intellectual freedom of the staff. Hence interpretations or conclusions in Brookings publications should be understood to be solely those of the authors and should not be attributed to the Institution, to its trustees, officers, or other staff members, or to the organizations that support its research.

In honor of Birdie

Foreword

AMERICAN complaints about foreign commercial unfairness have multiplied over the past dozen years. In response to requests for more relief from international competitors who underprice their products or whose governments subsidize exports or protect home markets, the U.S. government has devised elaborate programs to combat these unwelcome business practices.

This arduous regulatory effort to "level the playing field" is the subject of Pietro Nivola's study. The author, a senior fellow in the Brookings Governmental Studies program, argues that foreign protectionism, the passing of the cold war, and supposed American decline do not suffice to explain the heightened sensitivity to foreign trade inequities. The global trading system is not more restrictive now than it was earlier. Grievances about the rest of the world's trading methods have remained intense during recent years despite a surge in U.S. exports everywhere and (excluding oil imports) a marked improvement in the balance of trade. Regulation of so-called unfair trade has expanded not just because of new competitive pressures from the outside world, but also because the internal politics of trade have created additional incentives to complain about those pressures.

Nivola's study sounds an important cautionary note. Trade regulation now bears too much of the burden for remedying perceived economic failings. The resulting sense of frustration induces demands for still more regulatory intervention. While recognizing the need for an explicit and responsible commercial policy, the book concludes that such a policy must be based on realistic expectations and ought to complement, not take precedence over, a more basic agenda. Improvements in the national rate of saving and investment, better preparation of the work force, and containment of health care costs, for instance, are likely to be far more consequential than trade activism for the nation's long-term competitiveness and living standards.

This project received valuable advice and backing from several individuals and organizations. Barry P. Bosworth, Isobel D. Coles, Kenneth Flamm, Bill Frenzel, Robert Z. Lawrence, Edward J. Lincoln, Robert E. Litan, Thomas

E. Mann, and Warwick J. McKibbin were among the author's colleagues who contributed insights at various stages. Robert E. Baldwin, I. M. Destler, Gary N. Horlick, and Gary Clyde Hufbauer made helpful comments on earlier drafts of the manuscript. Michael Bosco, Renuka D. Deonarain, Helen Hall, Marina Niforos, Lisa Pace, Todd L. Quinn, Erik Riegler, Sandra Z. Riegler, Susan A. Stewart, Eloise Stinger, and Elizabeth O. Toy provided research and administrative assistance. Deborah Styles edited the manuscript, and Alison M. Rimsky checked it for accuracy. Celeste Newbrough prepared the index. Funding for the book was generously provided by the Lynde and Harry Bradley Foundation, Inc., and the Earhart Foundation.

The views in this book are solely those of the author and should not be ascribed to the persons or organizations acknowledged above, or to the trustees, officers, or other staff members of the Brookings Institution.

BRUCE K. MACLAURY
President

January 1993
Washington, D.C.

Author's Preface

AMERICAN trade policy has been busy battling the rest of the world's unfair commercial practices. The following study is not the first to observe this phenomenon, but it is one of the few that has tried to explain it.[1] The task has proved more difficult than I had anticipated.

If this book had been written a decade ago, the story to be told might have been relatively simple. Unusual conditions were severely straining the comparatively relaxed attitude of the United States toward the inequalities and vexations of foreign trade. The national economy had suffered its worst bout of unemployment and negative growth since the Great Depression. The effects of global economic competition on jobs and incomes loomed larger than at any previous time in the postwar period. As a share of GNP, the goods and services we bought and sold around the world now accounted for double the level of 1970. Increasingly, our imports vastly exceeded our exports. A number of major industries sensitive to these developments were battered by losses of market share at home and overseas. Payrolls were cut and real wages restrained in much of the nation's industrial heartland. Under pressure to slow or reverse the dislocation, the government moved inexorably to check the influx of imported products and to contest persistent constraints abroad that burdened our exporters and investors.

By the time I sat down to compose a manuscript, however, much had changed. Aided by better exchange rates and notable productivity improvements, American manufacturers of tradable goods were making a big comeback. Between 1986 and 1991, the volume of U.S. manufactured exports rose 90 percent, more than three times the average export growth in other industrialized countries of the Organization for Economic Cooperation and Development (OECD).[2] So strong was the resurgence that the U.S. share of the industrialized world's manufactured exports not only surpassed Japan's but helped reduce the U.S. trade deficit from almost $160 billion to $73 billion. This demonstration of commercial prowess did not look like that of an industrial weakling, stymied or no longer competitive in world markets.

Yet suspicions remained rife that Americans were "trade wimps," steadily losing ground to pernicious competitors. In the early 1980s the defensive tilt had manifested itself on several levels. Calls proliferated for protection from "unfair" imports, with such prominent industries as producers of steel, automobiles, lumber, and semiconductors demanding relief. Congress entertained a great many punitive legislative proposals. The Democratic party's presidential nominee promised to get "really tough" with trading partners.

While the mood during the past three years has not been so virulent, it has still been dreary. The volume of formal objections to foreign commercial misconduct was actually greater in 1990 than ten years earlier. Producers of steel, automobiles, lumber, and semiconductors have all filed new cases. Lawmakers have been drafting bills regulating imports of everything from jeeps to fresh-cut flowers. Presidential candidates in both parties spent most of last winter trying to exploit the trade issue. At one time it was thought that if only we could lessen the imbalance between the quantities of goods we imported and exported, self-doubts about American competitiveness, fears of Japanese high-tech dominance, and complaints about foreign unfairness would fade. As I print this page (on a Hewlett-Packard printer hooked to a DEC personal computer probably equipped with an American-made Komag disc, Seagate drive, Red-Rite magnetic head, and Intel microprocessor), the monthly trade gap is one of the narrowest in nine years—but the self-doubts, fears, and complaints continue.

This chronic sense of grievance has no easy, mono-causal interpretation. One cannot say that it has solely tracked business cycles, rates of growth in manufacturing productivity, or current account balances. Nor can one say it has simply been aggravated by worsening barriers and abuses in the international trading community—even though genuine abuses and barriers persist and may matter more to American entrepreneurs now than they have in the past. As I suggest in chapter 2, the proverbial playing field has not become less level than it was back in the happy days of U.S. economic hegemony and trade surpluses.

Up to a point, the heightened reaction to trade offenses, real or perceived, may reflect a "diminished giant" syndrome.[3] Our share of global markets is not what it used to be, and, more important, our standard of living no longer dwarfs everyone else's. Nevertheless, policymakers are not asinine; no one expects America's relative economic stature to be the same today as it was in the 1950s, when shell-shocked economies elsewhere were barely recovering from the Second World War. Granted, as other industrial powers revived, stiffer competition from them would eventually constrain real wages increases in this country. Yet family incomes, at least above the population's lowest quintile, continued to rise over the past two decades.[4] Properly measured (using purchasing power parity exchange rates), Americans have remained among the richest people on earth.[5]

The gradual dissolution of the Eastern bloc was bound to bring Western commercial frictions to the fore. Each year there would be less reason to indulge the economic misdemeanors of allies in the interests of broader security objectives, and the absence of a common threat would diminish incentives for deeper cooperation. Witness the seemingly endless foot dragging and acrimony that has beset the current round of multilateral negotiations on services and agricultural liberalization—a project that the United States has been pushing uphill ever since the ministerial meeting of the General Agreement on Tariffs and Trade (GATT) in 1982. Nonetheless, the post–cold war vacuum, along with the disarray in the Uruguay Round, can only account for some of our recent trade activism. The unstable setting may have accentuated disputes with Europe over farm subsidies, for instance, or with Japan over market access for certain critical industries. But how could it explain, say, the numerous antidumping petitions directed at other countries exporting items such as shopping carts, stackable patio chairs, roses, appliance plugs, kiwi fruits, martial arts uniforms, and key pads for woodwind instruments?

Much regulation of so-called unfair trade has little to do with grand geopolitical considerations or with strategic products. Instead, it performs a more mundane function that commercial policy, here or anywhere, has always performed: attending to the demands of anxious producers of all kinds for government support to defend or to improve their sales base, profitability, or jobs. This activity increased after 1980 not just because competitive pressures generally intensified but also because we have developed more ways and inducements to complain about those pressures. Unlike the tariff policies of an earlier era, our modern regulatory apparatus administers redress to an aggrieved constituency of victims. This tack offers at least a couple of important political assets. One is that it avoids touting raw protectionism, even though it may produce some of the same results. Another attraction, undeniably, is that it affords a measure of moral authority. If the U.S. economy was extraordinarily protected in the first third of the twentieth century, American markets in the last part of the century have been more hospitable than most. "Reciprocal access" is the battle cry of contemporary trade warriors. It is not a protest without foundation.

In addition to these factors, the promise of trade remedies has attracted more interest over the past decade as other forms of government aid for businesses and workers have run into fiscal constraints. Interest groups drawing less adjustment assistance, for instance, may well insist on greater import restraints. Such remedies, admittedly, have been cause for considerable frustration, because they often fail to deliver the types or levels of benefits imagined. But these shortcomings scarcely seem to diminish expectations. On the contrary, the limitations of existing remedial regulation have frequently evoked desires to impose more of it.

These reflections form the main themes of this volume. Although it is not my primary aim to derive from them a detailed list of practical recommendations, a portion of the concluding chapter is prescriptive. Its gist is as follows.

While the United States continues to be an industrial colossus, decidedly capable of holding its own in international competition, complacency is not warranted. Problems exist. Some are not of our own making. Americans cannot ignore foreign economic *dirigisme* when it clearly has a distorting and corrosive effect on the global trading system and on our own world-class companies. When the European Community refuses, after years of negotiations, to comply with rulings by GATT panels against subsidies that violate international obligations, the U.S. government has reason to threaten retaliation.[6] If vestiges of Japanese infant-industry protection continue to impede sales of superior American products (from supercomputers and satellites to cellular phones), affirmative action is in order. Realistically, it is also impracticable to remain aloof from the adjustment problems of some less competitive domestic industries.

The public interest is ill-served, however, when preoccupations with trade transgressions and the animus they generate divert our limited energies from other priorities that are more fundamental to the nation's long-term welfare. For all the political salience of foreign trade, the fact remains that the sum of all the goods and services we export and import still amounts to approximately 20 percent of our gross national product.[7] That ratio has stayed more or less unchanged since 1980, and it remains small compared with that of many other developed countries. It ought to give pause to politicians and pundits who declaim, year after year, that "trade is the most important issue we face."

The more insidious threats to the American economy continue to come from our comparatively low levels of saving and investment, glaring deficiencies in elementary and secondary education, excessive health-care costs, and oppressive litigiousness. Some of these self-inflicted disabilities (the saving and investment lags) are root causes of trade imbalances; all are a drag on national productivity growth, hence on future living standards. A challenge for the makers of foreign economic policy in Congress and in the executive branch is to help focus national attention on these uncomfortable realities instead of getting distracted from them. Exactly *how* will be much debated. The final pages of this book suggest some places to start.

Contents

CHAPTER ONE

Gulliver's Travails

THIS BOOK IS ABOUT an ambitious regulatory program: America's effort to combat objectionable trading practices of other countries. Early in the 1980s charges of foreign commercial improprieties began to proliferate. Sunrise industries, such as manufacturers of semiconductors and telecommunications equipment, joined older complainants, like steel and textile producers, seeking refuge from international competitors who priced their products too aggressively or whose governments subsidized exports or protected home markets. Both Congress and the president proved responsive to these claims, devising increasingly stringent rules to deal with offenders.

This activity marked a change. Through most of the period after the Second World War, policymakers had deemed it in the nation's economic and strategic interests to tolerate asymmetries and infractions in the international trading order. Now a new sensitivity to trade inequities and a growing conviction that the government should intervene, frequently and forcefully, to ensure a "level playing field" were lowering that tolerance.

The extent of intervention became significant. Even as American negotiators strove to liberalize trade in world markets, protection in the United States, which had affected less than one-tenth of import volume in 1975, covered more than one-fifth by 1985.[1] Regulated trade had long protected certain agricultural products, shipping services, and textiles and apparel. By the mid-1980s elaborate sectoral arrangements also governed steel, automobiles, and computer memory devices, and it looked as though they might spread to telecommunications, auto parts, and financial services. Some critics of American trade policy bemoaned a stubborn fealty to laissez-faire ideology and a refusal to experiment with alternatives when other countries were enjoying a free ride. But if these critics had in mind closer regulation of imports and attempts to secure market shares in selected sectors, they could look to a number of

1

experiments that were already on display. Thus the question at the end of the 1980s was no longer whether U.S. policy had become less conciliatory toward alleged unfair traders—and less willing to adhere unilaterally to a free market philosophy—but precisely how and why?

The Trade Issue

Earlier in the postwar period, the United States had dominated the world economy. Imports and exports amounted to a negligible fraction of the gross national product. With unparalleled industrial might, clear technological supremacy, and little need for capital from overseas, the United States seemed in command of its economic destiny. From its position of strength it could afford to make unbalanced concessions to other nations, turning a blind eye to their foibles. Since the overriding mission of American foreign policy was the worldwide containment of communism, economic sacrifices were considered worthwhile to ensure the prosperity and allegiance of allies.

Hegemonic Instability

Later decades brought big changes. Trade grew to account for a significant share of GNP, with imports outpacing exports by wide margins. The merchandise deficit towered to $159 billion in 1987, remaining above $100 billion until 1991, despite a sharp depreciation in the exchange value of the dollar after 1985. To finance this surfeit of consumption over domestic production, the United States rapidly became the world's largest debtor, losing some control of its economic sovereignty to outside lenders. The worsening trade performance and mounting foreign claims on U.S. assets came to be viewed with alarm, that is, as signs of economic decline. America's technological lead, productivity, and manufacturing base were being challenged by dynamic newcomers, most conspicuously Japan.

Although the end of U.S. hegemony was the inevitable result of long-term shifts in the global distribution of technology and of productive facilities, some of those shifts seemed to reflect the economic statecraft of competitors. With trade turning not just on relative factor endowments but also on the availability of capital and of technological capabilities nurtured by governments, the role of national commercial policies in creating comparative advantages could no longer be ignored. How could the foreign competition seemingly pick off, in rapid succession, one basic domestic industry after another? How could foreigners have amassed the wealth to buy so boldly into America? Apprehensive businessmen and politicians began looking for answers in the peculiar practices of advanced economies like Japan's, where the government seemingly provided safe havens for mature as well as for infant industries, securing for them the economies of scale, hence the financial strength, they needed for huge outlays for research and development, predatory pricing strategies, and extensive foreign investment.

Market Access

Concerns about import penetration and foreign ownership aside, the United States could be expected to begin pressing for greater access to overseas markets because the country was now more dependent on export-led growth. Reliance on currency depreciation to stimulate sales abroad would mean less favorable terms of trade (higher prices for imports relative to exports) and thus lower living standards. Seven rounds of multilateral negotiations under the General Agreement on Tariffs and Trade (GATT) had left the U.S. market more exposed than those of other countries. Their tariffs and quotas had come down, but many behind-the-border barriers seemed so refractory that efforts to discipline them in the Tokyo Round (1973–79) had comparatively little effect.[2] At the end of the day, the conviction on the American side of the bargaining table was that trade concessions were being inadequately reciprocated. Other governments had edged away from formal means of curbing competition but still resorted to less visible techniques, such as administrative guidance, underenforcement of antitrust laws, official cartelization of firms, and use of discriminatory standards and procurement codes.

Backdoor trade restraints continued—indeed, increased—in the United States also, but the rest of the world generally remained more restrictive. Patience with this fundamental inequity and with the GATT's enduring inadequacies wore thin—all the more so as tensions with the Soviet Union abated and the case for indulging strategic friends and associates became less compelling.

Public Indifference

But this perspective is not sufficient. To begin with, the public does not normally instruct its elected officials to seek complicated remedies to economic problems that the voters consider abstract and remote. Surely the nuances of current account deficits and international debt, industrial policies and comparative advantage, market access and terms of trade are not matters the general public comprehends. When the trade issue meant anything to people, it was because they connected it to what they really cared about: unemployment and inflation. During most of the 1980s, that connection was not easy to draw. With the U.S. economy basking in sustained noninflationary expansion at nearly full employment through the greater part of the decade, the storm clouds from the trade front were distant or scattered, and for the most part political leaders had to strain to get the electorate excited about them.[3]

Rational Voters

Complacency about the trade deficit was hardly surprising. Importing more than it exported, the nation was able to spend more than it produced and so to enjoy a higher standard of living than was warranted by national productivity. Granted, this avid propensity to consume had long-term liabilities. Americans sustained their spending by saving less for the future and borrowing massively from abroad. Interest payments on the loan would mount. If foreign creditors suddenly tired of lending us nearly $10 billion a month, the ensuing disruption in currency markets might risk global recession.

But while economists ruminated over these possibilities, it is hard to imagine that most voters did. The burden of repaying external obligations and of saving too little would fall chiefly on later generations. Consumers were not in the habit of forgoing present gratification for the sake of posterity, and even if they were, no one had made a conclusive argument that the nation's indebtedness had yet become unmanageable. America, after all, is not Sri Lanka. By the end of 1989, with an economy that turned out $5 trillion worth of goods and services annually, the country's net public indebtedness as a percentage of GNP and as a percentage of annual government revenues had approximately stabilized.[4] Hence, more of the foreign capital inflow could find its way to the private sector. The infusion of offshore funds augmented the capital available to service the national debt.

Public anxiety about the balance of payments might have been stirred by the risk of a financial crisis from excessive borrowing. If the stream of foreign capital had abruptly dried up, the dollar would have tumbled, inflation and interest rates would have risen, and a recession would have loomed well before 1991. Although the danger of a dollar strike existed, it never materialized. Financial markets withstood punishing blows year after year, including defaults by third world debtors, the collapse of the savings and loan industry, a colossal stock market crash in October 1987, and a similar shakeout on the Tokyo stock exchange. Eight years of solid economic growth were finally interrupted at the end of 1990, with the help of a new oil crisis in the Middle East. Until that point, the economy had seemed recession-proof despite intermittent currency fluctuations, comparatively high real interest rates, and other disturbances. Apart from continuing vulnerability to oil shocks, the United States seemed less, not more, susceptible to economic perturbations as a result of global interdependency. And it had become respectable to suppose that the circular pattern, with the United States running large external deficits and foreigners recycling dollars, could go on for a long time.

The pattern involved a transfer of U.S. assets to foreign owners. Americans were disturbed at the sight of Japanese buyers snapping up prominent cultural landmarks, like Rockefeller Center and Hollywood studios, and many would say they were afraid that strategically sensitive companies were falling into the wrong hands.[5] Realistically, however, how many citizens lost sleep over, say, Fujitsu's attempted takeover of Fairchild Semiconductor or Nikon's bid for Perkin-Elmer (a major manufacturer of chipmaking gear)? The majority of people were uninterested or, understandably, confused because foreign direct investment still amounted to only a little more than 2 percent of the national wealth. Moreover, a growing constituency realized that it had foreign investors to thank for its jobs.[6]

Although opinion polls registered awareness of America's relative decline and revealed unease about the efficiency and productivity of U.S. companies and workers, the polls did not turn up profound pessimism about the nation's competitiveness.[7] At the end of the 1980s, relatively few Americans were predicting that the country's competitive situation would worsen. When asked to evaluate the strengths and weaknesses of the United States relative to Japan and Western Europe, overwhelming majorities duly recognized the U.S. economy's comparative strong points: its overall standard of living, its scientific research, and its capacity for technical and engineering innovation. Even categories that had received much negative publicity did not seem to bother most respondents. A majority of respondents, for example, considered the United States strong in the "production of quality goods."[8] Furthermore, although a solid majority continued to think, as it always had, that rising imports endangered American jobs, an equally strong majority seemed to know that competition from imports forced domestic producers to become more efficient and to make products at a lower cost to consumers.[9]

Public Opinion versus Official Attitudes

While policymakers devoted increasing attention to the detrimental effects of unfairly traded imports and of impediments to entry in potential export markets, popular sentiment appeared to lag behind this emphasis. Approximately two-thirds of the population suspected that Japan traded unfairly but also that Japan was successful largely because of the quality and price of its products, not because of unjust trading.[10] When surveyed, government officials were much more inclined than the general citizenry to regard the trade policies not only of Japan but also of other partners—for instance, the European Community and South Korea—as unfair to the United States.[11] In sum, official discomfort with foreign commercial misconduct seemed appreciably more broad and intense than the public's concern.

Regulatory activity does not always need an immediate crisis as justification to expand. Sometimes the agenda has widened even when the objective conditions addressed by regulation were actually improving. In the mid-1960s, for instance, automobile safety standards were legislated during a long-term downward trend in the number of highway fatalities. The Occupational Safety and Health Act was enacted in 1970, when the rate of industrial deaths had been declining steadily for nearly twenty years. It was somewhat unusual, however, for combative economic regulation to advance without an acute and widely shared sense of urgency.[12] But this appeared to be the case with many governmental actions directed at foreign trade abuses.

Policy Dissension

In the absence of profound public angst that trade derogations abroad were causing competitive deterioration at home, a political preoccupation with these problems could still have intensified if policy analysts had generally concluded that the problems were closely related and deserved top priority. Instead, confusion reigned.

American Decline?

No one doubted that the economic preeminence of the United States was diminishing in relation to the rest of the industrialized world. But the nature and extent of this relative change, and whether it was cause for alarm, remained very much in dispute. Some asserted that America's economic clout had declined precipitously; others were quick to note that between 1970 and

1987 the U.S. portion of world output actually stayed in the range of 22 percent to 25 percent.[13] Some saw U.S. exports losing ground to the largest industrial rivals; others pointed out that the U.S. share of exports among the seven economic summit countries only slipped from 24 percent in 1970 to 23 percent in 1987 and that at the close of the 1980s the United States was again the world's largest exporter. Some claimed that the United States was deindustrializing; others rejoined that manufacturing continued to represent about 20 percent of GNP, the same percentage it had held for the past forty years.[14]

Whatever the change in America's weight on the global economic scales, the fact that other industrial powers were posting gains did not simply reflect failings on the part of the international trading system or on the part of the United States. On the contrary, it could reflect their success in rebuilding the world economy after World War II. Robust growth abroad and expanding trade meant not only that other countries gradually caught up but also that the welfare of Americans improved. Gulliver was not better off in a world of industrial Lilliputians. If the purpose of economic policy was to raise living standards, then relative U.S. decline was neither surprising nor indubitably disturbing.[15]

Revisionists took issue with this harmonious view of the postwar economic realignment. They warned that in the contemporary world economy, distinguished by industries trading on the basis of technological versatility rather than on the basis of immobile national endowments, the progress of some industrial countries was not always beneficial to the others. High-technology industries characterized by economies of scale, strong "learning" effects, and large research and development costs competed imperfectly: dominant producers acquired lasting advantages over small firms, and new entrants faced daunting hurdles. In conditions of imperfect competition, some of these industries might generate excess returns, hence higher wages and R&D expenditures, the benefits of which would spill over to the rest of the economy.

Foreign governments deliberately tried to exploit these dynamics, coddling domestic producers with subsidies and informal protection. A nation might enrich itself at the expense of others by enabling its firms to capture market share.[16] These beggar-thy-neighbor policies, which often fell outside the GATT's purview, could erode America's position in leading-edge industries and possibly imperil security and future national welfare.

The notion was not apocryphal. In some sectors a handful of foreign corporations seemed, in fact, well on the way to obtaining global market power. In the span of a decade, for example, six Japanese firms had squeezed the sales of U.S. microchip manufacturers to 40 percent of the world market,

down from 60 percent in 1977. The Japanese, moreover, were rapidly invent-
ing new chipmaking techniques and advancing downstream in product applications. By 1987 a study by a task force of the Defense Science Board had
concluded that the United States had remained ahead in only three of more
than a dozen critical semiconductor technologies.[17] Two years later the United
States was no longer the chief supplier of chip fabrication equipment.[18] Primacy in these areas positioned Japan to control the most critical components
in a broad spectrum of high-growth, high-tech industries, from computers and
telecommunications equipment to myriad scientific instruments.

The Japanese companies did not accomplish this feat entirely on their own.
The vertically integrated giants were thought to have accumulated large stocks
of capital for investment through their thriving consumer electronics divi-
sions. Earlier government tutelage had helped fill their war chests by providing a sheltered domestic market and stimulating exports.

Yet the semiconductor story, along with other tales of seemingly calculated
economic aggression against the United States, left many observers puzzled:
If the strategic commercial policies of other nations had turned international
trade into a zero-sum game, why did world commerce continue to prosper?[19]
By definition, trade among a group of nations could not take place if only
some of them profited while the voluntary transactions impoverished others.
There were grounds for concern about the long-term fortunes of some key
sectors sharply targeted by foreign industrial policies. But the resiliency of
American manufactures was often underestimated. Contrary to journalistic
commentary, overall U.S. exports of high-technology manufactured goods
held their own, even in the first half of the 1980s, when exchange rates were
extremely unfavorable. In 1984 the United States still accounted for 25 percent of world exports in high-tech products, which was close to the share it
had held in the 1960s.[20] Taking into account the strong dollar through much
of the period from 1980 to 1987, U.S. exports of high-tech manufactures grew
about as fast as world exports of comparable products.[21]

Notwithstanding persistent contentions that the United States was "trading
places" with Japan in high technology, much informed opinion still regarded
the United States as the dominant economic power and the overall technological leader.[22] Japan had staked out leads in certain sectors (including robotics,
metal alloys, commodity memory devices, optoelectronics, and various
advanced materials), but American companies still held an edge in others
(such as biotechnology, artificial intelligence, medical devices and diagnos-
tics, high-performance computing, sensor technology, and aerospace and
avionics).[23]

Would this gigantic trading nation be in a weaker position to maximize the benefits of its commercial relations with other technologically advanced contenders if it accepted coequal status with them in some important fields than if it tried to remain in first place across the board? Advocates of a comprehensive high-tech industrial strategy for the United States likened the modern economy to a food chain: the nation had to stay on top in all (or most) technologies because loss of one lead might cause the loss of others. But dissenters would reply that in the final analysis, the food-chain metaphor was tautological and implied autarky: since everything was related to everything else, and since each link in the chain was "strategic," a nation adhering to the food-chain logic might be foolish not to protect or to subsidize a very long list of industries producing sophisticated manufactured products.

While one group of analysts dramatized the competitive threat posed by foreign industrial targeting, another asked: How much of the contraction in certain U.S. industries—steel, automobiles, machine tools, consumer electronics, semiconductors—could ultimately be ascribed to the unfair advantages of foreign competitors? Governments had a hand in launching the export drives of foreign producers, but the bottom line was that many troubled industries in the United States would have had to retrench even without the manipulative economic policies of other nations. In almost every case the tribulations of these industries seemed closely associated with homemade handicaps—from macroeconomic conditions affecting the pool of investment capital to microeconomic factors involving industrial structure, managerial strategies, and the education of the labor force.[24]

If the advantage of many Japanese enterprises stemmed from uncontested control of their domestic market, especially during an earlier developmental stage, American business for most of the postwar period had gone unchallenged in a much larger mass market. The dominance had proved to be a mixed blessing. Several key industries (automobiles provide perhaps the clearest example) might have sharpened their competitive teeth sooner if their niches had been smaller and the international competition keener from the start.

Was the principal effect of severe import competition in the 1980s to wreck American manufacturing or to improve manufacturing productivity? For all the hand wringing about poor U.S. industrial productivity, output per hour of labor in manufacturing during the period 1979–86 grew at a yearly average of 3.1 percent, a rate greater than at any time in the past three decades and one that compared favorably with that of some other principals, West Germany, for instance.[25] Although Japan did better, the differential was narrowing.[26]

Slowdowns in productivity growth had occurred in every major industrial country since 1950. In many the growth rates had slowed more than in the United States.

The Trade Numbers

Because U.S. productivity appeared to have accelerated in the sectors that produced tradable goods, it was doubtful that the soaring trade deficits of the 1980s were only manifestations of America's ebbing growth in productivity. In fact, the cause of the deficits was one subject on which most experts concurred. At the root of the problem was the low national rate of saving, linked to large federal budgetary shortfalls after 1981. Dwindling domestic savings entailed relatively high real interest rates, increasing the global demand for dollars and thus the dollar's exchange value. In the first half of the decade a strong dollar sucked in imports and depressed exports—with an extra tug coming from the U.S. economy's comparatively high rate of growth and the virtual collapse of exports to debt-ridden Latin America.

But if exchange rates had played such an important part in enlarging the trade deficit, why did they not shrink it commensurately right after the dollar dropped from its peak in 1985? Disequilibrium, particularly in trade with Japan, persisted through the rest of the decade, leading some commentators to wonder whether dollar devaluation was "worse than useless" in righting imbalances and whether "structural" obstacles abroad were obstructing U.S. exports more than previously assumed.[27] Theories about exchange-rate hysteresis abounded, but the principal reason for the slow progress in fixing the trade figures lay in simple arithmetic. Before the dollar began to fall in 1985, imports exceeded exports by about $120 billion. Although the rate of importation slowed after 1985 while exports grew rapidly, imports still advanced from a much larger base.[28] Even so, thanks to a lower dollar, the disparity between imports and exports did close, from $159 billion in 1987 to $109 billion in 1989. Without the devaluation, the gap would have widened to roughly $200 billion by 1987.[29]

A more basic question was whether the remaining trade deficit was a grave ailment. Some thought the foreign debt associated with the deficit was burdensome: the heavy borrowing was not being used to finance additional productive investment, and it involved financial risks. Others regarded the deficit as sustainable and even a sign of American strength, not weakness. Logically the United States could not run a deficit on current account if foreigners lacked confidence in the U.S. economy and were reluctant to invest in it.[30]

Some complained that the lopsided trade surpluses abroad and negative trade statistics for the United States meant that other countries were "exporting unemployment."[31] But in the period when the trade imbalances reached extremes, the reverse seemed to be true. Between 1982 and 1987, 14 million new jobs were created in this country, and unemployment plunged from 9.5 percent to 5.7 percent, reaching its lowest level in fourteen years. Meanwhile unemployment rose 16.6 percent in Japan and 16 percent in the European Community.[32] To be sure, workers in particular industries were severely injured by a loss of market share here and overseas. But on the whole, economists stressed that international trade, however unbalanced, had resulted in more American gainers than losers. If the trade deficit shifted national employment among industries, eliminating the deficit would also result in sectoral dislocations with no guarantee of an increase in total employment.

One thing was certain about the movement of trade: ridding the world of exclusionary business practices, laudable as the idea was, would not by itself restore balance. In simplest terms, an overdraft of about $100 billion persisted because the United States continued to spend $100 billion more than it produced. Even if, say, all Japanese biases against American products were to end overnight and U.S. sales to Japan suddenly increased by $100 billion, a lopsided import-export picture would persist. The additional exports would be drawn from the domestic stock of goods. As long as our spending pattern remained the same, those exports would have to be replaced by $100 billion in goods from some other source—either by more imports from somewhere else or by fewer exports to somewhere else.[33]

Market Opening

The limited effect of external unfair trade barriers on the current account balance was acknowledged by trade officials and even politicians, not just by academic policy specialists. Despair in Congress over unfavorable trade numbers became acute in early 1985. That spring both chambers vented their anger on Japan by passing, among other things, near-unanimous resolutions that called on the administration to "obtain elimination" of various unjustifiable Japanese "acts" that blocked imports. Even this early outburst was tempered by recognition that misaligned exchange rates (the result of strong borrowing to pay for overconsumption), not just Japan's acts, were augmenting that country's bilateral surplus.[34]

Influential congressmen and administrators, while assailing the abusive trading methods of foreign countries, did not assert that stopping them would end America's trade woes. By far the largest part of the country's global deficit was "our own fault," admitted Representative Richard A. Gephardt during his ill-fated presidential campaign in 1988.[35] In the words of Senator Robert Dole (at the time the Republican presidential aspirant who spoke out most strongly on trade), "We all know that $60 billion [the 1987 deficit with Japan] is not all a product of unfair trade barriers in Japan. It is largely the product of bigger economic factors—like the incredible U.S. budget deficit."[36] U.S. Trade Representative Carla A. Hills repeatedly said the same thing: "Macroeconomic factors will have far more to do with the trade deficit than anything that comes out of this building."[37]

A sound justification for forcing open foreign markets and for pushing American exports into them was that such a policy would improve the nation's terms of trade, enabling Americans to buy more imports for each dollar earned from exports. Promoting exports in this way rather than by devaluing the dollar would add to the national income and help raise the standard of living.

Yet forecasters could not agree on what the income gains to the United States would be from greater access to particular markets. Some predicted that an offensive against foreign trade obstructions that averted a 5 percent depreciation of the dollar would net $15 to $20 billion annually for the nation.[38] Others calculated that a result that large could not be achieved even if the current account could be balanced by selling more abroad with a much stronger dollar. The United States was already the world's top exporter. Without sharply higher productivity growth, the need to produce the additional goods and services for export would constrain an improvement in living standards. Thus, according to one reliable estimate, averting a 10 percent decline in the value of the dollar might raise living standards by four-fifths of 1 percent by 1995.[39]

Analysts were also divided on how export campaigns would affect the adjustment problems and protective reactions of domestic industries. Larger footholds in various offshore markets would help exporting firms spread their overhead and R&D costs over a broader sales base. But what about firms that were competing against imports? Persuading other countries to buy more American goods would not reduce U.S. demand for imported products or diminish the capacity of other economies to produce those goods competitively. In fact, better terms of trade at home would draw in more imports; a reallocation of resources abroad, away from protected sectors producing import substitutes, could ultimately strengthen export economies such as Japan's.[40]

Weak industries in the United States might face stiffer competition, and if so, their calls for protection would increase.

Effects on the World Trading System

A whiff of unilateral coercion (like that wafting from the 1988 Trade Act) was useful to press the international community into playing by better GATT rules. World commerce might expand if the United States led an attack on economic systems that were more closed than its own. At some point, however, a program of aggressive unilateralism might be mismanaged. When foreign import policies were liberalized on an explicit most-favored-nation basis, new markets would be up for grabs; any entrant could enjoy the better commercial opportunities. But expectations in bilateral dealings conducted on behalf of particular plaintiffs and backed by the possibility of sanctions might be very different. Would the complainants, who took the trouble to instigate a negotiation in the first place, remain indifferent if they failed to win the expected business? Would the target countries, under the threat of retribution, reason that the safest way to ease bilateral tensions was to grease the wheels that squeaked loudest? Would these countries (assuming they could exercise quantitative controls over imports) not be tempted to grant some preferential franchises? Elaborate juggling would be required to use unilaterally decreed procedures and ultimatums to pry open foreign markets without violating agreed methods of settling disputes, at the same time satisfying aggrieved interests and guaranteeing that shared principles of nondiscrimination were never breached.

On the one hand, provisional defection from the GATT's deficient procedures would give trade reformers leverage as they strove to patch the deficiencies through new multilateral compacts. The rest of the world was more likely to take seriously the need for GATT reform if the alternative was an American lone-judge-and-jury approach to trade conflicts. On the other hand, what if the domestic political process was unable to give up the bargaining chip regardless of whether negotiators achieved many of their aims? Skeptics cautioned that a retaliatory commercial policy might acquire vested interests and prove difficult to roll back. If threats of retaliation were successful, their success might whet appetites. Threats that failed would necessitate meting out real penalties. Various domestic producers would thereby receive protection. These groups might organize to retain the windfall. Others, inspired by the example, might want to arrange their own schemes, lobbying to close the domestic market on the pretext that markets abroad were not offering symmetrical access.

Most thoughtful observers conceded that, like all forms of international organization, the GATT was flawed. As had been true since the system's inception, American stewardship and prodding were necessary to correct the flaws—especially since few other governments seemed capable of exerting much leadership or even of understanding the need for it. But, critics asked, what if (as seemed possible) new disciplines did not work the same magic as the early rounds of simple tariff reductions? Would malcontents then reassert that the GATT was "dead"? Or would they grant that living within the GATT's framework, warts and all, was still safer than setting possible precedents for member states to operate outside it? Entering the 1990s, American trade politics had reached a crossroad on these fundamental issues.

International Relations

Finally, the foreign policy establishment was at odds over the implications of the increasingly muscular U.S. trade regulations. On one side were theorists who posited, in essence, that continuous external pressure would eventually transform closed societies into better neighbors in the league of trading nations, thus making them more congenial colleagues of the United States. According to this view, for instance, the rivalry between the United States and Japan would ease if the Japanese could be talked into implementing a far-reaching agenda of structural reforms. Such reforms would be in the best interests of consumers and would be welcomed by other enlightened groups in Japan and in third countries sharing some of our frustrations. "Friends must sometimes help friends break destructive habits."[41] On the opposite side stood onlookers who suspected that, although applying pressure on friendly states to bring their economic structures into conformity with America's had become less inexpedient as the cold war receded, the perennial nagging and hectoring of these partners might one day exact a price in foreign relations.

Neither view was fatuous. Few would deny that U.S. businessmen had serious and legitimate objections to lodge with foreign governments. Understandably galling to these entrepreneurs was the attitude that apparently existed in some countries, particularly among the Japanese, that their producers were entitled to ride freely into the U.S. market while their own economies remained inordinately encrusted in bureaucratic or cultural restrictions against outsiders.[42] Insisting that these well-founded complaints be addressed was appropriate and could even solidify international partnerships. The deeper the integration among major economies, the lower the risk of dangerous economic or political rifts.

At the same time, the public interest and the interests of individual firms were not identical. The business of America, after all, was more than business. If policymakers entertained a bulging roster of private claims and treated them as if they merited national confrontations at the highest levels, they would expend diplomatic capital and strain ties with countries whose cooperation was needed over the long haul to advance other strategic goals—such as ensuring a stable military balance in volatile parts of the world, enlisting underwriters for fledgling democracies, or coordinating international efforts to check environmental degradation or suppress drug trafficking.

In the fall of 1990, Americans took note of the vacillations of various allies when their help was urgently needed. Slavishly protecting their local farmers, the French, German, and Japanese governments allowed the Uruguay Round to falter. Then, as war approached in the Persian Gulf, Tokyo engaged in lengthy, introspective reflection about its proper contribution to the common defense of world oil supplies; anti-American demonstrations erupted in Germany; and, for a while, officials in Paris created confusion. An ambivalent U.S. Congress, watching these equivocations, saw economic giants behaving too timidly. At the same time, few seemed to wonder whether the prospect of impelling these governments to shoulder their international responsibilities would be enhanced by more ministerial wrangles over issues such as the cultural value of television programs, the worthiness of aluminum baseball bats, or the rightful proprietorship of concession stands in national parks. Weighing and managing diplomatically the growing assortment of complaints about commercial malfeasance required more and more Promethean skill.

A Regulatory Paradox

Not only did much regulation of foreign trade practices take root amid a policy dissensus; it expanded during a period of growing awareness and sophistication about the limitations of other economic regulatory ventures. While the U.S. government was policing more international commerce, it curtailed its role in important sectors of the domestic economy, areas such as transportation, energy, and telecommunications. While policymakers relaxed the enforcement of antitrust laws, the trade statutes moved in the opposite direction, authorizing regulators to curb more business practices abroad. Domestic regulatory debacles (the disastrous system of price controls on crude oil and natural gas in the 1970s was the most vivid example) had taught law-makers and rulemakers an important lesson: attempts to apply therapy to market imperfections were often worse than the malady. But when it came to international trade, the same legislators and bureaucrats sometimes behaved as if their many medications for sore businesses, if cleverly concocted, would only be salubrious.

Business regulation is frequently characterized as a type of government policy that concentrates benefits on well-organized interests (namely, the firms and workers that are protected from competition) while dispersing the costs among ill-organized consumers. Schemes to regulate trade commonly fit this description. Whether the government's involvement takes the form of old-fashioned tariffs or of new administrative protection against unfair competition, policymaking that favors a particular clientele is often involved. Especially when imports are curtailed, particular producers collect rents at the public's expense.

Beginning in the 1970s, however, American regulatory politics took some unexpected twists. In a number of instances entrenched producer interests were bested by diffuse consumer interests.[43] Fares and fees for air travelers, for customers of the trucking industry, and for subscribers of long-distance telephone service were lowered through procompetitive deregulation. Utility ratepayers and shippers using freight trains enjoyed more flexible service and pricing structures as regulatory reform swept electric power companies and the railroads.

After the fiasco of the Smoot-Hawley tariff in 1930, the main direction of U.S. economic policy beyond the water's edge had been similar: toward lower costs for end users through rate reductions. But enough detours were taken over the years (an especially large number in the early and mid-1980s) to make for a complex travelogue. It was not easy to tell whether policy in the 1980s always promised a safe passage for consumers (for example, by bettering the terms of trade) or a choppy crossing, as the government sought to relieve a growing collection of petitioning industries by raising (or threatening to raise) the prices of imports.

Foul Is Fair and Fair Is Foul

Nowhere was the complexity in public objectives more striking than in the dual treatment of price discrimination, the practice of selling like products to different buyers at different prices. Benign neglect of the Robinson-Patman Act was now the unwritten rule in national antitrust doctrine.[44] Federal regulators were persuaded that the main effect of Robinson-Patman was to protect high-cost businesses that interfered with the efficient movement of resources to lower-cost sellers. Since the mid-1970s only rare cases of predation posing clear dangers of market concentration had been prosecuted by the Federal Trade Commission.

By contrast the U.S. International Trade Commission (ITC) became busier than ever adjudicating claims of foreign dumping (originally defined as sales of like products to the United States at prices below those in the country of origin), even when the differential pricing was not necessarily anticompetitive. Selective price discounts, in other words, were fair game when offered inside the domestic market but disagreeable from merchants transacting business across a border.

Partisanship

One might ask whether this apparent incongruity—trying to exert more control over the conduct of foreign trade while decontrolling domestic sectors—simply reflected divided party control and partisan politics. Perhaps the Democratic Congress sensed that trade was one realm in which patriotic incursions could be legislated against the will of Republican administrations that opposed big government. Though partisan motives were a factor at times (in the debate on the 1988 Trade Act, for example), the maneuvers between the legislative and executive branches were generally more complicated and confusing.

For the most part the drift toward trade strictures did not take the form of legislated tariffs or quotas. Ever since 1930, Congress had artfully avoided such traditional forms of protectionism. Instead, most of the recent intervention emanated from administrative actions even under the aegis of a Republican president who professed confidence in the beneficence of unfettered world market forces. The occasional irony here was hard to miss. The Reagan administration trumpeted the president's free trade instincts, but high officials simultaneously commended him for having "granted more import relief to U.S. industry than any of his predecessors in more than half a century."[45]

To a considerable extent, the politics of trade became bipartisan. While overtly protectionist laws remained out of favor in both parties, measures to penalize foreign unfair traders enjoyed very broad congressional support. Every four or five years, beginning in 1974, Congress adopted a massive piece of legislation aimed at deterring these delinquents. Each passed by wide margins, and not on party-line votes. Similarly, every candidate in the 1988 presidential race, Democratic and Republican, affirmed a need to fight commercial unfairness, even though few claimed that the endeavor would greatly alleviate the nation's trade troubles.

Summary

During a period of sustained economic prosperity, the goal of fair play in world commerce moved to center stage in Washington. It became a recurring theme in national elections and received broad backing in Congress, despite a lack of widespread public agitation to act. It also engendered a widening array of rules and regulations under a Republican administration that was dedicated to deregulation. Specific business interests could find these developments helpful, though seldom wholly satisfying. Some of the businesses that received help—for example, in the form of broader markets over which to spread their costs—might gain a better slot in the international economic race. Beyond that, however, no consensus existed on how much the national economy would gain from an increasingly exacting pursuit of fairness, while it was widely conceded that other reforms, such as boosting savings and investment, would make a much bigger difference in the national trade accounts and, in the long run, in the nation's standard of living.

The new trade activism forged ahead with some reasonable misgivings in full view. Dwelling on the fairness issue was a relatively safe strategy in domestic politics, but it could also become an irritant, rather than a constructive moral force, in international politics. Fears that it would rupture vital bilateral relationships and seriously corrode delicate multilateral institutions proved largely exaggerated. Nevertheless, while coping with unfair trade was an unavoidable concern of policymakers, the remedies—including hundreds of antidumping suits and countervailing duties and hints of other retaliatory sanctions—yielded mixed results, often giving rise to additional frustrations. And arguably, absorption with the countless aches and pains of foreign trade distracted national attention from other primary tasks, such as healing the budget deficit, resuscitating the national rate of saving, and rehabilitating the nation's human capital.

Overview of the Book

Economic decline, real or imagined, has not sufficed to explain the past decade's stiffening regulation of unfair trade. Nor has policy only reflected exasperation with foreign parochialism. American companies interested in entering markets like Japan's still needed inordinately deep pockets and patience. In an age that called for better international cooperation, exhausted negotiators endured long days listening to the implacable subsidizers of European farmers and protectors of overpriced Japanese rice. Presumably, one could not break deadlocked discussions with such parties by carrying nothing but olive branches. Yet the lengthening train of commercial regulations in Washington had started rolling well before the annoying delays in Brussels, in Geneva, and in other venues, and at times it seemed to maintain a head of steam irrespective of changing realities, including a brighter picture for U.S. exports almost everywhere. So this book is inclined to interpret the course of recent trade policy somewhat differently: it will factor in the role of domestic politics alongside loftier motifs like a national desire for economic balance and revival or a quest for global economic harmony. To be sure, the stresses and strains of the world economy informed domestic political perceptions and incentives. But in part the incentives and the perceptions also had a life of their own.

To a significant degree, I will suggest, contemporary trade regulation is old wine in new bottles. Like the commercial policies of the past, here or anywhere, they have aimed to bolster the competitive position of some firms or industries against other firms or industries. But more than the policies of earlier vintage, today's have invoked equity as their central rationale.

This has not been simply a ruse. Policymakers have been trying to rectify some genuine injustices. Their exertions have sometimes been encouraged by receptive constituencies abroad as well as at home. But steps against unfair trading have also had this distinct advantage: lacking a protectionist stigma, they afforded possibilities for servicing constituents and clients unobtrusively and at relatively little risk to elective officeholders. In an era of budgetary austerity, domestic regulatory retrenchment, and a simplified tax code, all of which have constrained the flow of other selective preferences and protections, reliance on trade remedies has grown. At the same time, because this activity has faced a tall order—to lessen the vulnerability of America's basic industries and high-paying jobs in a much more competitive world—there would be disappointments, demands for additional measures, and little rest for the weary.

These observations are set forth in chapter 3. The fourth chapter examines the theory and practice of correcting trade offenses. Chapters 5 and 6 explore the distinctive contributions of Congress and the executive. The final chapter makes some modest suggestions for improving the way trade decisions are reached in the American political system, or at least for clarifying the locus of responsibility for those decisions.

Before taking up these matters, however, we must consider the objective circumstances. The world's economic playing field has always been tilted against free traders, and few trading states have consistently been models of good sportsmanship. But was the slope getting steeper and the unsportsman-like conduct growing worse? The next chapter addresses this question.

CHAPTER TWO

The Lay of the Land

PARTICULARLY DURING SPELLS of unfavorable exchange rates, prominent parts of American industry and agriculture have been hammered by foreign competition. Inevitably this has given impetus to trade regulation. Consider the fate of steel producers during the period 1980 to 1985. Imports of iron and steel rose from 18 million to nearly 28 million tons, while exports plunged from 5 million to 1.5 million tons.[1] Steelmakers suffered losses totaling $5.6 billion, some large corporations went bankrupt, and thousands of workers lost their jobs. All the ills of basic industries could not be imputed to foreign trade. Nevertheless, as their competitive position deteriorated, more and more of them ran to the government for relief from imports or for assistance in pushing exports.

But this simple interpretation is incomplete. While hardship may explain rising pleas for help, it does not account for the prevailing form of those pleas. Established channels for requesting trade relief did not require proof that competitors were wrongdoers. The right of beleaguered industries to gain temporary respite from import surges or of governments to ensure unimpaired access to markets was always recognized in the General Agreement on Tariffs and Trade (GATT). The escape clause (under U.S. law, section 201 of the 1974 Trade Act) afforded temporary safeguards for petitioners injured by imports, while the GATT provided means for its members to investigate virtually "any measure" or "situation" that obstructed the free exchange of merchandise between the signatories.[2] Yet among the numerous trade casualties the U.S. government attended to, very few were treated through the escape clause. Most sought relief on grounds that, under other U.S. statutes outlined in table 2-1, the competition was not only injurious but unjust.

Table 2-2 displays the pattern. Of the 1,155 trade cases entered between 1980 and 1990 only 20 (fewer than 2 percent) were based on the escape

21

Table 2-1. Principal U.S. Trade Law Provisions

Statute	Principal focus	Remedy	Investigative agencies	Decisionmaker	Override
Section 201[a] Escape clause	Increase of fairly traded imports deemed to cause or threaten serious injury to a U.S. industry	Temporary tariffs, quotas, negotiated restraints, and/or Trade Adjustment Assistance	U.S. International Trade Commission (ITC) determines extent of injury and makes recommendation to the president	President decides what, if any, action to take	Congress can override within 90 days if president rejects an affirmative ITC recommendation
Section 232[b] National security	Imports that threaten to impair the national security	Remedial action at president's discretion	Department of Commerce (no ITC injury test required)	President decides what action to take	None
Section 301[c] Trade barriers	Foreign practices deemed in violation of U.S. trade agreements; unjustifiable, unreasonable, or discriminatory practices deemed to burden U.S. commerce	Negotiated settlements, backed by remedial retaliatory actions (such as the suspension of trade concessions or the assessment of import restrictions) if a satisfactory agreement is not reached	Office of the U.S. Trade Representative (no injury test required)	U.S. Trade Representative (President, prior to 1988 Trade Act)	President can waive remedial action citing effects harmful to the national economic interest

Statute	Practice covered	Remedy	Decisionmaking	Administration	Presidential role
Section 337[d] Unlawful marketing	Infringements of patents, trademarks, or copyrights; false advertising; misdesignation of origin; trade secret misappropriations	Exclusion orders; cease-and-desist orders	ITC decides on remedy (ITC injury determination was required prior to 1988 Trade Act)	ITC issues orders	President can waive ITC orders for policy reasons
Section 701[e] Unfairly subsidized imports	Targeted production or export subsidies deemed to cause or threaten material injury to a U.S. industry	Countervailing duties (CVDs) to offset margin of subsidy; negotiated adjustments	ITC determines extent of injury; International Trade Administration (ITA) of Commerce Department calculates subsidy margin and determines remedy	ITA administers remedies	None
Section 731[f] Dumped imports	Imports, sold below fair value, deemed to cause or threaten material injury to a U.S. industry	Antidumping duties (ADs) to offset margin of unfair pricing; negotiated adjustments	ITC determines extent of injury; ITA calculates margin of unfair pricing and determines remedy	ITA administers remedies	None

Source: Author's compilations from sources as follows:
a. Section 201, Trade Act of 1974, as amended.
b. Section 232, Trade Expansion Act of 1962.
c. Section 301, Trade Act of 1974, as amended.
d. Section 337, Tariff Act of 1930, as amended.
e. Section 701, Tariff Act of 1930, as amended.
f. Section 731, Tariff Act of 1930, as amended.

Table 2-2. Number of U.S. Trade Cases, 1980–90[a]

Type of petition	1980	1981	1982	1983	1984	1985	1986	1987	1988	1989	1990	1980–90
Escape clause												
Section 201	2	1	3	0	7	4	1	0	1	0	1	20
Unfair trade actions												
Section 301	0	5	6	7	2	5	6	5	7	10	4	57
Section 337	18	18	23	43	33	25	24	18	11	19	13	245
Section 701	14	22	140	22	51	43	27	8	11	7	7	352
(Steel)	(0)	(3)	(115)	(10)	(23)	(16)	(5)	(5)	(4)	(1)	(0)	(182)
Section 731	21	15	65	46	74	66	71	15	42	23	43	481
(Steel)	(8)	(6)	(47)	(14)	(49)	(23)	(3)	(0)	(4)	(0)	(0)	(154)
Total	53	60	234	118	160	139	128	46	71	59	67	1135
Total minus steel	(45)	(51)	(72)	(94)	(88)	(100)	(120)	(41)	(63)	(58)	(67)	(799)

Sources: I.M. Destler, *American Trade Politics*, 2d ed. (Washington: Institute for International Economics, 1992), p. 166; I.M. Destler, "United States Trade Policymaking in the Eighties," in Alberto Alesina and Geoffrey Carliner, eds., *The Politics and Economics of the Eighties* (University of Chicago Press, 1991), p. 262; United States International Trade Commission, unpublished data; Office of the United States Trade Representative, unpublished data; and Institute for International Economics, unpublished data.

a. Frequencies based on countries cited by date of petitions filed with the ITC. Totals do not include 751 (b) review investigations of CVD and AD orders/suspension agreements.

clause. The others involved claims about violations of trading rules. Returning to the steel industry example, although Bethlehem Steel Corporation submitted a section 201 petition in 1984, the industry's main line of defense was a truckload of requests (162 of them filed in 1982 alone) for sanctions against improperly priced imports.

The onslaught of trade cases diminished after 1985, when American industry became markedly more price competitive. Exchange rates had now made it easier to sell American exports overseas and harder to buy imports here. Thus from 1986 through 1990, after the dollar had fallen 45 percent against the Japanese yen, the average annual frequency of cases dropped to 74, down from 127 between 1980 and 1985.

Still, caseloads in later years settled on a relatively high plateau. Throughout the decade complaints about commercial misconduct exceeded the volume registered in previous periods, and no fewer grievances were recorded in the last two years of the 1980s than during the first two. Subtracting the great number of cases from one industry, steel, more complaints were recorded between 1988 and 1990 than in 1980–82, three years in which a truly severe recession had exacerbated protectionist pressures.[3] For the most common type of case, petitions for penalties against "dumped" imports, the figures (steel industry excluded) were nearly 23 percent higher from 1987 through 1990 than during the five-year period 1980–84.

Foreign trade derelictions were no fiction; there were (and would always be) plenty to be uncovered. However, a tide of protests about them surged to extraordinary heights in the first half of the 1980s, and, though it subsided sharply in 1987, it did not ebb steadily thereafter.

Had international trade suddenly become that much more unfair?

Backsliding to Closed Markets?

Measuring the extent and severity of unwarranted foreign trade distortions is for all practical purposes impossible. We would have to scrutinize every national policy that directly or indirectly determines export pricing and the contestability of markets, making many debatable judgments about what was unreasonable. Tax laws in Japan inflate urban land prices, crowding citizens into cramped dwellings in which comparatively few consumer durables will fit. Japan's tax policy, in other words, constricts the market for spacious housing, household appliances, and furnishings. But consider the effects of the following unique policies in the United States: minimal gasoline taxes, local zoning ordinances that favor single-family homes, mortgage interest deductions on those homes, and grants-in-aid heavily earmarked for highways. Such policies not only skew trade balances (by inducing demand for automobiles and dependence on imported oil); by influencing the modal choice of urban commuters and intercity travelers, the policies may also be limiting a potential market—in this case, for mass transit equipment and other nonautomotive ground transportation. The tally of national policies (or lack thereof) that might be construed, in some sense, as trade-distorting can range far and wide.

Yet, short of dragging the kitchen sink and the home mortgage into the analysis, systematic efforts to study the commercial constraints of the past decade provide little basis for believing that the world after 1980 had become, all of a sudden, a more malicious environment for merchandise trade—or that discrimination against American products worsened as the U.S. current account turned negative.

Nontariff Protection

For some twenty years, as traditional tariffs were lowered, observers have stressed the prominence of other kinds of encumbrances. As one writer put it at the end of the Kennedy Round, "the lowering of tariffs has, in effect, been like draining a swamp. The lower water level has revealed all the snags and stumps of non-tariff barriers [NTBs] that still have to be cleared away."[4] The question is whether the snags and stumps were mostly swamp residue or malignant new growth.

Scholars who contend that the trading world has been experiencing a "rising trend in trade restriction" typically cite estimates of nontariff restrictions that appear to show an increase in protection.[5] For example, surveying a group of sixteen industrial countries, researchers at the World Bank counted a net increase of no fewer than 2,486 NTBs between 1981 and 1983 alone.[6] Tracking the proliferation of "hard-core" NTBs in major industrial nations from 1981 through 1986, the World Bank found that imports subject to restrictions generally increased from about 15 percent to nearly 18 percent (table 2-3).

While this was the best quantitative information available on trends in identifiable protection, it could be misleading in at least two respects. First, the figures were estimates of import coverage (that is, the percentage of a country's imports, in value terms, reached by NTBs), but not of *restrictiveness*. Today's product-specific trade controls were often more permeable than the high comprehensive tariffs of the past. Exporters had figured out ingenious

Table 2-3. *Share of Total Imports (by Value) Subject to Hard-Core Nontariff Barriers by Individual OECD Countries, 1981, 1983, and 1986*[a]
Percent unless otherwise noted

	Coverage[b]			1981–86 change (points)
Importer	1981	1983	1986	
Belgium-Luxembourg	12.6	15.4	14.3	1.7
Denmark	6.7	8.0	7.9	1.2
Germany, Fed. Rep.	11.8	13.6	15.4	3.6
France	15.7	18.8	18.6	2.9
Greece	16.2	21.0	20.1	3.9
Great Britain	11.2	13.4	12.8	1.6
Ireland	8.2	9.7	9.7	1.5
Italy	17.2	18.7	18.2	1.0
Netherlands	19.9	21.4	21.4	1.5
EC (10)[c]	13.4	15.6	15.8	2.4
Switzerland	19.5	19.6	19.6	0.1
Finland	7.9	8.0	8.0	0.1
Japan	24.4	24.5	24.3	−0.1
Norway	15.2	14.7	14.2	−1.0
New Zealand	46.4	46.4	32.4	−14.0
United States	11.4	13.7	17.3	5.9
Total	15.1	16.7	17.7	2.6

Source: Sam Laird and Alexander Yeats, "Quantitative Methods for Trade Barrier Analysis," Washington, World Bank, 1988, pp. 33, 130, 133. Computations based on data compiled by the United Nations Conference on Trade and Development (UNCTAD).

a. Hard-core nontariff measures include variable import levies and product-specific charges (excluding tariff quotas); quotas; prohibitions (including seasonal prohibitions); nonautomatic import authorizations, including restrictive import licensing requirements; quantitative "voluntary" export restraints; and trade restraints under the Multi-Fiber Arrangement. Not included are measures such as health and sanitary regulations, packaging and labeling requirements, technical standards, minimum price regulations, and tariff quotas. Trade data exclude EC intratrade. Australia, Canada, and Sweden were excluded from the computations because of technical problems experienced in compilation of the NTB files of these countries.

b. In computing the ratios, 1981, 1983, and 1986, nontariff measures are applied to a constant 1981 trade base. This allows one to examine the influence of NTB changes while holding the effects of trade changes constant. Petroleum products have been excluded from the calculations.

c. Excluding Spain and Portugal.

ways to increase the value of their foreign sales by assembling their goods in different locations, by switching from restrained categories of components to categories not yet restricted, and by transshipping goods through unrestricted third countries.[7] So despite an increase in nontariff restraints, their porousness meant that the industrialized countries increased their dependence on imports from the rest of the world, even in sectors that were vigorously regulated, such as footwear, textiles, clothing, and steel.[8]

Second, the effects of NTBs must be weighed against the effects of continuing tariff reductions. A precise assessment of the net effect of nontariff measures would require estimating their tariff equivalents—an impossibly complex task. But even with no such assessment, the growth of NTBs in the

1980s was almost certainly being offset by multilateral tariff reductions. Throughout the decade, world trade expanded more rapidly than income. The world's protectionists generally seemed to bark more fiercely than they were willing or able to bite.

Who's Doing What to Whom?

If markets were closing anywhere, it was not in the Far East. Taiwan, Singapore, Malaysia, Hong Kong, Indonesia, and South Korea were among the fastest-growing U.S. export markets of the 1980s.[9] Although trade frictions with Korea increased in the 1980s, Korean tariffs, formerly among the highest, were rolled back an average of nearly 50 percent between 1979 and 1986. After 1987, when Seoul announced further tariff cuts and allowed the won to float upward against the dollar, Korea's trade surplus began to dissipate.[10]

Even the region's bête noire, Japan, had become more receptive to imports. After 1986 Japan's overall current account surplus declined by a third. From 1985 through 1990 American exports to Japan increased 119 percent, while exports to the rest of the world rose by 79 percent.[11] By 1990 the Japanese were importing more U.S. products than did the three largest economies in Western Europe—those of Germany, France, and Italy—combined.[12] Japan imported over a third more American goods per capita than did the Europeans.

As table 2-3 suggests, nontariff barriers in the European Community were inching upward in the 1981–86 period, and observers feared that the trend might worsen amid the politics of economic integration. Emergent policies, such as the antidumping measures the EC was adopting as a protectionist device and earlier directives calling for strict reciprocity in banking services, were not reassuring.[13] In addition, it remained unclear how far Europe would be prepared to go in scaling down its most egregiously protectionist edifice, the Common Agricultural Policy (CAP).

Despite the problem of agriculture (where every stage in the development of the CAP seemed to come at the expense of U.S. farm exports), American exports to "Fortress Europe" stormed ahead in the second half of the 1980s, rising from $49 billion to $76 billion between 1985 and 1988. While 29 percent of our exports to Japan in 1988 were classified as high-technology goods, fully 45 percent of our exports to the EC were in that category.[14] On balance, the process of regional integration in Europe was not likely to stifle the expansion of transatlantic commerce; lower internal regulatory barriers promised to stimulate more than to divert trade by generating growth.

If it was difficult to make a case that rising protectionism in Europe and Asia had choked off an increasing proportion of international trade or constricted the flow of exports from the United States, it was harder to argue that protectionism had become a growing problem in the relationships with Canada and Mexico, the other principal trading partners of the United States.

Almost a quarter of all U.S. foreign commerce is with Canada. At the outset of the 1980s, there were irritating inequalities in U.S.-Canadian trade: even with Tokyo Round tariff revisions fully in force, only about 20 percent of Canada's exports faced duties entering the United States, while 35 percent of American-made goods incurred duties going north, and the Canadian duties were higher.[15] By the end of the decade, however, a bilateral trade pact was eliminating these and other obstacles.

On the southern border was the fourth largest purchaser of U.S. goods (after the EC, Canada, and Japan). Mexico had clung, in effect, to a policy of zero-net-import quotas: import increases had to be matched by export increases.[16] By 1988, however, Mexico had unilaterally liberalized many of these controls, allowing billions in additional imports from the United States. That year the Mexican government also committed itself to creating a North American free trade zone.

Developing nations continued to be a challenge for U.S. exporters and investors. The competition from low-wage economies, many of which violated the standards of the International Labor Organization, was deemed lamentably "unequal."[17] Imports from developing countries penetrated the American market with relative ease. Nonetheless, the percentage of manufactures imported from these countries remained stable: during the years when the U.S. trade deficit ballooned to $140 billion, 1981 to 1986, manufactured goods from developing nations increased only from 25.0 percent to 25.9 percent of total U.S. imports.[18] The greatest competitive threat facing American business was not from nations with low wage rates.

The tendency of industrializing countries to practice more protection than fully developed countries was nothing new. At one time or other, every nation shielded infant industries; U.S. tariffs in the nineteenth century, indeed well into the twentieth, had done so notoriously. In the 1980s, moreover, the third world debt crisis added involuntary limits on the ability of the worst debtors to take in more imports. In this context, more remarkable than rampant protectionism among the developing countries and the newly industrialized countries were the decisions of prominent ones such as Brazil to reduce voluntarily their import barriers.[19]

The United States remained less protected by trade barriers, including nontariff measures, than many other countries. As of 1986, according to the World Bank survey, approximately 17 percent of imports to the United States faced major NTBs, whereas in Italy and France the share exceeded 18 percent, and in Japan more than 24 percent. The difference is almost certainly understated because the percentages do not tell us how restrictive the barriers have been. For example, the United States, France, and Italy had each negotiated limits on imported Japanese autos. But the French and Italians limited the imports to less than 3 percent of domestic sales, compared with a U.S. quota of about 25 percent.[20]

Nonetheless, a distinctive development during the 1980s was the widening reach of observable NTBs among such champions of free trade as Germany and the United States. Judging from table 2-3, while the scope of measurable NTBs continued to be extensive but at least stable in Japan, by 1986 it had expanded by more than 30 percent in West Germany and more than 50 percent in the United States. Thus the coverage of hard-core nontariff protection in the United States appeared to be converging on the average for the Organization for Economic Cooperation and Development (OECD) sample.

It does not follow from this that the United States was well on its way to erecting the same trade walls as those in some European countries, Japan, or other traditional harbors of defensive commercial policy.[21] By the same token, the data lend no support to the notion that the variance between America's open market orientation and the restrictivist proclivities elsewhere had increased.

Dumping

Much of the new trade regulation in the United States was a reaction to an apparent menace: wrongly priced imports. If, during the 1980s, more imports were being artificially underpriced as a result of increased foreign subsidies or other subterfuges, domestic industries were entitled to greater protective intervention.

Fair, Fairer, Fairest

More than any other commercial offense, foreign traders were accused of dumping—undercutting the price of U.S. products by selling exports at "less than fair value." The number of dumping complaints filed with U.S. authorities in the 1980s averaged about three times the annual caseload in the

1970s.[22] This was not just because the absolute volume of imports had increased; definitions of what constituted fair prices had changed, making it easier to complain.

Enacted in 1916, the original U.S. antidumping law had a limited aim: to bar discriminatory pricing where intentional harm was being done to an efficiently operated industry. Domestic producer interests found this formulation impractical, however, since prosecution required not only evidence of injury but a demonstration of injurious intent (the dumper had to be purposely "destroying or injuring an industry in the United States").[23] New legislation in 1921 broadened the scope of antidumping enforcement by eliminating the requisite proof of predation. Further adjustments in 1954 ordered regulators to commence dumping investigations before establishing that injury had occurred.[24]

The most important statutory revision came with the Trade Act of 1974. Until then, dumping had been defined as export sales at prices below the prices of comparable products in the country of origin.[25] The 1974 act, however, introduced a novel concept: the notion of proper cost recovery. Henceforth, if investigators determined that selling prices in the exporter's home market fell below fully allocated production costs averaged over a given period, such sales would be considered abnormal even if the home price and export price did not differ.[26] In time, not surprisingly, a majority of cases would charge that imports were being priced below average cost—and the Commerce Department's International Trade Administration would confirm these charges in most instances.[27]

The idea that pricing below-average cost is a pernicious practice that somehow falls outside "the ordinary course of business" may seem peculiar. Periodic discounts are normal, efficient business behavior for firms with substantial fixed costs and fluctuating demand. (It is worth recalling that the first antidumping law was enacted in 1904 by Canada against the U.S. Steel Corporation for periodically unloading surpluses at cut rates.) Domestic antitrust policy had all but ceased to challenge local price discrimination, and when it acted, the relevant question was whether sales were below variable, not total cost.[28] Why firms should be enjoined from practicing in international markets what they could freely try in their domestic market remained a mystery to economists.

Strategic Dumping

The double standard might be easier to understand if it could be shown that price discounting in international trade was mostly anticompetitive—that is, used effectively to knock out competitors, to gain market power, and ultimately to extort monopoly profits. Although this has always been a central premise of antidumping rules, there were few examples of such methodical predation in which dumping succeeded in eliminating enough competition to impose monopolistic pricing.[29] Why?

Firms engaging in price warfare must take protracted, subnormal profits or losses.[30] If the marauding firms are able to absorb these prolonged losses, and if their ultimate objective is to acquire their victims, national antitrust law can generally step in to prevent mergers that form dominant market shares. In industries in which the costs of entry are modest, the dominant firms would have to collude to prevent new entrants, domestic or foreign, from returning to the captured market.[31] The would-be cartel would have to coordinate its actions perfectly, maintaining profitability but also shaving prices whenever necessary to discourage upstarts. In industries where entry costs were high, the victors would still need to ensure that no member of the cartel broke ranks.

Detractors objected that these were only fanciful assumptions of economic theory and that, particularly in technically advanced sectors, the prospect of foreign monopoly power was imminent. Japanese dominance in electronics, for example, has been compared with the stranglehold on the world's energy supplies maintained by the Organization of Petroleum Exporting Countries (OPEC). Guarding the U.S. industrial base in electronics was like preserving a healthy domestic oil industry: it would provide "anticartel insurance," maintaining access to an essential resource "at reasonable and stable prices."[32]

A continuing difficulty with the "anticartel insurance" rationale (apart from the fact that OPEC in the 1980s was a textbook case of an unstable cartel), was that the supposedly extortionate prices remained largely conjectural, even where outside sellers had swept entire markets. In the 1980s, for example, the share of the domestic market held by American-owned firms declined from 90 percent to 10 percent for color televisions and from 90 percent to 1 percent for stereos. With plenty of entrants muscling into the business, the prices of these items went down, not up.[33]

The Semiconductor Scare

The most celebrated dumping controversy of the decade was the low-ball pricing of semiconductors from Japan. By the mid-1980s, leading Japanese manufactures had managed to drive a number of U.S. producers out of the market for basic integrated circuits (primarily 64-K and 256-K DRAMs). Few domestic chipmakers reentered even after prices recovered. The merchant field was largely left to a half dozen Japanese corporations who, after 1986, were able to jack up prices and rake in large profits. Those profits were then plowed back into research and development and into new equipment, allowing Toshiba, Fujitsu, NEC, Hitachi, Mitsubishi, and Oki Electric to leap ahead in the fabrication of future generations of products.[34] Increasingly dependent on these suppliers for key components, the U.S. computer industry and other customers bore higher costs.

These outcomes were worrisome. Whatever the effects of Japanese machinations, however, they were hard to disentangle from the consequences of the regulatory scheme devised to correct the situation. At the insistence of U.S. chip manufacturers, which were trying to stanch an influx of dumped chips in the mid-1980s, the government of Japan signed the Semiconductor Trade Arrangement in 1986 (STA). Prior to the STA, Japan's producers had been competing energetically not only against their American counterparts but with one another, and in so doing had incurred substantial losses. But the STA seemed to enable the Ministry of International Trade and Industry (MITI) to organize a producer cartel.[35] Had there been no MITI-ordered production cutbacks and pricing "suggestions," profitability in Japanese DRAM production might not have been so readily restored and then sustained. Competition among the Japanese firms would not have ground to a halt as easily as it could under the government's mandatory guidance. In the absence of supranormal profits, Japan's manufacturers might not have been so well positioned to meet challenges from a corps of American companies developing more advanced or specialized memory devices.[36] And the squeeze on American computer manufacturers in need of inexpensive microchips might have been less severe.[37]

Of course there was no guarantee that the discipline of market forces would have held sway, improving the competitiveness of American firms, even without an antidumping plan. Perhaps the Japanese semiconductor industry would have been able to set cartel prices on its own. Some U.S. computer manufacturers might have faced a greater risk of being cut off from cheap chips or of being otherwise at the mercy of Japanese monopolists.

Although these were possibilities, the counterproductive side effects of the antidumping action were more than possibilities; they happened. While the STA may have managed to keep in business a few domestic producers still manufacturing commodity memory devices, the arrangement did not enhance (in fact, for a while it seemed to impair) the competitive edge of other, more numerous and equally important U.S. firms. In short, by apparently facilitating formation of a foreign cartel, this adventure in trade policy seemed to ensure that some dreaded prophecies would be self-fulfilling.

In the semiconductor dispute, a case could be made, on national security grounds, that some form of trade measure was needed to ensure the survival of a critical industry. If protection was necessary, however, levying an explicit import fee would have been preferable in some ways to the STA. A tariff, ordered under the national security provisions (section 232) of the 1962 Trade Expansion Act, would at least have avoided years of bickering about the "right" price for semiconductors and would also have collected some helpful revenue instead of sending shortage-induced rents overseas. (An obvious disadvantage of a tariff, however, would be that, by taxing an essential input, it might force the domestic manufacturers that depend on those inputs for final products to shift more of their production offshore.)

An Antitrust Test

Although dumping could cause damage, its prevention could, too. The regulatory cure, in other words, was often no better than the disease. Sometimes, as when low-priced imports actually had procompetitive effects, the cure was distinctly worse. Suppose, for instance, that the low-priced goods were widely sourced inputs that enabled producers in the receiving country to compete effectively with firms in the exporting country and elsewhere. Or suppose that inexpensive imports helped break down administered prices in key domestic industries.

At the core of the general dilemma about antidumping enforcement was that the U.S. International Trade Commission has had no mandate to take into account broad economic trade-offs when determining injury: jobs and earnings lost to low-priced imports are not weighed against the jobs and earnings those imports may generate (not to mention the savings to users and consumers). The commission was charged with deciding whether the profits and jobs in an "industry" (sometimes amounting to very few firms and employees) were affected, but the fate of other industries and workers using or distributing the imports in question would not be counted. The narrow calculus could mean that a petitioner's victory would make utilitarian fairness stand on its head: the greatest good going to the smallest number.

In sum, the post-1974 course of antidumping administration, not only in the United States but also in a growing number of countries tightening their regulations, raised troublesome questions. If antidumping regulation, in its current form, was altogether fair, then fair in what sense, and to whom? Did the social benefits of blocking below-cost imports exceed the burdens? Impairment of certain domestic industries vital to security interests could, over the long haul, create broad and serious dangers. But the preponderance of dumping cases did not involve strategic industries. In too many cases, the extent of injury caused to some Americans may not have outweighed the gain for other (often more numerous) Americans.

Equity presupposes that like cases are treated alike.[38] At a minimum, therefore, policymakers needed to explain—not just to take for granted—the conventional distinction between intraterritorial and extraterritorial price discrimination (where one was deemed undesirable only in rare instances, while the other was considered wrong even in the commonplace form of "sales below cost"). A fairer test for dumping allegations, conforming to modern interpretations of antitrust principles would make a reasonable attempt to differentiate between effects on the economy as a whole that were favorable or unfavorable to competition. This standard would direct attention toward secondary-line harm to intermediate producers and end users, not just primary-line damage to direct competitors.

Such a test was daunting. There was little reason to suppose that Congress would want to devise it or that any regulatory authority, no matter how well staffed and organized, could easily administer it. But in the absence of procedures for thinking through the systemic implications of dumping, the number of complainants bringing antidumping suits was capable of swelling regardless of whether the foreign price competition was really harmful.

Subsidies

If predatory price cutting is sustainable, it is only feasible for firms with deep pockets. Discriminatory pricing of commodities and financial cushions provided by government subsidies might thus be linked. The U.S. public sector is smaller than that of most other advanced economies, and it has bankrolled fewer native industries. But, agricultural trade aside, exactly how wide this disparity remained and, more important, what difference it made in international competitiveness were not simple matters.

Defining the Offense

Barring some breakthrough in identifying and measuring "subsidy," comparative estimates of subsidization, not to mention its net effects on competition, are complicated. How to distinguish between supposedly innocuous domestic support programs and illegal subsidies that buoy exports, for instance, is not obvious. As an extreme example, a country could even assist its exporters by subsidizing imports. Such may have been the case in the 1970s, when the U.S. petroleum price and allocation controls in effect subsidized imports of crude oil, providing a short-term benefit to petrochemical producers and some other industries using petroleum-based feedstocks. Practically any government action can be regarded as a subsidy for someone, and many such actions can affect exports. As one analyst has written, "Even a requirement that domestically manufactured flags be flown on government buildings provides assistance for flag makers. By giving a secure home market and promoting economies of scale, such a regulation may assist potential exporters." [39]

Definitional dilemmas thus make it difficult to compare subsidy levels in different countries. Discrepancies narrow or widen depending on which categories of governmental involvement are included. If defense funding of research and development and National Aeronautics and Space Administration projects are assumed not to have underwritten important commercial ventures, American developmental policy shrinks in comparison with the efforts of Great Britain, France, Germany, and Japan. But if, as is well known, such programs serendipitously helped create some vibrant export industries, from commercial aircraft and satellites to computers, the role of government in the United States looks less anemic.

For this reason, the debate about comparative governmental assistance has shifted from a focus on whether certain countries spend more on industrial promotion than others to whether some spend their money more cleverly. Presumably, while Japan's lean R&D subsidies select and hit specific targets, costly Pentagon programs or NASA projects, with other primary missions, achieve only accidental commercial spin-offs. But the truth is, no one really knows whether American aircraft or computers would now command stronger export potential if a hypothetical civilian economic planning bureau rather than the Department of Defense had been left to nurture such industries. Imaginably, the winners might not have been picked, or if picked, would have received less sustained support, absent the cloak of national security.

Disharmonic Convergence

Whatever the organizational issues of industrial policy, in the 1980s evidence did not point to a growing subsidies gap. The growth of industrial subsidies generally seemed to slow down in Europe and decline in Canada and Japan. [40] Foreign-tied aid programs, the practice of conditioning financing for overseas development on the purchase of products from the donor country, may have been costing U.S. exporters of capital goods as much as $2.4 to $4.8 billion in lost sales.[41] Because of the overall trend in net resource flows to developing countries, however, it was hard to tell whether this aspect of the export-subsidy problem was worsening. Through most of the 1980s, export credit flows declined, and official development assistance from major donors (adjusted for inflation and exchange rates) was not substantially greater in 1988 than it had been in 1980.[42]

Agriculture was still plagued by uncontrolled spending. With more farmers, the European Community subsidized farming more than the United States did, and the EC's programs distorted far more trade. In 1987, the EC's direct export subsidies were *ten times* higher than those of the United States.[43] But in terms of the estimated average producer subsidy equivalents (PSEs), which measure the percentage decrease in gross farm revenue that would occur if all of a nation's agricultural subsidies and border measures were removed, the picture was as follows. In 1979 the PSE of the United States had stood at the low end (11 percent), near the level of Australia (7 percent).[44] Europe's PSE was much higher (38 percent). By 1986 the EC had moved up to 41 percent, but owing in no small part to additional federal commitments, such as those authorized by the Food Security Act of 1985, the PSE of the United States had tripled, reaching 34 percent.[45]

Throughout the 1980s, the U.S. government took the lead in calling for an international halt to the ruinous contest among major producing nations to bloat their agricultural exports. The response to this initiative was ponderous. The EC at first refused to participate in any new multilateral discussions on the issue. Later, when the Uruguay Round was launched, the EC's proposals seemed conceptually cramped, defensive, and introspective in comparison with serious American efforts to address the underlying questions.[46] Even after the budget reconciliation of 1990 conditionally committed the United States to an estimated 25 percent cut in farm aid over the next five years, the Europeans proposed only a 15 percent reduction in expenditures by the year 2000. The EC's negotiators crept toward the U.S. position in certain areas (for example, on restructuring of variable levies), but continued to insist on rebalancing duty reductions in some commodities with increases in others.

Despite the glacial pace of the agricultural trade talks, however, time seemed to be on the American side. Each year, the scope of European farm spending was becoming more unsustainable. Indeed, with the recent appreciation of the European Currency Unit against the dollar, Europe's PSE rose again, from 41 percent in 1989 to 48 percent in 1990, while the U.S. PSE settled at 30 percent.[47] By early 1991, when the EC was confronted with a record increase of nearly $11 billion in projected costs of the CAP over the next ten months (plus an obvious need to offer Eastern Europe better market opportunities in agriculture), there were renewed hopes that the European delegation would move toward a binding schedule of deeper reductions in internal and external subsidies.[48]

Buying Competitive Advantage

Subsidized firms may be more likely to export their products at discounted prices. Why a nation on the receiving end of such bargains should want to fence them out may seem puzzling; the providers are offering, in Milton Friedman's phrase, "reverse foreign aid." In the real world, however, governments cannot afford to be oblivious to foreign subsidies. When producers abroad receive special assistance, domestic industries have a stronger claim on similar subsidization (otherwise the favored foreigners can move with impunity to undercut their competitors). One nation's pork barrel is likely to be matched, to a disturbing degree, everywhere else. Just as theft may be abetted by accepting contraband, raids on the public fisc may spread by permitting importation of subsidized goods.

But evidence has been mixed on the extent to which subsidies conferred increasingly ominous advantages in pricing and market power. Agricultural trade clearly presented a problem. So has some foreign targeting in high-technology sectors such as aeronautics, telecommunications, and electronics that has helped some manufacturers gain competitive strength. Twenty-one years of subsidized loans to Europe's aircraft manufacturing consortium, for example, finally helped move Airbus Industrie into second place, where it holds 30 percent of the global aviation market. McDonnell Douglas, and even Boeing, could not be expected to compete indefinitely against a government-propped combine that had operated unprofitably for nearly two decades but still managed to corner much of the market with promotional sales.

In general, though, more public financing seemed to be squandered on antiquated, high-cost industries that had the greatest difficulty earning normal rates of return.[49] Grants or equity infusions for the French, Belgian, and Italian steel producers, for instance, did not result in major expansions of capacity or in highly competitive export prices in the 1980s. Instead, they frequently sustained inefficient management, uncompetitively high wages, and mounting debt payments.[50] Often heavily subsidized industries were associated with prices higher than competitive levels. High ticket prices on European airlines were an obvious illustration.

The theory that the comparative commercial capacity of nations rested on the lavishness of their industrial aid programs was unsubstantiated. Take France, a notorious practitioner of industrial promotionalism. Not long ago, a reputable study of French export targeting found that, for the most part, "export-credit subsidization wastes France's scarce public resources in the promotion of the wrong industries exporting the wrong products to the wrong markets." In Germany, according to research at the Kiel Institute of World Economics, "subsidization policy mostly redistributes money from structurally strong sectors to weak ones."[51] The Japanese lesson was more complicated, but even in this instance, there was no proof that industrial policy remained the engine of Japan's commercial success.

Japan, Inc.

Japan has been described as a developmental state, a system of state-led capitalism, a structure of guided free enterprise, and, most recently, an enigma.[52] It is not always clear from these descriptions whether one ought to conclude that central administrative organs have been the primary orchestrators of Japan's economic growth, or whether, as Karel van Wolferen has suggested, the Japanese system is more like a headless horseman: "a complex of overlapping hierarchies [that] has no top."[53] Nor is it clear whether the telling thrust of Japanese economic planning has come primarily at the macro level (reducing the cost of capital, for example, by fostering a high rate of national savings), or at the micro level (by steering investment toward specific sectors and firms).

A scholarly feud has raged over how much the virtuosity of government has generated outcomes at variance with those that ordinary economic forces might have produced.[54] On one side, studies of several successful industries— including automobiles, steel, machine tools, computers, and semiconductors—have concluded that the government's contribution was critical or decisive.[55] On the other side, a growing body of research, some of it on the same industries, has reached a different conclusion.[56] "In the machine tool case . . . ," David Friedman discovered, "the state exhibited neither the ability to plan effectively or independently nor the capacity to force private interests into compliance." Even in robotics, the machinery industry's leading edge, Michael E. Porter found that the Japanese government played only "a modest role." In his analysis of the energy sector, Richard J. Samuels observed that the pervasive developmental state actually "does not lead, guide, or supervise private interests." And in the automobile and electronics industries, observers have cited well-known examples of bureaucratic misjudgments, some so basic that key firms such as Honda and Sony may have prospered in spite of industrial policy, not because of it.[57]

How the score card for industrial promotion in Japan compares with that of the United States has not been easy to figure out. Japanese efforts to create world-class industries in aluminum, chemicals, pharmaceuticals, and commercial aircraft have been rated failures in comparison with their U.S. counterparts, several of which have received varying degrees of government support.[58] Japan has increasingly targeted areas in which the United States has held the highest levels of technological capability. This trajectory of Japanese industrial strategy, away from the technological low end (textile mills and rice paddies) and toward the high end (computers and biotechnology), frightened many American industrialists. Yet the record of Japan's high-tech megaprojects has by no means been an uninterrupted series of miracles.

In its quest for excellence in computer technology, MITI's Very Large-Scale Integrated Circuit Program was a success. It helped give electronics companies the basic skills they needed to enter and, within a decade, to dominate the memory chip business. On the other hand, the so-called Fifth Generation project, initiated at the beginning of the 1980s to develop computers with artificial intelligence, fell far short of its original goals. Likewise, the Superspeed enterprise, an attempt to develop the hardware and software for parallel processing machines that use many processors at once, accomplished little in Japan that companies in the United States have not been able to achieve by themselves.[59] In the much-publicized race to develop high-definition television, the jury was still out on whether Japan, which began research on high-definition television twenty years ago, chose the optimal technology or has locked itself into a nondigital system that is less than state of the art.[60]

By the late 1980s, two facts about Japanese industrial policy were being widely recognized by scholars. One was that, with the economy well beyond the catch-up stage, Japan's vaunted economic bureaucracy still played a significant coordinating role but exerted less control and managed less systematic planning than it had earlier in the postwar period.[61] Not the least of the reasons for this change was that Japan had become a technological leader, no longer a mere follower, in a number of fields. Inevitably, it was easier for planners to borrow winning technologies invented elsewhere than to pioneer in them.[62]

The other fact was that market closure, not subsidies in the normal sense, was a distinctive feature of Japanese industrial strategy.[63] The home market would be reserved not just for traditional domestic products (like rice), but for nascent modern industries. Particularly irksome was a pattern of exclusion in key advanced technologies, such as satellites and supercomputers, that were protected by discriminatory procurement.

Yet the overall trend of officially organized protection in Japan since the 1970s has been downward, and less of the country's remaining resistance to imports can be attributed to deliberate trade or industrial policies.[64] This transition has had significant implications. If the competitive advantage of Japan's industrial powerhouses derived from a protected home market, much of it seemed to reflect the residual effects of earlier formal restrictions coupled with continuing informal constraints such as the *keiretsu* system, which made it difficult for newcomers, foreign and domestic, to compete successfully on price.[65] Outsiders continued to face barriers when trying to burrow into the Japanese marketplace, but the reasons for the obstacles were more deep seated and complex than a bureaucratic plot to bar imports.

Consequently, the case against "Japan, Inc.," which began as a complaint against official protectionism, increasingly came to resemble a complaint about de facto trade distortions that often had less to do with the intrusions of government than with the *lack* of suitable policies (antitrust enforcement, for instance). In some instances, the argument also seemed tantamount to an affirmative action suit, aimed at compensating victims for the de jure discrimination they had suffered in the past at the hands of the Japanese bureaucracy and from which Japanese businesses presumably continued to benefit.[66]

Grievances of this sort could be sources of considerable friction and frustration. It was arduous enough to do battle year after year with discriminatory practices that were rooted in deliberate and identifiable commercial policies. But how readily could "structural" biases (that were distortionary but not always discriminatory) be eradicated? And how easily, and nonarbitrarily, could past wrongs be righted?[67] As trade negotiators moved on to an increasingly ambitious agenda, expectations rose—and so could mistrust and irritation when the negotiations failed to produce quick results.

The Japan Conundrum

If the global contest in merchandise trade was not increasingly unfair in the 1980s, it was still being played on a field that was not smooth. Trading on Japan's economic terrain was especially wearing.

Asymmetrical Access

The Japanese trading pattern remained unusual—and not just because of the large surpluses associated with it. At times Germany's trade surplus, for instance, was larger than Japan's, yet German commercial practices drew far less fire. One reason was that Japan's level of intraindustry specialization appeared to be unusually low, so imports of manufactured goods have remained lower than might be expected (in 1989 they were still only 3.4 percent of total domestic output, compared with 16.6 percent in Germany).[68] Some of this difference could be passed off as the result of geography. Japan is poor in resources and more isolated geographically than other industrial countries; it imports raw materials and processes them into higher value-added exports, minimizing two-way trade in manufactured products.[69] Controlling for these determinants is difficult, and even sophisticated analyses leave questions about what ratios of imported manufactures and of intraindustry trade are theoretically appropriate for a processing economy like that of Japan, which, unlike Germany's, is not inside a customs union. Nevertheless, there was little doubt that the Japanese market remained comparatively impenetrable to foreigners.

Japan remained comparatively closed not only to manufactured imports but also to new direct investment.[70] American companies might have been less angered by Japan's large trade surpluses if more of the companies had benefited by establishing subsidiaries in Japan. U.S. multinationals in Germany, for example, profited handsomely during the 1989–90 boom in German and European sales and exports. While foreign investment accounted for 17 percent of German assets, foreign companies held only about 1 percent of Japan's national assets.

Such limited external penetration and control did not befit a modern economy as large as Japan's. This condition created some unacceptable difficulties for competitors. The burden could be especially serious for high-tech businesses, in which economies of scale, learning-by-doing, and technological externalities are maximized by selling voluminously in global markets. A condition in which the U.S. market remained disproportionately more accessible than the Japanese market could deprive American firms of the returns on investments that Japanese firms obtained.

The trouble was that the sources of this disproportion had become harder, not easier, to come to grips with. At one time it was possible to draw up very long lists of technical measures administered by Japanese government agencies expressly intended to thwart foreign competition. At first the counts included onerous duties, quantitative restraints, and direct controls on foreign investment and capital. As more of these roadblocks were cleared, attention turned to less visible hindrances: licensing procedures, product standards, testing and certification requirements, patent delays, and public procurement. Bureaucratic barriers of this sort remained. But even as they became more flexible, another sobering realization sank in: the modifications produced few big breakthroughs, and somehow even the breakthroughs seldom fulfilled hopes. The process of trade liberalization in Japan, it seemed, was like peeling an onion, where the core of the onion was not quickly reached as layers were removed.

Hence, by the end of the 1980s, the level of analysis had shifted again.[71] Amid signs that some Japanese ministries were urging businesses to accept more imports (even offering multibillion dollar incentives for that purpose),[72] the problems of perverse administrative guidance and red tape began to seem less central than did the underlying, systemic impediments to a more open economy. Public expenditures, land use policies, retailing patterns, and *keiretsu* relationships, among other fundamentals, came under inspection.

Plus Ça Change . . . ?

While the critique of Japanese economic comportment continued to widen and deepen, however, trade flows did not remain static. The changes were not trivial.

Since the mid-1970s, Japan had largely eliminated official restrictions on direct foreign investment, partially deregulated financial institutions, and privatized Nippon Telephone and Telegraph. It had relaxed its import regimes for medical instruments, pharmaceuticals, computer software, telecommunications equipment, forest products, tobacco, beef, and other agricultural products. In 1985 the yen began to appreciate sharply against the U.S. dollar, a process that affected the import-export balance. More recently, the government promised to curb the rigging of construction contracts (the *dango* system) and to permit more open bids on some public works projects.[73] Agreements were eventually reached to improve the sales of U.S.-made supercomputers, satellites, wood products, and semiconductors.

A number of these accommodations yielded returns. The pace of American direct investment accelerated toward the end of the 1980s (albeit less than the rate of Japanese investment in the United States).[74] Exports to Japan more than doubled from 1985 to 1990, with sales of manufactured goods rising 160 percent. Although a considerable part of the increase reflected affiliates of Japanese multinationals shipping products back to their parent companies, the share of this intrafirm trade was declining.[75] Gradually the bilateral trade deficit shrank from a record $56 billion in 1987 to $41 billion in 1990.[76] Critics dismissed the 27 percent drop over four years as too little too late or as masking a still improper composition of imports and exports. Nonetheless, reversing the direction of the trade statistics was an accomplishment, given the magnitude of the initial imbalance. In 1987, for example, U.S. exports to Japan were one-third the size of U.S. imports from that country; thus our exports would have had to grow three times as fast as our imports just for the balance to remain unchanged. Helping to narrow the bilateral gap was the fact that the dollar value of U.S. exports to Japan not only rose rapidly, but rose more rapidly than U.S. exports in general, while U.S. imports from Japan grew less quickly than U.S. imports in general.[77] The bottom line was that Japan accounted for a growing share of American exports of manufactures and a declining share of America's imports of manufactures.

Nor were most of these gains extracted by saber rattling. The much-maligned market-oriented sector-selective (MOSS) negotiations of 1985–87, which carried no mandatory threats of retaliation, actually generated a combined 47 percent increase in exports to Japan for the sectors involved (telecommunications, medical equipment, pharmaceuticals, electronics, and timber products), well above the increase in total U.S. exports to Japan over the same period.[78] The tenacity of American negotiators was a factor in these talks. Judicious pressure helped spur progress in several disputed areas, partly because it could provide embattled Japanese pragmatists with a pretext to force adjustments that they would not have been able to try on their own. Yet the most consequential Japanese trade adjustment of the 1980s, *endaka* (yen appreciation), was an act of cooperation with the finance ministers of the world's largest economies more than a surrender in a bilateral confrontation.

Near the end of her first year of bilateral discussions, U.S. Trade Representative Carla A. Hills told Congress that Japan had "moved further this year than perhaps any other country" in meeting American demands.[79] Skepticism appeared to be the main reaction among lawmakers. Some reflexively pointed to past agreements with the Japanese that "haven't worked." Others adopted a wait-and-see attitude. Still others felt that any forward motion would stop, or go into reverse, if Japan were not again chastised as a leading unfair trader. Hardly two months had elapsed before congressional oversight committees expressed renewed dissatisfaction.[80] These sentiments were not just a feint, intended to keep the heat on negotiations that were progressing with the usual fits and starts; they reflected continuing displeasure that the desired degree of commercial parity had remained maddeningly elusive.

New Issues

An increasingly vigilant U.S. trade policy concentrated on more than foreign predatory dumping, barriers against merchandise exports, and distortions wrought by government-sponsored industrial projects; it sought to solve additional problems. The GATT umbrella did not cover trade in services, nor did it offer adequate safeguards for intellectual property. Furthermore, the process of appealing to the GATT to settle disputes needed improvement. In part, the importance of directing international attention to these matters justified a more assertive American trade stance, even a willingness to act unilaterally.

Mondo Cane

One-fifth of global commerce was in services, an area in which U.S. industries have been highly competitive. Obtaining more room for these industries to maneuver in world markets inevitably became a priority. Service trade introduced legal issues different from those associated with tradable goods. For example, because local production is often required, questions of investment and right of establishment are involved. GATT principles of national treatment and nondiscrimination held only that an imported product should receive the same treatment as a domestic product once it entered the importing country. International rules did not extend to foreign providers selling services inside another country's boundaries. For the United States, the world's largest exporter of services, this omission would be increasingly problematic.

Patent and trademark infringements also became a growing concern. Continuing creativity in advanced technologies required adequate reward for innovation. Firms would lose their incentive to innovate if the payoff was too easily pirated. Foreign counterfeiters might steal a march on the competition by simply being able to devote less capital to develop new products, copying proven successes but rarely absorbing the costs of failures. A number of governments even used their national intelligence services to purloin industrial secrets.[81] In the mid-1980s, inadequate international protection of intellectual property was costing American companies an estimated $20 billion in sales a year.[82] The stakes could only mount as other countries moved into a better position to capitalize on U.S. research investments.

These shortcomings of the multilateral institutions could no longer be over-looked, nor could the often protracted and cumbersome procedures for mediating disputes through the GATT, even in areas in which it had clear jurisdiction. GATT panels sometimes handed down their verdicts much too slowly, and the defendants could then block the decision. In one ludicrous example, a U.S. complaint about European pasta subsidies languished for twelve years. When the case was finally "resolved," the EC refused to accept the adverse panel report.

The United States had long sought correctives through a multilateral forum. Progress came grudgingly. At a 1982 GATT ministerial meeting, an American proposal to negotiate an extension of GATT legal disciplines to include services and intellectual property was only recommended for further study by "countries that were so inclined."[83] Not until 1986 did the international body agree to place the new issues on the agenda for the Uruguay Round. In the meantime, partly to stimulate these negotiations and partly out of sheer frustration, U.S. complainants and policymakers began deploying the national trade laws more aggressively. Section 337 cases (defending patents, trademarks, and copyrights) multiplied, and so did actions with another increasingly powerful weapon, the unilateral investigations and sanctions of section 301.

The Problems in Perspective

Some of this impatience was misplaced, however. Service industries are often government-owned or intensely regulated. Inevitably, harmonizing national regulatory systems to equalize ease of entry cannot be accomplished overnight. The case of telecommunications illustrated the difficulty. So much conflict centered on telecommunications trade that a separate provision of the 1988 Trade Act required the government to inspect the telecommunications policies of foreign countries and determine which were most offensive. If bilateral treaties failed to modify the offending policies, the law authorized retaliation by executive order.

The divestiture of American Telephone & Telegraph transformed a regulated public utility, making telecommunications in the United States a more openly competitive industry. This independent decision inevitably conferred some nonreciprocal benefits on foreign firms, particularly because the procurement practices of publicly owned enterprises (or of publicly regulated monopolies) tend to be less open than those of competitive private firms.[84] In one stroke, telecommunication services in the rest of the world were rendered "more protectionist." Was the more open American regime now entitled to call for compensatory liberalization everywhere else for an inequality that had been substantially self-imposed? The answer could be yes, but the legislation Congress wrote also seemed to say, "and on our watch, or else!"

Securing intellectual property rights also raised sensitive issues. Devising an enforceable multilateral code that afforded sufficient security for intellectual property to avoid underinvestment in R&D but did not stifle an efficient diffusion of innovations would take time. The American economy might benefit from ensuring that more of the technological rents from inventions stayed at home longer, but it could also benefit through trade if foreign producers commercialized those inventions rapidly. Moreover, differences between developed and developing countries had to be carefully taken into account. It was clearly annoying for American subsidiaries in Japan, for example, to wait, as they did, an average of three times longer for a patent to be issued than Japanese subsidiaries in the United States had to wait.[85] But was global well-being enhanced if, for example, protection of trade secrets for pharmaceuticals inflated the cost of medicine in the third world?

A certain amount of civil disobedience using techniques such as section 301 might nudge the international trading system toward new and better protocols.[86] Parts of the trade laws were designed to pick up where the GATT left off, covering agricultural and service trade and intellectual property violations. Indeed, the preponderance of section 301 cases dealt with disputes in these categories; others merely supplemented formal GATT proceedings. Contrary to a common perception, however, international trade had not degenerated into a dog-eat-dog environment in which the GATT's dog-catching apparatus had largely broken down. American companies were making impressive inroads in sectors in which the GATT was deficient. They exported over $100 billion of services in 1989, for instance.[87] The majority of the world's trade conflicts that had come to the GATT, for all its faults, either were settled or were dropped by the complaining country.[88] A number of cases dragged on when the parties to them refused to comply expeditiously with rulings, but the U.S. Congress also failed sometimes to abide by the timetables it expected of others.[89]

48 *Regulating Unfair Trade*

Conclusion

For nearly two decades politicians had decried the way "the rest of the world hides behind variable levies, export subsidies, import equalization fees, border taxes, cartels, government procurement practices, dumping, import quotas, and a host of other practices which effectively bar our products."[90] By the middle of the 1980s, this litany had reached a stentorian pitch—and the decibel level stayed high even when many of the world's disharmonious trading practices were objectively grating less (or at least not more) than before. Despite some increase in nontariff barriers among major industrialized nations, global merchandise trade burgeoned, expanding at more than 6 percent annually after 1982 and surpassing $3 trillion a year at the close of the decade. In this environment, U.S. industry performed well as the exchange value of the dollar improved. In 1988 and 1989, export shipments of goods such as aircraft, electrical machinery, small manufactured goods, computers, and office equipment soared, accounting for almost a third of the increase in real gross national product.[91] This performance did not comport with the suspicion that American manufacturers were increasingly throttled in international competition. Yet the level of anxiety remained high, and although the volume of trade actions abated after 1986, it never faded back to its pre-1980 level.

Inequities or imbalances continued to mar foreign trade. Yet the most frequently cited injustice, dumping, reflected redefinitions of "unfair" pricing rather than a higher incidence of predation and price-gouging. Complaints about commercial subsidies were often problematic, too. Some foreign subsidies were clearly destabilizing. Europe's Common Agricultural Policy fit that description, and so did the tireless efforts of governments to create or nourish certain sensitive industries that seemed incapable of turning a profit on their own. Hothouse programs such as the European Airbus or Japan's protection of supercomputers and satellites, which threatened important U.S. export industries, could not be left unchallenged. By and large, however, levels of subsidization among the most important trading nations did not appear to be pulling apart during the 1980s. For every sly subsidizer who might be sharpening a comparative advantage, there were more who chiefly wasted their money or who may have boosted our living standards by lowering the costs of the goods we imported.

If laments about unequal trade remained very much in the air even as export industries and the national economy prospered, maybe the complaints were having their intended effects. Perhaps, in other words, the additional grievance procedures mandated by recent trade laws had finally persuaded other countries of the need for concerted negotiations to arrest protectionism, thus opening up major business opportunities. American pressure did lessen resistance to imports and investment in Japan and some other trouble spots, and it may yet help to bring another multilateral trade round to a reasonably auspicious conclusion. But to contend that recent trade policy, struggling to level the world's commercial playing field, has been largely responsible for the remarkable growth of commerce during the past decade is no more plausible than to argue that the condition of the field had generally deteriorated. The U.S. export boom began long before the end of the Uruguay Round. The overall effect of sectoral market-opening actions was small in comparison with the effect of currency realignments, improvements in U.S. manufacturing productivity, and other macroeconomic forces. Although the specter of additional import regulations may have driven some of our trade adversaries to the negotiating table, another consequence was the proliferation of similar regulations elsewhere. Whether the world trading system would remain better off after more countries adopted punitive antidumping rules, for example, was far from certain.

These and other measures against unfair trade did not just sway with changing economic conditions, or only fill gaps in the GATT; to some extent they moved with a political rhythm of their own.

The Politics of Remediation

AMERICAN FIRMS AND WORKERS over the past decade faced greater foreign competition combined with tighter government fiscal limitations, including cutbacks in adjustment assistance.[1] Predictably, calls for help were answered in the form of protective or promotional trade interventions. But why were more and more of these actions based, in one manner or another, on claims of unfairness? That certain domestic industries were in trouble was clear (particularly in the early 1980s); that an increasingly lawless trading system caused most of their troubles was not clear at all. Whatever else induced a growing emphasis on rectifying economic wrongs, the following considerations seemed to contribute.

While trade policy was being summoned to support commercial interests as other governmental resources drew taut, a focus on correcting or offsetting unfair business practices could enter the breach with a serviceable justification: as long as the U.S. economy generally remained more open than others, restitutions appealed to an intuitive sense of justice—and smacked less of special pleading or "protectionism." With fairness dominating the terms of debate, the trade issue had elements in common with other policy dialogues in American politics and facilitated the building of coalitions. Further, the pursuit of fair trade appeared to gain momentum from its complications and frustrations as well as from its rewards.

Trade Policy to the Rescue

In the absence of a significant change in national rates of saving and investment, the many microeconomic measures taken to correct trade problems during the 1980s did not restore balance between imports and exports or noticeably raise American living standards. But if the correctives had not mattered at all, petitioners would not have requested them, and policymakers would not have labored to deliver them. Parts of the trade laws (section 301, for instance) were used, with some success, to reinforce broad American objectives in multilateral negotiations. Others served somewhat narrower tactical purposes, such as the need to keep some beleaguered industries from protesting concessions that would have to be made during those negotiations. Not least, the trade remedies could simply confer specific benefits.

Dividends

For their immediate beneficiaries, restraints on unfair imports sometimes amounted to significant off-budget subsidies. (Quotas on imported carbon steel were the equivalent of a $113,600 transfer per job saved.)[2] What of the remedies for exporters? Aid through import restrictions was by definition more narrowly gauged and calculable than the individual gains from efforts to penetrate overseas markets. All comers could profit from freer access to those markets. As a practical matter, though, bilateral negotiations on market access, like import remedies, tended to be selective. Negotiators were expected to defend the interests of, or seek targets of opportunity for, specific industries with export potential. If these industries were politically sensitive, there was added incentive to go to the mat.

Why, for instance, did a squabble over feed-grain sales to Europe turn serious in 1986? When Spain and Portugal joined the European Community (EC), they raised their tariffs on imports from non-European suppliers, giving an advantage to suppliers from the south of France. The United States threatened an extensive retaliation to prevent this substitution. The dispute was viewed in Europe as one of the most acrimonious in decades. When the EC partially relented, protests broke out in the streets of Paris.[3] If mainly the exports of third countries (rather than nearly $1 billion in U.S. sales) had been riding on the outcome, it might have been quixotic to press the case so vigorously. But a significant principle was involved: the right of injured parties to receive compensation from trade-restrictive effects of EC enlargements. The injured parties, moreover, happened to be corn growers in states like Iowa and Indiana, and the context was a volatile election year in the farm belt.[4]

Congress directed the U.S. Trade Representative (USTR) to brandish the threat of retaliation against countries accused of placing unjustifiable burdens on U.S. commerce. The idea, however, was to liberalize markets on the basis of most-favored-nation (MFN) trading status, not to guarantee a sales base for particular vendors. Proceeding on MFN principles (as most section 301 cases did) had the distinct advantage of interesting other potential entrants who might ally themselves with the U.S. position. When Japan began to loosen its quotas on beef imports, consignments from the United States increased, but so did shipments from Australia. A liberalization instigated at the behest of U.S. cattlemen soon found McDonald's of Japan frying Australian hamburgers. Odd as this sort of result might seem, it was almost always more acceptable than a bilateral deal without side benefits for others. Disputes over market entry gained legitimacy when they amounted to more than the mere propitiation of powerful lobbies.

At the same time, complainants who took pains to litigate closed markets naturally did so in the hope of hearing the ring of their own corporate cash registers, not just to enrich third-country competitors. Target countries occasionally seemed to respond to this expectation by extending special privileges.

At the end of a clash with South Korea on behalf of the insurance industry, the Koreans did not "open" their insurance cartel; they simply granted licenses to a couple of aggrieved companies.[5] Sometimes the mere rumble of congressional wrath about trade imbalances seemed to induce preferential adjustments. Nervous about its bilateral surplus with the United States in 1987, Seoul began switching agricultural imports away from various other suppliers.[6]

In short, complaints about unequal trade could assist firms that were competing against imports and firms that were oriented toward exports. When the benefits were generalized (as in most market-access negotiations), the complaints often appealed to some attentive publics abroad as well as at home. When the spoils were particularistic (as in cases of import regulation and some market-access outcomes), the recipients could still claim they were being compensated for handicaps, rather than receiving special favors.

More with Less

Reliance on trade dispensations seemed to increase in the 1980s as other sources of assistance were pinched by budgetary constraints and, in some cases, by less regulatory protection in the domestic economy.[7] The sugar program adopted at the end of 1981 exemplified the type of affordable subsidy devised by legislators. To help domestic sugar growers, Congress required the secretary of agriculture to support the price of sugar through the purchase of surpluses whenever the price fell below a specified level.[8] "To avoid the adverse budgetary consequences" of such purchases, however, the Senate Agriculture Committee's report accompanying the legislation urged the president "to make timely use" of his authority under section 22 of the Agricultural Act of 1933 to impose import fees on foreign farm products.[9] Timely use of section 22 followed within weeks. As international sugar prices sagged, the Reagan administration ordered higher duties and later reinstated binding country-specific quotas that had not been in effect since 1974.

Plans to boost exports also offered opportunities for creative financing. A variety of mechanisms relying on minimal appropriations had long been available to underwrite exports. The Export-Import Bank (EXIM) provided loan supports, guarantees, and insurance coverage to exporters and foreign buyers. A lesser known agency, the Overseas Private Investment Corporation (OPIC), bolstered foreign procurement of American goods by extending many of the same services to U.S. investors overseas. In addition, the Department of Agriculture (USDA), through the Commodity Credit Corporation (CCC) and Title I of the 1954 Agricultural Trade Development Act, operated major concessional sales and financing programs.

These instruments were not scaled back, despite attempts by the Office of Management and Budget to curtail EXIM in 1981. On the contrary, most found a greater raison d'être, and several expanded. The USDA acquired additional mandates, including a $2.5 billion Export Enhancement program and some new commodity-specific projects (for sunflower seed oil and cottonseed oil, for example). To counteract countries like France and Japan, whose volumes of export credits surpassed those of the United States in the early 1980s, the Trade and Development Enhancement Act of 1983 authorized the Export-Import Bank and the Agency for International Development (AID) to begin arranging tied-aid credit packages. Three years later, these efforts would be supplemented by an EXIM "war chest." The purpose, again, was to support defensive transactions that might convince other practitioners of tied aid to curb their activities. Although some progress along these lines was made within the Organization for Economic Cooperation and Development (OECD) in 1987, it was not enough to justify closing the war chest. In 1990, its resources, blended with grants from AID, were redeployed in an attempt to recapture spoiled markets in Indonesia, Pakistan, the Philippines, and Thailand.

A common assessment of initiatives like these was that they were "basically peanuts" in comparison with the lavish mixed credit operations of major international rivals.[10] In terms of budgetary outlays, this was largely true. (Japan's expenditures on Indonesia, Pakistan, the Philippines, and Thailand were projected to be four times the U.S. total.) But the beauty of key export subsidies was that they were indirect (in the form of loan guarantees, for example). Some were big and getting bigger. In the 1985 farm bill, for instance, Congress found two complementary reasons to authorize an additional $5.5 billion annually in CCC guarantees through fiscal 1990: a need to move the EC into international talks on agricultural subsidies and a desire to relieve farm indebtedness through greater export earnings.[11]

Some modest programs, moreover, apparently succeeded in making limited dollars go a long way. The Trade and Development Program, a small organ created in 1980 to fund planning studies in potential export markets, was able to claim an estimated $2.8 billion in U.S. exports from only $113 million obligated through fiscal 1988.[12] The OPIC, whose direct loans, guarantees, and insured projects increased appreciably between 1986 and 1989, had managed to spin off an estimated $20.8 billion in direct procurement and follow-on exports during the 1980s.[13] For individual recipients these activities were sometimes very helpful. A $6.5 million OPIC loan to support the expansion of machinery distributorships in Egypt generated some $20 million in orders for U.S.-made equipment. Two relatively small grants, totaling $1.25 million from the Trade and Development Program, helped U.S. companies win $200 million in contracts to build a coal-fired power plant in China.[14]

In short, interest groups and policymakers increasingly leaned on compensatory trade measures to lend a helping hand. The measures were relatively easy to justify: they busted no budgets, and they claimed to even the playing field.

Limiting Liability

Alongside these advantages was another: less risk. Trade policy often entailed costs as well as benefits. Sometimes the downside was minimal or nonexistent, as when an external market was truly opened (without having to resort to sanctions). At other times, as with some minor import duties, the burdens might be so light and widely dispersed as to go virtually unnoticed by voters or other salient audiences. But commercial history also abounded with trade decisions that went seriously awry. The Smoot-Hawley Tariff Act of 1930 was one such disaster, and although Congress had some sixty years to live it down, the lesson was not easy to forget: more than twenty-five nations had dropped their purchases of U.S. exports by two-thirds, thereby deepening the Great Depression. Today, with some $590 billion worth of foreign sales on the line, even limited retaliations would inflict pain, or at least agitate much opposition.

Notes of Caution

No recent blunders on the grand scale of Smoot-Hawley had occurred, but lesser mishaps were vexing. In 1973 the Nixon administration embargoed exports of soybeans. Countries such as Japan, which depended almost entirely on imports of American soybeans, soon questioned the reliability of their main supplier and proceeded to diversify their sources. Other producers, like Brazil, were thus handed an opportunity to expand. It took years for U.S. soybean sellers to recover their lost markets.

In the spring of 1986, the Reagan administration underestimated the Canadian reaction to a 35 percent increase in American duties on imports of cedar shakes and shingles. Canada counterpunched by restoring high tariffs on a range of products, including books, periodicals, semiconductors, and computer parts. The producers of these goods soon complained to Congress. Prominent congressional trade guardians began speaking about the need for caution. "Obviously, we don't want a trade war with Canada," allowed Senator Max S. Baucus, Democrat of Montana, and a watchful monitor of import competition from Canada.[15] Counterretaliation was ill-advised, he added, urging the administration "to let the dust settle and think through what the best next step should be." Trade actions ran risks. Few officeholders wished to be Pyrrhic warriors, held responsible for a loss of exports, inflated prices on critical inputs, or other economic and political embarrassments.

Major multinational corporations with extensive intrafirm trade flows counseled prudence. They had become particularly wary of higher trade barriers at home that could disrupt global production strategies, raise input costs, and possibly bring retribution against exposed fixed assets abroad.[16] Increasingly, these powerful corporations would join export-dependent domestic manufacturers and agricultural producers who had long been sensitive to trade reprisals. Even in trade with Japan, where import penetration and foreign investment were so low in some sectors that few American hostages could be taken, unbridled commercial strife would pose hazards.[17] The United States was stuck with an overhang of debt, now totaling about $4 trillion. No nation dependent on foreign capital inflows to help meet borrowing needs of that magnitude could afford to give financial markets, or its creditors, large jolts.[18]

A delicate task for legislators and presidents was to relieve hard-pressed constituents without reverting to heavy-handed protectionism.

Electoral Vicissitudes

Contrary to what might be thought, electoral politics often confirmed this imperative. Candidates usually had nothing to lose from appealing to economic nationalism—unless those appeals began to sound reckless. Presidential campaign trails of the 1980s seemed littered with the wrecks of candidacies that crossed the boundary. On the eve of the 1980 primary in South Carolina, John B. Connally, a presidential aspirant and former secretary of the treasury, railed, "It's time we said to Japan: 'If we can't come into your markets with equal openness and fairness as you come into ours, you had better be prepared to sit on the docks of Yokohama in your little Datsuns . . . while you stare at your own little TV sets because we've had all we're going to take.'"[19] Connally was promptly trounced by Ronald Reagan, there and elsewhere, and ended up at the Republican convention with one delegate.

In subsequent years, the militant oratory, playing on supposed fears of American decline and unhappiness with rising imports, became repetitious. So did its futility. Walter Mondale's attempt to strike the familiar chord ("If you try to sell an American car in Japan, you better have the United States Army with you when they land on the docks") proved ineffectual.[20] In 1988, following record-breaking trade deficits, the trade hardliners in both parties— Richard Gephardt, Robert Dole, and Pat Robertson—were routed in the early primaries.[21] The situation was essentially the same four years later. Even a stubborn recession did not enhance the messages of two Democratic presidential hopefuls, Tom Harkin of Iowa and Robert Kerrey of Nebraska. Senator Harkin, who said he was "proud to be called a protectionist," was driven from the race by early March.[22] Senator Kerrey, who had looked to be a serious contestant at the start of the political season, fared no better. In New Hampshire Kerrey ran commercials showing him in an open hockey goal, promising to play "defense" against foreign traders. "The truth," Kerrey reflected later, "is the hockey spot drove my numbers down and not up."[23]

Meanwhile, on the Republican side, the insurgent candidacy of Patrick J. Buchanan ("America First") failed to win a single primary.

Congressional races were less inhibited, but there, too, the trade issue was no silver bullet. For every candidate who reportedly scored hits with it, another found it hard to exploit. In a 1991 special election, Democrat Harris Wofford, campaigning against a prospective free trade agreement with Mexico, retained his Senate seat from Pennsylvania. But a year earlier, in a telling example, former Senator John A. Durkin did not do as well in his bid for Gordon J. Humphrey's vacated seat from New Hampshire. Durkin, a Democrat, accused his Republican opponent, Robert Smith, of receiving campaign support from "a front for the Japanese auto industry" and reportedly referred to him by such names as "Bob Sushi Smith."[24] (The Smith campaign had received financial backing from the Auto Dealers and Drivers for Free Trade Political Action Committee.) Despite a sharp regional slump, and no mighty incumbent to unseat, the Democratic candidate's plea—"We need a senator from New Hampshire, not a senator from Yokohama or Tokyo"—failed to resonate. Bob "Sushi" Smith ran away with 65 percent of the vote.

In fact, few leading trade activists in Congress could be characterized as indiscriminate antagonists of liberal trade. The most zealous protectors of specific industries would fret that others might try to "piggyback."[25] In general, there seemed to be sufficient constituent cross-pressure to produce rather mixed records. Senator Donald Riegle of Michigan was probably Congress's most vocal proponent of trade relief for Detroit, but he would oppose, for example, restrictions on the use of imported cement for federal highways.[26] The late Senator John Heinz of Pennsylvania favored requiring the Department of Defense to buy American coal for shipment to U.S. bases in Europe, but he was also careful to draw the line at amendments of the trade laws that would scare away foreign investors by requiring full disclosure of their U.S. holdings.[27] House majority leader Richard Gephardt, who had campaigned strenuously for mandatory retaliation against countries with "excessive and unwarranted" trade surpluses, later defied organized labor by tolerating a controversial open trade initiative with Mexico. Ernest Hollings of South Carolina and Ed Jenkins of Georgia regularly sponsored legislation that would impose strict quotas on textiles and clothing, but they voted for open commerce with Canada.

The prudent way to dissent from free trade orthodoxy was not to wax xenophobic and trumpet protectionist proposals at every opportunity, but to promise soberly more shelter for the casualties of unjust competition.

Delegation

The desire of Congress to hedge its liabilities in trade policymaking also took the form of delegating authority. While the Constitution explicitly assigned to Congress the role of regulating commerce with other nations, lawmakers learned to regard this mandate as a mixed blessing: it conferred great power, but with the exercise of that power came responsibility—and blame for decisions that backfired.[28] Scores of incumbents were driven from office in the tumultuous elections of 1932. Among them were Senator Reed Smoot and

Representative Willis Hawley, the authors of the 1930 tariff. Starting with the Reciprocal Trade Agreements Act of 1934, the legislative branch began entrusting more of its constitutional prerogatives to the executive. Presidents gained new discretion to negotiate tariff revisions, to grant or deny escape clause relief, and, through cabinet appointees, to decide how vigorously to perform other administrative duties. Legislators retained some ability to aid constituents, but with less exposure to the temptation and the sting of protectionism.

Of course, as presidents held more sway over policy and could be credited for leadership in successful trade initiatives, they would bear a heavier political burden if their activities proved awkward. And because they now made more decisions, they attracted a large audience. Closely watched by distressed or dissatisfied groups and their backers in Congress, the administration in power would have to cope with more demands for assistance. Presidential policymaking came to be influenced, at least in part, by incentives familiar to congressmen: the desire to retain control but also to gain a measure of immunity. Like the legislature, the executive began tying more of its actions on trade to concepts of equity and reciprocity. Indeed, in a revealing speech toward the end of 1985, President Reagan described the evolution of his hands-on commercial agenda largely in terms of aid to the "victims of unfair trade."[29] Since "victims" existed, and unfair trade was not a phony issue, such a formulation could claim moral authority. But sometimes, even when questions of fairness were peripheral, they would be moved front and center. When the International Trade Commission (ITC) concluded in 1984 that the steel industry had been injured, but not primarily by unjustly priced imports, the administration nonetheless cited "massive unfair trade practices" to explain the comprehensive restraint agreements it set out to negotiate.[30]

How would the victims of unfairness be relieved and the perpetrators brought to justice? As later chapters of this book will show, the preferred modes were often indirect: rarified revisions of statutes, for example, and plea bargains (so to speak) negotiated at the administrative level under congressional prodding and presidential auspices.

Redress versus Relief

A different way to assist industries battered by imports would have been to speak less of unjust trade and rely unabashedly on the escape clause. This safeguard could protect some trade-afflicted producers, but without raising questions of whether the competition was right or wrong. Industries in need

could turn to a reasonably impartial arbiter—the ITC—that would only determine whether imports caused or threatened economic harm. Yet few parties
used the escape clause compared with actions against unfair trading, partly
because its political profile was higher.

It was not as though important or persistent petitioners who elected to make
use of section 201 always came away empty-handed. The received wisdom
has been that presidents routinely rejected major petitions, but the record is
less clear-cut. Sometimes the ITC would be overruled but then the USTR
would be instructed to negotiate informal voluntary restraint agreements for
the same commodities. President Reagan did just that for carbon steel in 1984.
Some important petitions during the past twenty years were resubmissions—
cases in which an industry was turned down the first time but later received a
favorable decision. For instance, though the nonrubber-footwear industry
failed to persuade Gerald Ford to endorse an affirmative ITC opinion in 1976,
it persuaded Jimmy Carter to reach restraint agreements with Korea and Taiwan a year later. The real success rate in section 201 determinations was
somewhat higher than if the basic caseload were measured as a series of dis-
crete actions involving different complainants.

Still, presidents had discretion in section 201 cases. When, as in an appeal
by copper producers in 1984, awarding protection would incur clear economic
penalties and political censure, the ITC's affirmative recommendations were
not necessarily final.[31] Technically, the White House did not have the last
word; Congress reserved the right to reverse presidential decisions. But the
legislative vetoes were never cast.[32] Doing so would mean resuming full responsibility for explicit acts of protection, something most congressmen, like
most presidents, would rather avoid.

A major reason for the meager application of section 201 seemed to be the
greater reliability, and lower visibility, of seeking relief through alternative
avenues, especially the antidumping law. This bias reflected internationally
accepted codes. Under article 19 of the GATT, safeguard protection was per-
missible only if an industry could show it had been "seriously" hurt by imports. Industries seeking antidumping rulings or countervailing duties had
only to prove "material" injury—meaning harm that is not "inconsequential."
The somewhat easier test, as well as the lack of presidential veto power in
these cases, inevitably encouraged greater use. In addition, Congress abetted
the shift from a system that simply weighed reprieves from trade pressures to
one that promised redress for inequities. Gradually, access to shelters from
unfair trade was facilitated through small but significant adjustments in the
legal mechanisms for processing complaints.

Terms of Debate

A policy that sought to redress the grievances of discontented groups rather than one that simply considered bailing them out accorded with basic axioms of American political discourse in a wide range of public issues. One of these axioms has been that pleas for help, whatever their merits, carry greater force when they invoke fairness.

Earlier in the century, most bids for trade restraints seemed to require few moralistic arguments; businesses did not have to say that they were underprivileged, disadvantaged, or oppressed to be eligible for high tariffs. Indeed, the tariff was extended to countless producers as a matter of course.[33] Subsequent trade regulations became more discriminating. Safe harbors would be available, but not guaranteed, for industries rocked by international competition. Not every business that wished to moor in these sanctuaries could do so, only those that demonstrated they had been mistreated. While this convention has kept the extent of restricted trade to a fraction of the 1930 level, it has also legitimated a considerable amount. Proof of mistreatment would not be hard to turn up in an ever-disorderly transnational economy in which, one way or another, trading partners still played by different rules. Those who demanded and those who supplied solutions to unfair trade were able to adduce sufficient grounds to regard their remedies as just deserts, not mere excuses for favoritism. Thus, perhaps even more than the clients and custodians of farm policy, who preferred price supports to handouts, trade lobbyists would gain greater respectability asking legislators to officiate trade for the sake of fair play than when importuning the government simply to dole out relief.

A Smaller "Bargaining Tariff"

Earlier in the postwar period, the task of trade negotiators consisted of reaching mutually agreed reductions in tariffs.[34] These reductions were comparatively simple and satisfying to discuss: each nation's duties were transparent and measurable, and it was relatively easy to figure out how to trade off one nation's concessions against another's. In these early negotiating rounds, in order to take, each party would also have to give in kind.

After the Kennedy Round, however, the possibilities for deep tariff cuts in the developed countries were rapidly being exhausted. As the focus shifted to nontariff issues, the questions of what the negotiable trade obstacles were and what would constitute mutually balanced steps to eliminate them became murkier. Some countries now came to the bargaining table with fewer entice-

ments. What could the United States offer, for example, in international negotiations over telecommunications services? Its own telecommunications
market was already less regulated than any other, and major service providers
had come to believe that it was now entirely up to the other side to make the
next move. The other side, in turn, had its own ideas as to what a commensur-
able set of concessions might be. The Europeans, for instance, expected the
U.S. government to force AT&T into open procurement in exchange for opening procurement of their state-owned monopolies.

As conceptions of equivalence in trade talks became more subjective and
the stock of palpable carrots diminished, the salience of foreign trade
transgressions that appeared to justify the use of sticks increased. Moreover,
American companies were not alone in encountering residual barriers in parts
of the trading system. On issues such as Europe's agricultural policy or high-
technology trade with Japan, an impulse to inveigh against unfairness, and
even to strike back unilaterally, could develop an international following.

Coalition Building

One could not simply say of the contemporary emphasis on commercial
equity and reciprocity what Gladstone had said of the British reciprocity
movement a century earlier—that it represented nothing more than "our old
friend Protection" in disguise.[35] Nonetheless, members of Congress who
needed to perform an old service, serving constituents, often found improved
opportunities to do so in the struggle against unfair trade.

Members who wanted to legislate constraints on imports that competed
with industries in their districts faced an increasingly laborious task. Few industries have lobbying muscle in hundreds of congressional districts (the textile industry is perhaps the best-known exception), so intensive logrolling was
usually necessary to broaden the base of support for a pet import restraint. But
as the number of industries covered by the measure increased, so would the
opposition. Legislators whose constituents included producers dependent on
exports or on crucial imports would mobilize to defeat the bill or at least to
uphold a presidential veto. More representatives may have experienced such
dissonance now than in the past because an increasingly sophisticated lobbying network, organized by foreign producers, could also contribute to the
backlash.[36]

Thus congressmen interested in assisting needy firms or industries fared
better fine-tuning the existing regulatory vehicles, for example, by amending

the antidumping and antisubsidization statutes. The amendments tended to be arcane, except to specialists, and sometimes even the experts did not fully appreciate the policy implications until later. Even when the sleepers were detected and scrutinized, they were often difficult to assail because particularistic advantages were being mixed and matched with a collective good (ridding the marketplace of discriminatory pricing, fixing distortions caused by subsidies, and so on). In sum, as Robert E. Baldwin aptly concludes, "Not only does this procedure enable members to promote the interests of different industries in an unobtrusive manner, but it enables the group to appeal for support on grounds that are widely accepted as desirable for the nation: protecting industry and labor from unfair foreign competition."[37]

Export Politics

Although export-oriented agricultural and manufacturing lobbies have worried that protectionist policies could invite retaliation, their support of unfettered trade was not unconditional. Expansion in world markets was always critical to American agriculture, but it was now increasingly essential to numerous other producers. Domestic consumption alone did not suffice to realize an attractive return on investment for some high-tech manufactures such as the makers of semiconductors, telecommunications equipment, or commercial aircraft, all characterized by scale economies, heavy research and development requirements, and steep learning curves. Producers of these goods began to advocate sectoral reciprocity, making access to the U.S. market contingent on wider beachheads overseas for American entrepreneurs.[38]

Fair trade rallied, at the same time, local industries battling imports and enterprises eyeing additional foreign sales. In fact, it was no longer easy to draw a sharp distinction between remedial import controls and what I. M. Destler has called "export politics";[39] nor was it certain that pursuit of the latter would quell demands for the former. The two kinds of regulatory endeavors could be complementary; both invoked similar shibboleths, and each hoped to secure a market presence for firms.

Throughout the 1980s, legislators sought to strengthen the rules against iniquitous trading practices, not infrequently at the behest of particular interest groups. Especially in the events leading to passage of the 1988 trade bill, these legislators attracted new allies. By packaging tighter provisions against unfair imports with a tougher stance against uncontestable foreign markets, they brought erstwhile skeptics on board.

Complications

The commercial corrections did not always perform as intended. Many seemed to have a way of attaining fewer, or different, results than their sponsors expected. That, however, did not necessarily slow their forward motion. On the contrary, the uncertainties and frustrations could stimulate requests for more remedies.

Setbacks

Not only did skirmishes over foreign trading practices score no decisive victory in the war against the overall trade deficit; domestic industries buffered from import competition often failed to expand, even if they received enough relief to feel that petitions for protection were worth filing. In 1986 legislators were disappointed to learn from the Congressional Budget Office that protection of four perennial favorites—the automobile, steel, footwear, and textile industries—had failed to enhance significantly their international competitiveness.[40] Another study, which examined sixteen American industries that were granted some form of import relief between 1954 and 1988, revealed that only one, the bicycle industry, actually grew after it had been protected.[41]

The main voluntary restraint agreements negotiated in the early 1980s had ambiguous effects on employment. According to one analysis, the restraints on steel imports saved 17,000 steelworkers their jobs, but they may have idled 52,400 workers in other industries.[42] The restraint agreements on Japanese autos did not prevent almost 30,000 layoffs in the automotive industry during the first half of the decade.[43] Later, joblessness among autoworkers was alleviated, but thanks in part to transplants, which circumvented the quotas and intensified the competitive challenge to the Big Three U.S. automakers. Not surprisingly, many of the protected industries returned with new complaints and additional pleas for help.[44]

On the export side, wider openings to sell goods and services abroad fell short of fetching the volumes of business imagined. Sometimes, after much huffing and puffing, a few more doors might be pushed ajar, only to run into stiff competition from new sources. In March 1988 the United States and Japan concluded an agreement permitting foreign construction companies to participate in some Japanese public works projects. Five months later, it appeared that the builders bidding aggressively on a number of major contracts were not Americans but South Koreans. "We opened up the market for Koreans, which is what we do all the time," groaned Commerce Secretary C. William Verity.[45]

Some trade experts remained convinced that freeing the Japanese market for rice imports would do a great deal "to restore bilateral harmony and create a favorable atmosphere for real Pacific Rim cooperation."[46] Ending Japan's ban on imported rice would be a positive step in the context of world trade talks, which were stalled over agricultural protectionism. But only in this sense might it help defuse the U.S.-Japan "powderkeg." How an end to Japanese rice protection would greatly gratify rice growers in California, when the big winners would be farmers in Thailand, remained unclear.[47]

The drive to push exports had its ups and downs. Late in 1981, the Agency for International Development established a special Trade and Finance Facility for Egypt to match other countries' offers of credit tied to aid in that market. A year later, with the assistance of $5.9 million in grants from the AID and $34.5 million borrowed from the Export-Import Bank on standard credit terms, Egypt bought electric generators valued at $53 million from Westinghouse and from General Electric.[48] In 1984, however, the Egyptian government turned down a U.S. proposal to use the Trade and Finance Facility in the case of a lucrative thermal power project that was subject to international tender competition. French, Canadian, and Japanese suppliers got the contract.

The toughest measures, retaliations against foreign market closures, did not always achieve their intended effects. Four years after retaliatory tariffs were slapped on an assortment of Japanese electronics products to enforce compliance with a market-sharing agreement for semiconductors, the desired sales targets in Japan had not been reached.[49] In the 1986 struggle to recapture lost orders from Spain and Portugal for feed-grain, the United States threatened a reprisal, managing to win compensation valued at about $400 million annually for four years. But American corn exporters felt that the concession scarcely offset their losses.[50]

Repeatedly in recent years, the Senate Banking Committee has proposed reciprocity legislation for banks and securities firms: regulators would be authorized to halt expansion in the United States of foreign competitors if a company's home market did not offer reciprocal national treatment. The lawmakers tried to word their proposals carefully, to provide a flexible, wholly discretionary negotiating lever, not a wrecking bar. But merely obtaining reciprocal national treatment among the world's financial superpowers might not adequately address a more basic issue: differing national regulatory regimes that were becoming nondiscriminatory but that still created uneven competitive conditions. Enforcers of a Fair Trade in Financial Services Act were likely to discover, for instance, that the main problem with Japan's financial market was not preferential treatment of domestic over foreign firms;

other regulatory norms, such as the slow pace at which the Japanese approved the introduction of new financial products (a forte of many U.S. firms), caused difficulty. To flatten that type of bump in the competitive playing field required more than a retaliatory national-treatment policy. It remained to be seen whether the insufficiency of such a policy would stir moves to impose a more radical standard for reciprocity. (Any shift toward mirror-image reciprocity would, of course, lay the United States open to a European attack on the Glass-Steagall and McFadden Acts, which put Europe's universal banks at a disadvantage in the U.S. market.)

Finally, as real as were the trade-inhibiting practices in foreign markets, so were the differences in consumer preferences and purchasing power that delimited the marketability of many exports. It was not always easy to figure out where foreign unfair trading left off and the influence of tastes or incomes set in. By mid-1988 Japan had formally agreed to relax quotas on a variety of imported processed foods, from ice cream to chewing gum. Consumers there, like almost everywhere else, had developed larger appetites for these things, but if the imports did not show a sufficiently striking increase, did the problem lie with protectionist distributors or diets? Similarly, perorations of the 1988 presidential election notwithstanding, it would have taken a miracle for Chrysler Corporation to sell many $10,000 "K" cars in South Korea, even if tariffs were bashed to nothing. Korean trade barriers were high, but with an average per capita income of less than $3,000 in 1986, only eight of every 1,000 inhabitants had automobiles.[51]

Who Gets What?

When trade officials successfully facilitated additional foreign sales on behalf of U.S.-owned corporations, the companies did not necessarily export from the United States. Some mainly manufactured their wares overseas to serve local markets. Making the "global factory" hum by freeing more of those markets did not guarantee busier plants in Allentown or Akron.[52] To the companies, in other words, the place of origin of products was beside the point; what counted was the freedom to produce and sell them in any profitable location. To people who kept an eye on the export column of the trade balance sheet, however, it presumably mattered whether more foreign purchases would or would not translate into more shipments from U.S. shores.

The same was true in some other kinds of cases—the complaints by U.S. discount retailers against Japan's Large-Scale Retail Store Law, for instance. The question was not whether these American businesses had legitimate grievances (they did); rather it was whether, in an overhauled Japanese distribution system, a lot of American-made consumer goods would constitute the stock on the shelves. Toys 'R Us would finally be able to establish an outlet in Tokyo, but its inventory might be made in Hong Kong or Taiwan.

Underlying these complications has been a certain amount of regulatory zigzagging in a chase to catch up with the ever-changing permutations of economic globalization. Trade policy would be judged by whether, at a minimum, it helped the intended producers. But which producers was it supposed to help, those who employed American workers, or those who, in Robert B. Reich's phrase, simply flew the American flag?[53] At times, the emphasis seemed to be on the former, regardless of who owned the shop. The EC would be warned against limiting imports of U.S.-made Honda and Nissan automobiles. Foreign machine-tool companies with facilities in the United States would invoke U.S. trade laws to defend their investments and products from external competitors, including competitors from their own country.[54] At other times—in parts of the trade arrangements for computer memory devices, for example—the government backed some U.S. companies that produced mainly abroad while withholding support from some foreign subsidiaries that operated in the United States.[55]

The configurations of gainers and losers in modern commercial policy were becoming complex. When the outcomes (whether tallied in terms of trade flows, employment, profitability, or competitiveness) were uneven, the sense of being cheated increased.

Conclusion

Trade policy during the past ten years has been called upon to back up industries under sharp competitive pressure. Indeed, as fiscal conditions in the 1980s constrained the ability of government to oblige constituents and clients by other means, trade programs took more of the wear and tear.

The consequences in a globalized economy, however, were often complicated and unpredictable. Techniques of managing risk and minimizing political costs would be sought. Among the methods were extensive power-sharing arrangements between governmental branches and negotiated restraints instead of tariffs. Most notably, identification of alleged injustice, not only actual injury, frequently motivated trade actions.

Defensive steps, including most import controls and various kinds of export enhancement, were easier to explain when deemed instrumental to obtain a fair share of world commerce. In part this was because real inequalities, particularly with respect to market penetration, persisted. Whatever the trend in foreign trade malpractice, some countries were still presenting inordinate commercial barriers long after the high U.S. tariff had been negotiated away. Pointing to inequities like this, the defenders of various industries could mobilize support for measures correcting or regulating trade without seeming to embrace discredited policies of protection or crass promotionalism. Moreover, the language of fairness was a familiar refrain in domestic politics, as more groups seemed to claim grounds for thinking of themselves as victims of discrimination, old or new.

Finally, the search for a fairer playing field, in trade as in social policy, produced disappointments as well as payoffs. Both could spur demands for greater fairness—and for more action to secure gains or to alleviate unwanted side effects.

CHAPTER FOUR

War Stories

THE REGULATORY APPARATUS that handled complaints about foreign commercial transgressions could help lower some political risks in trade policymaking. But this is not to say that pressures on the political system have been consistently marginalized. In fact, institutional arrangements that were supposed to insulate the policy process have been shaken. To see why, it is helpful to examine in greater detail how some specific grievances were actually managed. The picture that emerges when we get down to cases does not match the model that public administration theorists, beginning with Woodrow Wilson, had in mind: a framework that would keep the lid on trade antagonisms and advance the public interest because politicians would delegate responsibilities to persons "capable of looking at the whole economic situation of the country with a dispassionate and disinterested scrutiny."[1]

Sanitizing Trade Policy

It is true that after the debacle of the 1930 Tariff Act, Congress began to share with the president a keen desire to hold renewed protectionist reflexes in check. A prudent solution was for the legislature to surrender some of its authority to other parts of the government. Henceforth, distressed or discontented groups would be escorted to regulatory agencies and the courts: the International Trade Commission (ITC), the International Trade Administration of the Commerce Department (ITA), the Office of the U.S. Trade Representative (USTR), and the Court of International Trade (CIT). Operating under clear rules, these bodies would adjudicate claims and in legitimate instances extend limited protection. By drawing demands away from Capitol

Hill, the various administrative and judicial interlocutors would help lawmakers avoid repeating the mistakes of the Smoot-Hawley era.

This accommodation was also agreeable to the White House. Enough trade relief would be supplied to keep injured parties off the president's back but not so much as to approximate the degree of protectionism that Congress might otherwise legislate and that the president would be forced to veto in deference to international obligations.

Most observers would place the past decade's concern with trade redress squarely in this context; the legal remedies merely ensured due process for aggrieved petitioners and offered a means of mollifying them with enough token payoffs to mute calls for much more drastic measures.[2] So even if the remedies did less than expected for the nation's overall economic performance, they indirectly advanced the cause of world trade by restraining inimical forces in domestic politics.

This analysis has considerable merit. To some degree the agitation to crack down on foreigners engaging in unfair trade practices was only posturing, as congressmen and trade officials played to the gallery or jockeyed to strengthen their negotiating hands with one another and against interested parties abroad. The play would unfold predictably. After hearing from enough unhappy constituents or lobbyists about the invidious commercial tactics of the latest Pacific tiger, Congress might decide to send a signal to the other end of Pennsylvania Avenue: it would hold hearings, adopt strongly worded resolutions, and even come close to passing some hard-nosed bills. In the meantime, under section 301 of the 1974 Trade Act, an investigation would be requested of the "unjustifiable, unreasonable, or discriminatory" behavior in question. A delegation from the appropriate regulatory bureaucracy—in this case the USTR—would take up the dispute, warning the offending nation of dire consequences ("Congress might take matters into its own hands!") if concessions were not forthcoming. After months of tedious talks, the tiger would make a few ceremonial gestures—enough to calm Congress and, however briefly, silence the aroused constituents and lobbyists—but not the kind that substantially narrowed its bilateral trade surplus.

Notice the tacit rules of the game. The American negotiators would gain a tactical edge by talking up the shots Congress had fired across their bow, and the legislators also got to claim credit for their labors. But every player was aware that, except for an unlikely settlement that offered no face-saving results whatsoever, the cannonades from Capitol Hill were mostly blanks: the hearings attracted fleeting media attention, the resolutions were nonbinding, and the bellicose trade bills were guaranteed to be tamed in conference or to fall short of commanding sufficient support to override a veto. Thus the furor was harmless and would conclude with a collective sigh of relief when the threat of draconian legislation and of trade warfare receded.[3]

Note also the helpful role of the trade ombudsman. An intermediary (here, the USTR) would step in, respond to the protest, and administer palliatives. Politicians could cheer or chide the process, but from a safe distance, in the grandstand, where they could do little real damage.

This characterization, in which policy is more symbolic than consequential, partly conforms to the data on administrative trade cases. Between 1980 and 1986, the number of formal requests for enforcement of section 301, antidumping penalties, and duties to countervail export subsidies reached unprecedented frequencies. Well over one-half of the cases during this period resulted in the imposition of import fees, quotas, or other identifiable sanctions.[4] Yet the quantity of imports successfully challenged amounted to only a small fraction of the total, suggesting to some analysts that the outside world still considered the U.S. trade actions little more than a nuisance.[5]

This perspective seems consistent also with the original theory of corrective trade regulation: that a neutral system of legal recourse for trade litigants would not interfere with the general flow of commerce. After all, if trade relief was "run" on the basis of objective "economic law" by "depoliticized" administrators and jurists rather than suggestible elected officials, interference would presumably be held to a minimum.[6]

Tokenism?

The argument, however, can be overdrawn. The trouble with surmising, as a former chairman of the ITC did, that the U.S. trade statutes have had "an imperceptible impact on our trading partners" is that many of them have found the impact anything but imperceptible.[7] In the negotiations over the U.S.-Canadian free trade treaty, by far the thorniest issue was Canada's "security of access to the American market as measured by relief from the operation of U.S. trade remedy laws."[8] Now, with discussions under way for an open trade zone with Mexico, the same thorn would protrude. Incessant legal wrangles over dumping and subsidies have bedeviled U.S.-Mexican trade relations.[9] Although the European Community could sound like the pot calling the kettle black when it complained that our trade regulations caused "a considerable loss for European business," the loss of business that they perceived was not imaginary.[10]

Table 4-1. *Cross-National Frequencies of Antidumping and Countervailing Duty Actions, 1980–86*[a]

Country	Number of actions
United States	631
Australia	436
European Community	287
Canada	241
Chile	140
Japan	1
Other GATT code signatories	12

Source: J. Michael Finger, "Antidumping and Antisubsidy Measures," in J. Michael Finger and Andrzej Olechowski, eds., *The Uruguay Round: A Handbook for the Multilateral Trade Negotiations* (Washington: World Bank, 1987), pp. 259, 265, other GATT code signatories, p. 158.

a. Operations of the Trade Agreements Program (OTAP), U.S. International Trade Commission, 1981 through 1986. The data are based on actions reported by signatories to the GATT Committee on Subsidies and Antidumping Practices and GATT's semi-annual reports on antidumping and subsidies measures, 1980–86. The 1986 data for Canada, Australia, the EC, and Chile are obtained from GATT reports. They are thus incomplete because the GATT data do not contain the actions taken against nonsignatories. The reports were available for the first half of 1986 only.

The reasons for these concerns have been plain. Duties or quantitative re-straints that have seemed small in relation to total imports could present seri-ous difficulties for foreign vendors who depended heavily on the U.S. market. Canada exports approximately one-third of everything it produces, almost 80 percent of it to the United States; however, only 20 percent of U.S. exports go north. Thus the effect of a 5 percent tariff on Canadian products would be the equivalent of a 20 percent Canadian levy on American products. Tolls that might appear moderate on one side of the border might seem onerous on the other.[11]

Petitioners resorted to more antidumping and countervailing duty actions than in other major trading nations (table 4-1). If the numerous investigations that were forestalled or discontinued through preemptive price undertakings (anticipatory price increases on the dumped or subsidized goods) were added to the number of cases that culminated in official import fees, antidumping and countervailing duty administration might be casting a much longer eco-nomic shadow than casual viewers realize. The frequency with which the in-struments of litigation were used suggests that the domestic private interests they served thought the actions worth paying for. The millions of dollars in legal and lobbying fees paid by American businesses to press charges of unfair trade probably bought more than just an even chance of hitting competitors with formal sanctions; they could blunt indirectly, by harassment, a larger quotient of unwanted competition.

Finally, it was misleading to assess the amount of trade inhibited through these means without recognizing that the outcomes of big cases were often extensive restraint agreements (or other strong medicine), not narrowly gauged duties or price adjustments. In 1983 a countervailing duty petition aimed at textile imports from China resulted in tighter supervision of East Asian textiles in general. The following year a barrage of complaints filed by the steel industry about dumping and subsidies resulted in negotiated restraints on exports from virtually every major producing country. In 1986 a determination that the Japanese were selling computer memory chips below fair value spawned not only a "voluntary" scheme to control prices but an attempt to designate a just market share. The same year, an antisubsidy suit against Canadian lumber was concluded not by imposing a simple duty on Canadian lumber imported into the United States, but by persuading the Canadians to levy upon themselves a $400 million annual export tax.

How did such cases escalate? A closer look at episodes like the Chinese textile and the Canadian lumber conflicts suggests a sequence: What began, seemingly, as a technical administrative exercise involving a few low-level participants and limited stakes, gradually drew in the rest of the government, raising tempers, altering expectations, and sometimes extending the conflicts. This pattern, furthermore, appeared not only in the outcries about foreign invasions of the U.S. market but in some complaints that foreign markets were not open for U.S. business. A continuing dispute over access to construction contracts in Japan was a case in point.

The Textile Tangle

Early in September 1983, a coalition of textile and apparel companies and unions petitioned the Department of Commerce to act against subsidized products from mainland China. The petition was interesting because it claimed that the illegal subsidy stemmed from China's dual exchange rate. The plaintiffs contended that in a nonmarket economy, where currency was not freely convertible into dollars and where exchange rates for trade payments were set arbitrarily by government fiat, certain exports could be systematically undervalued. Imported Chinese fabrics, valued at $121.8 million in 1978, had moved up to $857 million by 1982, contributing to a growing deficit in U.S. textile and apparel trade.[12] The litigants—the American Textile Manufacturers Institute, the American Apparel Manufacturers Association, the Amalgamated Clothing and Textile Workers Union, and the International Ladies Garment Workers Union—seemed to have a simple and limited case:

they believed that they were entitled to relief from this latest source of unfairly priced foreign-made cloth and clothing.[13]

Needling the System

But limited and simple the affair was not. In August 1983 trade negotiators had concluded an accord with Peking restricting the annual growth of textile and apparel shipments to between 2.5 percent and 3.5 percent—a range less stringent than the quotas on the world's largest producers, but considerably tighter than the 6 percent limit set for smaller producers under international agreement. The bilateral agreement had been difficult to attain. During the many months of talks, China had sought to gain the upper hand by curtailing purchases of American grains. Wheat exporters and their representatives in Congress had leaned on the administration to accommodate the Chinese on textiles. Under the circumstances, a number of trade officials and diplomats were surprised that the two countries were able to negotiate a relatively restrictive quota, controlling two-thirds of the textile and apparel imports at levels well below the standard of the Multi-Fiber Arrangement.[14] The textile and apparel lobby, however, promptly denounced the deal, calling it "a disaster."[15]

The antisubsidy suit filed in September, whatever its merits, was part of a larger strategy to unravel the August agreement and to induce the administration to tighten import controls. The case was designed (and timed) to apply maximum pressure. Countries such as China that were not signatories to the Tokyo Round's subsidy code could not avail themselves of an ITC injury test before any countervailing duty was ordered on disputed imports. In an ITC hearing it might not have been easy to prove that Chinese textiles were materially injuring American producers in 1983. The recession of the previous year was over; domestic textile production was up 20 percent; mills were operating at more than 90 percent of capacity; and imports from China did not command a large share of the market. But because, in the case at hand, an affirmative ruling by the Commerce Department's International Trade Administration was all that was required to impose a duty and because the ITA usually found in the affirmative in antisubsidy cases,[16] the domestic industry stood a credible chance of winning the additional protection it desired—and of creating a diplomatic embarrassment for the Reagan administration.

Throughout the fall the proceedings would tie up the ITA in a complicated investigation involving hundreds of separate categories of imported materials and uncharted legal questions such as the meaning, if any, of "subsidized" pricing in a command economy. President Reagan had scheduled a major state visit to Peking the following spring. The ITA's deliberations would reach a critical stage not long before his trip. The case also threatened to spill into the politics of the 1984 election.

The latter concern was uppermost. Reagan was vulnerable on the textile issue because of campaign promises he had made in 1980. At that time he had written to Senator Strom Thurmond of South Carolina, "The fiber-textile-apparel manufacturing complex provides 2.3 million vitally needed American jobs, including a high percentage of female and minority employees. As president, I shall make sure that these jobs remain in this country." [17] In addition, to shore up support from members of the House Textile Caucus for other priorities in the administration's legislative agenda in 1981, the president had committed himself to extending the Multi-Fiber Arrangement in a manner that would "allow us to relate total import growth to the growth in the domestic textile and apparel market." [18] Congressmen from textile-producing states did not remain silent bystanders while the Chinese subsidy investigation ran its course. Early in December several of them paid a call on the White House to remind the administration of its assurances.

Political Settlement

At about this time the Commerce Department was due to issue its preliminary finding. After a last-minute appeal by Secretary Malcolm Baldrige, however, the petitioning industry abruptly suspended its complaint. [19] Following consultations between a deputy assistant secretary for import administration and the chief attorney for the petitioning industry, the industry agreed to shelve its petition in return for a broader import-relief program to be worked out at the highest level, in the cabinet. If no such program could be developed within ten days, the industry would reopen its case.

A cabinet-level group met repeatedly in the following days. The contours of its deliberations were largely defined by a proposal Baldrige made that would automatically trigger tighter quotas in response to surges in imports of third world textiles. On the afternoon of Friday, December 16, only minutes before the industry's case was to be reactivated, presidential aides Edwin Meese and James A. Baker signed off on a modified version of Baldrige's plan. Under the compromise, temporary import surges from Hong Kong, South Korea, and Taiwan, as well as China, were to be systematically monitored and, on a discretionary basis, controlled according to "more timely and predictable" guidelines. [20]

Industry groups were generally pleased. The American Apparel Manufacturers Association called the new rules "a step forward in dealing with the problem of disruption of the American textile and apparel market by imports."[21] What had started out as a request to impose additional regulation on imports from one place had ended up as a decision to oversee more trade with four nations. A bonus was that the Chinese government, no longer singled out as the sole target, did not, for once, react apoplectically.

Temporary Relief

If this outcome had been the end of the textile saga, policymakers might have rejoiced at having pacified a politically powerful domestic industry and halted its quest for protection. But the December settlement was not the end, nor the beginning of the end, only the end of the beginning. Exactly two years later, textile interests would confront the president with legislation that called for a comprehensive system of import licensing and a rollback of imports to lower levels. To make sure a veto was sustained, the administration followed up by negotiating new bilateral agreements with the largest Asian suppliers. The result in 1986 was a set of more restrictive quotas, limiting the annual growth of imports from these countries to 1 percent or less.[22]

These efforts also were not enough. In 1988 the president had to veto a measure that codified the 1 percent limitation and extended it to all countries. Two years after that, the bill resurfaced, with as much congressional support as ever. Again a veto was cast and upheld, but not before Congress had rattled the U.S. negotiating stance at a sensitive stage in the Uruguay Round.

Starting with the "short-term" restraints on imported cotton in 1961, domestic textile and apparel manufacturers had been protected by a widening net of trade restrictions. By 1990 more than 1,000 quotas had been arranged with thirty-eight nations, covering three-quarters of all imports. Moreover, the average duty on these products remained nearly 20 percent (compared with 4 percent on all manufactured goods). This ongoing escapade in managed trade had become equivalent to a 50 percent tariff, costing American consumers an extra $20 billion a year for the clothes they bought.[23] Trade remedy cases, like the one in 1983, had not done much to hold down these costs.

The Hard Line on Softwood

In the fall of 1986, the Department of Commerce reversed a position it had taken in 1983; it determined that Canadian provincial fees for harvesting timber on government land were artificially low, constituting an improper subsidy to lumber exporters. The finding was complicated. On the premise that only earmarked subsidies distort comparative advantage among traders, norms established by the GATT do not contest generally available subsidies, only narrowly focused ones. Technically, several Canadian industries besides lumber (for example, pulp, paper, plywood, and furniture producers) benefited from the low fees. Initially, mostly on these grounds, the Department of Commerce had rejected an appeal for relief by a group of U.S. forest product companies. By 1986, however, the department had come to regard Canadian timber as a case of industrial targeting, with that country's lumber industry as the chief beneficiary of subsidized timber and other kinds of producers as nominal users.

Having established the "specificity" of the subsidy, the Commerce Department measured it by estimating what it cost the provincial governments to supply the trees. The department concluded that costs to the provinces exceeded their revenues from timber cuts and that the price of saw logs fell short of true market value by 14.542 percent. In a negotiated settlement at the end of December, the government of Canada agreed to make up the difference with a 15 percent tax on exports.

Numbers Game

Much fuss surrounded the Commerce Department's attempt to estimate a production function for provincial forests. On top of direct expenditures by the forestry ministries (logging roads, reforestation, administrative overhead, and so on) was added the "intrinsic value" of standing timber, the sum of which would be the full cost of supplying logs to commercial users. Canadian critics objected that the ITA's analysts had crudely imputed a value to trees in Ontario and Quebec by using as proxies the prices of some limited private sales in New Brunswick. The ITA, for its part, operated as if the degree of provincial underpricing (revenues minus real production costs) could be calibrated with pinpoint accuracy, down to three decimal places.

That some Canadian provinces were indirectly subsidizing their softwood industry may have seemed difficult to refute.[24] Ninety-five percent of Canadian woodlands are publicly owned. In most provinces the fees charged to private logging companies were not based on competitive bidding aimed at recovering full market value. Some forests were probably undervalued, and in some areas, such as British Columbia, officials admitted as much.[25] But exactly how bad the undervaluation was and, more important, what economic harm it caused the American economy were by no means clear.

Whether the contested subsidy had much to do with a bulge in Canadian lumber exports was also hard to determine. The exports had grown from 26.9 percent of the U.S. market in 1980 to 31.6 percent in 1985, but the increase tracked exchange rates so closely that other causes appeared to pale by comparison.[26] Moreover, whatever the wounds inflicted by Canadian competition on the U.S. complainants, the proposed cure—a 15 percent price hike—might jeopardize many more jobs in wood-using American industries like construction than would be salvaged in the domestic lumber industry.[27]

Getting to Yes: 1983 versus 1986

The most intriguing aspect of the lumber decision was that it contradicted a ruling, reached only three years earlier, that the disputed subsidies were de minimis and not sharply targeted. Although that ruling was questioned from the start, neither its statutory basis nor the substantive evidence for it changed fundamentally over the ensuing months. Imports as a percentage of U.S. softwood consumption had peaked in 1985 along with the U.S. dollar. During the following year the percentage declined. Two conditions were significantly different in 1986, however. One was the body of case law that lawyers for the petitioning industry could cite. The other was the intensity of lobbying activity and political advocacy surrounding the petition. Pressure groups were energized, not sidelined, by the administrative and judicial proceedings that had commenced in 1982.

The 1979 Trade Act had upgraded the old Customs Court to the Court of International Trade, a tribunal with more extensive powers of judicial oversight. Soon the court ceased to be a bit player in the trade policy game. Congress had envisioned not only more recourse for disaffected parties pressing their claims but a reliable arbiter. By 1984 few doubted that the CIT was living up to expectations. Earlier, the judges had adhered to a relatively exacting standard of specificity for actionable subsidies. As late as 1983, they turned down as "absurd" an appeal by American rubber manufacturers, who argued that "benefits from government programs are countervailable even if they are generally available."[28] But in a major 1984 steel case, the court began taking a different tack, hedging the principle "that, as a rule, generally available benefits are not subsidies."[29] The following year the court remanded a case in which the Department of Commerce had declined to countervail Mexican pricing policies for carbon black feedstock and natural gas. The court urged the ITA to ignore the "nominal" general availability of the rates the government had set, and instructed the agency to consider "the question of what aid or advantage has actually been received" by the export industry in question.[30] In the ensuing administrative review of its order on carbon black, the ITA now felt that it had "placed excessive emphasis" on general availability of the subsidized feedstock rates and that the recipients of the below-market rates were specific.[31] The reassessment in the Mexican carbon black case provided a precedent for the about-face on Canadian softwood later that year.

While legal interpretations of unfair subsidies were in flux, political passions were rising. Lumber companies in the United States had been complaining about Canadian practices since the early 1960s, but it was not until the mid-1980s that their organization, tactics, and congressional allies became a force to be reckoned with. Smarting from the defeat in 1983, the companies regrouped two years later with fresh recruits—Georgia-Pacific Corporation, for instance, among other giants in the industry—and this time retained the services of prestigious Washington and New York law firms specializing in trade litigation. With the help of these experts, the companies mapped out a dual-track strategy: they would instigate a second unfair trade suit, accompanied by a systematic campaign to rivet governmental attention on the lumber question.

Animated by the lumber lobby and sensing a chance to take the lead on a hot trade issue, entrepreneurs sprang into action in both the House and the Senate. In 1985 a dozen members introduced legislation to counter the ill-effects of Canadian stumpage practices. At least one of these measures, a wide-ranging natural resource subsidy bill, had to be taken seriously (it had been crafted by Representative Sam Gibbons's Ways and Means trade subcommittee). Then a series of "timber summits" on Capitol Hill, organized by Representative Larry Craig of Idaho, brought scores of congressmen face to face behind closed doors with U.S. Trade Representative Clayton K. Yeutter, Commerce Secretary Baldrige, White House aide Max Friedersdorf, and other principals. In February 1986, during a special order day in the Senate arranged by Max Baucus of Montana, some forty senators spoke out against Canadian timber pricing.

All of this set the stage for the Senate Finance Committee's hearings in April 1986 on a long-discussed proposal to liberalize all trade between the United States and Canada. The 1986 countervail case could not have been more perfectly timed; it arrived on the scene when the administration was already a *demandeur* before the Finance Committee with other pressing business (comprehensive tax reform, for instance) and a request to maintain fast-track procedures for ratifying the U.S.-Canada free trade negotiations. The point of the fast-track suspension of usual procedures was to force an up-or-down vote, without revisions, on a finalized trade treaty. Clearly, the executive could not negotiate a treaty that would be open to amendments on the Senate floor. Finance Committee consent to fast-track was therefore considered indispensable to fashioning a free trade deal with Canada—in essence, a vote of confidence on the negotiations.

Finance was well stocked with members from lumber-producing states—a total of eight, including the new chairman, Bob Packwood of Oregon, who was up for reelection in the fall. The committee was thus strategically situated and politically motivated to throw its weight behind the lumber industry's forthcoming request for countervailing duties. Only after an exchange of correspondence with administration officials, who vowed to "get lumber fixed" and "expedited," did the committee uphold fast-track authority.[32] And only then, with these assurances in place, did an alliance of American lumber firms, called the Coalition for Fair Lumber Imports, formally petition for protection.

The rest of the story unfolded within these policy parameters. In June the ITC affirmed in a preliminary inquiry that Canada's timber exports were materially injuring the U.S. industry. In October the Department of Commerce issued the initial results of its investigation, affirming probable cause for sanctions. At the end of the year, after a series of high-level exchanges (including the intervention of Secretary of State George Shultz, who made an eleventh-hour trip to Ottawa), the United States waived the threatened duty when Canada agreed to raise prices by taxing exports.

The Collision over Kansai

In the textile and lumber conflicts, interest groups had initiated complaints. But when the exclusion of American contractors from Japanese construction projects flared up as a major trade issue, the relevant interests—the Associated General Contractors of America, the National Construction Association, the International Engineering and Construction Industry Council, the American Institute of Architects, and various individual firms—were not the first to enlist. Instead, the opening shots were fired by an enterprising commercial consular officer stationed in Osaka.

Reconnoitering the region for American business opportunities, he began making inquiries with the Ministry of Transportation in Tokyo to ascertain how foreign firms could take part in the building of Kansai International Airport. The smoke signals emanating from the Japanese bureaucracy were not reassuring. Public construction in Japan operated under a discriminatory and corrupt system of designated bidding.[33] Only licensed firms, and firms ranked highly by the government according to past performance in Japan, were invited to bid on projects. Because hardly any foreign company could claim extensive prior experience working in Japan, hardly any were eligible to register as bidders.

Early in the summer of 1985, the Osaka consulate began alerting Washington about the obstacles for American builders who might be interested in obtaining Kansai contracts. A deputy USTR, later joined by an undersecretary from the Department of Commerce, presented the Ministry of Transportation with a series of requests to change the contracting practices for the airport project. They were told repeatedly that the Kansai airport was a private corporation over which the ministries in Tokyo had no control.

The infelicity of this contention (private money constituted only a fraction of the airport budget) was not lost on Congress, where hearings on the Kansai question were held in June 1986 by the Foreign Relations subcommittee on East Asian affairs chaired by Alaska Senator Frank H. Murkowski. When Murkowski and other Republican senators followed up with a request to U.S. Trade Representative Clayton Yeutter to consider a section 301 investigation, the Japanese government respecified its position: Inclusion of foreign contractors in the airport's first phase (reclaiming land and building a seawall) was impossible because of the construction schedule; but, within the traditional designated-bidder framework, efforts would be made to entertain foreign bids in later stages of the project.

For a time, U.S. negotiators seemed to respond chiefly by adjusting their sights and demanding transparency in the bidding process for the most suitable contracts. During a visit to Tokyo in July, for instance, Commerce Secretary Baldrige pressed mainly for involvement in the construction of runways and terminals, but not in the landfill and breakwater operations.[34] Later in the fall, an assistant secretary, leading a special presidential trade delegation at a meeting of government and industry representatives in Osaka, also deemphasized first-stage participation. The American agenda was relatively specific, including such items as better information for American firms that wanted to work as subcontractors; specification of contract orders; public notification of bidding results; and a role for AT&T in providing communication facilities. The airport was the focus of these requests, which stressed equitable access at the technological high end, where a number of American construction companies excelled.[35]

Escalation

As congressional interest in the case mounted and more industry spokesmen began to stir, the Reagan administration found itself broadening the scope and upping the ante. Toward the end of the year, an industry group had submitted to Baldrige a report recommending restrictions on Japanese contractors in the United States if U.S. firms did not receive a piece of the action at Kansai and on other major construction jobs. Senator Murkowski, traveling to Tokyo that December, similarly warned of possible retaliatory measures by Congress if Japan did not liberalize the contracting procedures. Kansai had come to symbolize something much larger: Japan's restricted market.

The new year began with a Commerce Department emissary returning to Tokyo to revive the issue of participation in the landfill and seawall operations, this time in the form of American entry through joint ventures and subcontracts. The Japanese reiterated that Phase I was closed; work was already in progress.

Reopening the question of Phase I participation may have been just a bargaining chip. Nevertheless, it was curious. No U.S. companies seemed anxious to bid on this component, and the Japanese had considered the matter settled.[36] While the American construction industry was probably never eager to "move dirt" in Japan, some elements may have begun to recognize a different opportunity: the possibility of barring Japanese builders from the U.S. market on the grounds that Japan's was closed.[37] The Kansai dialogue did not quickly degenerate into an excuse to bring down sanctions. Politically, however, the longer the discussions fastened on Phase I, where the bulk of the airport's $8 billion construction cost lay and where no foreigners shared the prize, the more they dramatized Japan's market closure.

By the spring of 1987, the quarrel had been hauled up to the level of summit diplomacy. Airport construction contracts were among the topics at meetings between Prime Minister Yasuhiro Nakasone and President Reagan in April–May and again in September. With the rumblings of retaliatory legislation growing louder on Capitol Hill, the Japanese cobbled together a set of concessions during the summer. They offered to apply GATT-approved procurement procedures to the second phase of work at Kansai—publishing construction orders, allowing contract specifications to be open for inspection, and granting a forty-day period in which estimates could be tendered. They also promised to explain publicly any decisions to exclude particular enterprises from being designated to bid.

The U.S. negotiating team countered with demands for the estimate period

to be lengthened to sixty days and for adoption of the American "perform-
ance-style" method for procurement of equipment (giving contract winners
more discretion in matters of design). In anticipation of Nakasone's September trip to Washington, the Japanese government accepted these conditions.

But even as details like these were being ironed out, people in the administration and in Congress who followed the negotiations closely were becoming increasingly suspicious that the other side's guarantees were only cos-
metic. One reason was that the catch-22 in Japanese bidding procedures
remained unresolved: how could foreign candidates qualify without a record
of prior accomplishments in Japan? Another was that, while the Japanese
thought they were negotiating for American participation in the construction
of Kansai airport and possibly a few other sites, the Americans were interested in more than a sui generis agreement; they wanted a general set of rules
extending to a range of public works in the future. So just days after Nakasone's visit in September, the U.S. Senate turned up the heat. It approved a
measure sponsored by Murkowski excluding from U.S. military construction
projects competitors from countries that did not give American contractors
"fair and equitable access."

Soft Landing?

Through the rest of 1987, Tokyo temporized as control of the government
passed from Nakasone to his successor, Noboru Takeshita, who had close ties
with the native construction industry. Meanwhile, an inflamed U.S. Congress
moved inexorably toward retaliation. Late in December, the axe finally fell,
in veto-proof style: an amendment, coauthored by Senator Murkowski and
Representative Jack Brooks of Texas, was attached to a fiscal 1988 omnibus
appropriations bill. It withheld funds from public works projects that employed any Japanese contractors or suppliers.

With diplomats in both countries now fearing an appreciable deterioration
of relations, the construction controversy became a major preoccupation of
the foreign offices. In January 1988, on the eve of another summit in which
the subject of construction would be on the agenda, Secretary of State Shultz
and Foreign Minister Sosuke Uno unveiled a compromise. Japan would retain
its designated-bidder system, but international experience outside Japan
would be counted as equivalent to experience inside Japan for foreign applicants. In addition, special arrangements would be made for Americans to bid
on specified public projects in joint ventures with Japanese firms.

Reaction was mixed. A major stumbling block, the prior experience re-

quirement, had been partially cleared. Some large American construction out-
fits welcomed the possibility of more joint ventures; a day after the Uno plan
was released, two of them separately announced plans to link up with major
Japanese companies. At the same time, a representative of the International
Engineering and Construction Industry Council warned that the firms he represented would not be satisfied until there were "market results."[38] And on
Capitol Hill, lawmakers were contemplating legislation to bar Japanese firms
from *private* construction.

Matters grew worse when the Japanese announced the list of projects in
which U.S. firms could participate: there were eight, including the Kansai
airport and a bridge across Tokyo Bay. The Americans had wanted fourteen.
Of the eight, two were expansions of airports near Tokyo and Hiroshima. On
both of these the Japanese offer did not include participation in the design and
construction of terminals, apparently on the theory that these buildings were
strictly private ventures, not public works.

For two years members of Congress and a subcabinet-level interagency
coordinating body had been recommending a broad indictment of Japan under
section 301 to expose the full extent of the construction quagmire. This course
of action had been deferred, in part because the U.S. industry had never filed
a formal petition. But by mid-March U.S. officials had reached the limit of
their patience. A cabinet-level group headed by Treasury Secretary James
Baker set a two-week deadline for concluding a settlement of the dispute.
After that, section 301 would presumably be invoked with or without an industry request. The ultimatum worked—at least for the time being. Before
the end of the month the Japanese had revised their proposal. In addition to
counting non-Japanese experience in evaluating applications for licenses and
designated-bidder status, the new offer provided for U.S. access to fourteen
projects, including terminal buildings at several airports and some local jobs
that had previously been omitted.

For a short time this deal, finalized by an exchange of letters between the
new Commerce Secretary William Verity and the Japanese ambassador in
Washington on March 25, looked as though it would lay the construction
problem to rest. But soon new doubts arose that the truce would hold. The
Commerce Department noticed that American firms were slow to respond to
the openings supposedly arranged in the agreement. Whether this hesitancy
was mostly the result of continuing obstacles to doing business in Japan or
reflected the possibility that, as Verity observed, most U.S. contractors "are
still not oriented to a world market" remained an interesting question.[39] With
the Japanese supplying some provocation, Congress would not leave it unan-

swered. Through a special provision of the Omnibus Trade and Competitiveness Act enacted in August 1988, the USTR was ordered to conduct a continuing section 301 investigation of the Japanese construction and engineering market. Over the next three years, the trade combatants were snarled in another torturous series of negotiations, replete with renewed threats to ban Japanese contractors from federally funded construction. An eleventh-hour cease-fire, at the end of May 1991, offered American builders a little more room in the minefield of Japanese public works. How long this latest pause in hostilities would last was anybody's guess.

Some Lessons

These three examples illustrate several attributes of major trade cases in the past decade. First, the cases tended to slip out of prosaic administrative forums and into a stormy political arena. Starting at low echelons, a Washington law firm might set the process in motion by submitting a section 701 petition on behalf of a feisty client. Or, as in the Japanese construction flap, an inspired official in some remote recess of the trade bureaucracy might open a Pandora's box. Soon, boisterous congressional voices would join in. Sometimes the chorus was orchestrated by an effective lobby (as in the lumber and textile examples); at other times particular lawmakers, having found an egregious trade abuse, chimed in on their own (as in the Kansai fracas). If legislators or interest groups were quiescent in the early rounds, they were roused in the course of the proceedings. Eventually, because the cases frequently rubbed sensitive political and diplomatic nerves, some became serious. Cabinet officials, and even presidents and prime ministers, were forced to devote attention to them.

This, in fact, was a second characteristic: the cases were not always trivial pursuits for politicians. Substantial resources and risks could be involved. In the forestry fight, for example, the U.S. lumber coalition showered many millions of dollars on lawyers, lobbyists, and consultants. The fruits of these efforts were a hefty impost on Canada's timber exports, perhaps the largest self-imposed tax ever levied anywhere to penalize exports.[40] To obtain this result, the U.S. Congress went to the brink, at one point jeopardizing an immensely beneficial North American free trade zone. On the Canadian side, where the forestry industry was the country's largest employer, the trade dispute became a national obsession, making headlines week after week. The final compromise, derided by the parliamentary opposition as a sellout, helped fan the inflammatory rhetoric of Canadian politicians wary of the U.S.-Canada treaty. In the months leading up to the fateful parliamentary election of 1988, Canadian voters seemed worried that the colossus to their south would declare open season on every manner of public subsidy, from old-age pensions to medical insurance. On both sides of the border, public officials at all levels—state governors and provincial premiers, cabinet secretaries and ministers, scores of congressmen and members of parliament, even heads of state—got involved, spending time and political capital on softwood for many months.

Complaints like these were not false alarms or small brush fires that were readily smothered. They often burned for years or reignited with more intensity after a "settlement." The textile tangle was illustrative. "You can bet they'll be back again," grumbled a senior administration official, referring to the domestic industry after an action against Chinese imports had been resolved in its favor.[41] And in fact, return they did, year after year, pressing policymakers with new needs or wants and securing more favors. Few trade debates have raged longer than the one about textile protection, but even in narrower disputes, like those involving Canadian lumber and the Kansai contracts, the tendency was for hot coals to keep smoldering even after the main blaze was thought to have died down.[42]

The trade cases, in short, could create a good deal of regulatory commotion, sometimes with no end in sight. Particular industries or firms received support in coping with objectionable competition, but the help they got often fell short of expectations or failed to make a meaningful difference. They then asked for more, sometimes at considerable cost to the public and to other industries or firms. This was an unstable state of affairs, regardless of whether the petitioners' specific grievances were sound.

The textile and apparel industry, for instance, had a reasonable claim against the Chinese dual exchange rate. U.S. forest products companies may also have had a plausible claim against the stumpage programs of some Canadian provinces. American contractors who were serious about doing business in Japan had every reason to suspect that they were being systematically shut out of the Japanese market. Yet the textile and apparel industries were already much sheltered. Their petition in 1983 was just one aspect of a seemingly interminable campaign to enlarge the shelter. By the end of the 1980s, the annual cost of the industry's import relief was averaging nearly $238 for each American household. Protection of domestic lumber was not so expensive, but it still may have cost more jobs in the economy than it saved. Perhaps this outcome was the only practicable solution to an explosive trade complaint. Critics, however, took notice of the case's fluid legal doctrine, political imperatives, and the inevitable element of methodological pseudoscience in calculating the magnitude of the injurious foreign subsidy.

Even the strife over Japanese contracting seemed, at times, to promise uncertain net benefits. To be sure, few bilateral trade disputes seemed more stark: Japanese construction firms enjoyed some $2.5 billion worth of contracts in the United States, while U.S. construction work in Japan totaled around $300 million. American companies remained understandably diffident about making a big move into the thicket of Japanese contracting practices. In time, indefatigable teams of negotiators from the Commerce Department might help more Western pioneers pick their way through the brambles, but no one seemed to be able to cut a very wide swath. Even the threat (and use) of retaliation, as in the showdown of 1988, failed to clear much of an opening. The Murkowski-Brooks amendment may have prevented public works projects in the United States (like the new rapid transit system in the capital) from accepting some economical bids, but despite the year-long sanctions, the Japan construction issue continued to fester into the 1990s.

Politics and Administration

Administration of the trade laws was substantially in the hands of independent bureaucratic organizations operating through regularized procedures. Try as they might, however, these organizations could not "take trade law enforcement out of politics."[43] Through much of the 1980s, an administrative system intended to deflect protectionist storm winds was buffeted by political gusts blowing into and out of Capitol Hill and the White House.

In 1985 trade investigators in the bureaucracy rolled up their sleeves. Suddenly a half-dozen countries suspected of dealing unfairly in goods ranging from supercomputers to sweaters, pasta, and motion pictures were the subject of detailed inquests. These cases, like the one over Kansai airport, were not prompted by formal petitions outside the government; they were self-initiated.

But only in part. Although some spirited administrators—like Baldrige and newly appointed U.S. Trade Representative Clayton Yeutter—led the charge, the trade offensive was still substantially a reaction to interest group pressure and congressional advocacy. Against the backdrop of widening trade deficits, which exceeded $100 billion in 1984, worried lawmakers were looking for ways to defend the economic rights of American manufacturers and farmers. Hundreds of bills were introduced between 1981 and 1985, with one chamber or the other eventually adopting several that contained strict reciprocity standards or provisions to beat back competition in the domestic market through buy-American and local-content requirements. By early 1985 the calls to ensure equitable market opportunities had reached a high pitch. The House and Senate each passed virtually unanimous resolutions urging the administration to curb Japan's mercantilist policies. Later two major pieces of legislation began wending their way through the Capitol: a measure to expand textile quotas and a proposal to levy a 25 percent surcharge on imports from Japan, Taiwan, Korea, and Brazil. Hoping to head off such developments, the administration resolved, in Yeutter's words, "to deal vigorously and decisively with trade problems" through available administrative mechanisms.[44]

Were the ensuing initiatives at the USTR and from Baldrige's strike force a sudden "turnaround" in President Reagan's benign neglect of trade policy? Or were they, more accurately, the latest moves in a series of affirmative actions intended to deflate congressional measures and sometimes to meet other political needs?

The administration had chosen in 1981 to negotiate limits on imports of Japanese automobiles. The voluntary restraints were meant to forestall a move widely supported in the Senate to set mandatory quotas. The restraints also fulfilled a presidential campaign pledge to slow the "deluge" of Japanese cars into the United States.[45] In 1982 the administration reimposed import quotas on sugar, a concession that was part of a deal with southern Democratic House members: the president agreed to support the price of sugar in exchange for votes on the 1981 budget reconciliation.[46] In 1983 the administration raised quotas on specialty steel and sharpened regulations on textile imports. In the latter case, Republican senators from textile states, up for reelection in 1984, had made their wishes known. The White House listened, making good on an earlier commitment "to moderate the growth of textile imports."[47] Reagan also heeded a cry from the motorcycle industry for "a little breathing room" and ordered a tenfold increase in duties on heavy bikes.[48] The action was unusual because the domestic industry in this instance consisted of a single company, Harley-Davidson. In the elections the previous fall, however, the Democrats had picked up twenty-six House seats and were now stressing the growth of imports as a sign of weakness in the administration's economic policy.[49]

In 1984 the administration answered the pleas of carbon steel producers, promising to seek more restraint agreements with steel-exporting nations. The political exigency this time was to prune a comprehensive trade bill bristling with neoprotectionist amendments for steel and a half dozen other products. Moreover, 1984 was a presidential election year. The Democratic candidate,

Walter Mondale, had stumped the Rust Belt vowing to "get tough, and I mean really tough" on trade. Calling for more limits on imports, he declaimed, "We've been running up the white flag when we should be running up the American flag. What do we want our kids to do, sweep up around the Japanese computers and spend a lifetime serving McDonald hamburgers?"[50] The White House played it safe by stealing some of Mondale's thunder.

In 1986 protection was extended to three more major industries: microchips, machine tools, and lumber. In each instance congressional or electoral tremors reverberated through the decisionmaking process. A trade panel of the Joint Economic Committee, steered by Senator Pete Wilson of California, held lively hearings on the Japanese practice of selling memory chips below average production cost.[51] When machine tools became a candidate for negotiated restraint, the president timed his announcement to dilute support for another disagreeable trade package nearing a vote on the House floor. And in one of the most politically charged cases of all—the drive to impose countervailing duties on Canadian timber—the Commerce Department found provincial stumpage programs to be a form of export targeting. Canadians suspected that the verdict was a price exacted by members of the Senate Finance Committee, which had come within a hair's breadth of denying the administration fast-track negotiating authority for the U.S.-Canada free trade pact.[52] The decision, reached in mid-October, was welcome news to several Republican senators in lumber-producing states—for example, Steven D. Symms of Idaho and Mack Mattingly of Georgia—who were facing uphill reelection fights in November.[53]

Conclusion

The management of demands for trade succor and safeguards did not consistently remain an autonomous exercise in administrative law, with politicians remaining mere spectators. Petty cases were justiciable through a bureaucratized set of procedures, but important ones were less easily dispatched. In more than a few instances, damage control, the central function of the administrative machinery, seemed to falter. Disputes droned on; relations with some trading partners were sorely tested; and sometimes significant costs and frustrations accreted in deference to rather narrow commercial gains. If the system was intended to perform as a shock absorber for the nation's liberal trade orientation, at times it appeared to administer as many shocks as it absorbed.

How much did these malfunctions matter? Trade policy came under considerable stress, but it did not lurch into rank protectionism, wholesale abandonment of GATT principles, or unrestrained economic conflagrations. Although there were examples of regulatory breakdown, some cases may have had positive effects. For instance, the years of negotiations over Japanese construction contracts, however exasperating, became an object lesson in a broader subject, competition policy, that seemed destined for a place on the international trade agenda of the future. If the upshot of lengthy conflicts like this was to underscore the need for global ground rules governing anticompetitive practices—and to clarify the kinds of rules needed—the ordeal was worth enduring.

Yet the system was strained. A volatile legacy of the 1980s was that more complainants had acquired more ways to complain. Whether institutional safety valves would continue to decompress the political steam that these developments had helped generate or would someday let it build up again remained a nagging question.

CHAPTER FIVE

Legislative Activity

CONGRESS WAS OF TWO MINDS about its part in trade policymaking. On the one hand, the lawmakers were vested with an unambiguous constitutional charge "to regulate commerce with foreign nations." The importance of facing up to that responsibility had increased as the national economy became more dependent on world trade and as other levers of economic policy—the ability to tax and spend, for instance—became less flexible. On the other hand, those in Congress who devoted serious attention to trade issues did not wish to relieve the executive branch of its front-line duty. From time to time, they might try to channel or to circumscribe the commander in chief's tactical discretion, but they would never revoke it. In large part this was because enough lawmakers continued to recognize that trade was the sort of seductive political subject that was best managed when the legislature denied itself a completely free hand. Also, many legislators had come to realize that, with their hands partly tied, they could still attend to the local or national concerns they deemed important.

The most promising path for congressional influence was inside the maze of rules and regulations about unfair trade. Here, without retaking control from the executive, Congress periodically intensified the enforcement of trade remedies by making bold noises and then legislating with considerable subtlety. Interest in concrete lawmaking was episodic, swelling when requests to renew presidential negotiating authority were pending or when Congress was asked to ratify major trade accords. Flamboyance and bluffing tended to accompany the legislative process but were also used to apply pressure at critical stages in commercial disputes, or merely to express solidarity with various disaffected domestic groups, particularly during election years. Both forms of influence, the theatrical gestures and the substantive enactments, have animated trade policy. The latter warrant top billing, however. While the

91

statutory decisions often seemed unobtrusive and technical, they were bolting significant new regulatory fixtures firmly into place.

The Trade Act of 1974

Modifications of the trade laws had been a quid pro quo for nearly every extension of delegated negotiating authority since 1934, but the Trade Act of 1974 marked a watershed. When the Nixon administration, reeling from the Watergate scandal, requested permission to open the Tokyo Round of talks on reducing nontariff barriers, Congress took the opportunity to tuck into its authorizing legislation important, if obscure, legalistic refinements to "promote the development of an open, nondiscriminatory, and fair world economic system." [1]

Section 301

One such innovation broadened the basis for possible retaliation against foreign trading practices that were alleged to have an adverse effect on U.S. commerce. The Trade Expansion Act of 1962 had granted the president authority to impose duties or other sanctions in cases where certain types of U.S. products were unjustifiably barred from foreign markets. "Unjustifiable" meant unlawful—that is, in direct violation of the General Agreement on Tariffs and Trade (GATT) articles. [2] The 1974 legislation extended the scope of market-access investigations to "unreasonable" as well as GATT-illegal practices. It also encompassed trade in services, which was not yet in the GATT's orbit. [3]

Section 301 later became a much-used crowbar in the trade-policy tool kit. At first, however, even astute academic chroniclers of the legislative history of the 1974 act gave little scrutiny to section 301. [4]

The New Math of Dumping

Under the provisions of earlier legislation, sales of products to the United States were considered unfair only when there was evidence of international price discrimination (when the products were being priced lower abroad than in the home market). The 1974 act allowed imports to be actionable if they were sold below cost, even if the domestic and foreign prices were the same. [5] This notion was introduced by permitting a particular procedure for calculating the difference (or margin) between U.S. prices and "fair" prices. It became the standard practice to compare each sale in the United States to an average ("fair") value: only foreign sales above total costs of production were to be included in the average, and only U.S. sales below the average would be used to calculate the margin of dumping. If, during a period of investigation, sales above cost in the home market (or in third countries) were insufficient to provide a basis for comparison, regulators would "construct" a foreign market value by reviewing a suspected offender's average fully allocated unit costs and attaching an arbitrary 8 percent minimum for profits.

As a consequence of these methods, administrative authorities began finding that goods were being dumped in the majority of the complaints they investigated. Indeed, they could find positive dumping margins as long as prices varied over the period of observation, even when prices at home and abroad were identical.[6]

No spritely legislative debate attended this novelty. It seems to have been quietly masterminded by Russell B. Long of Louisiana, chairman of the Senate Finance Committee, who had come to the rescue of Freeport Industries, a Louisiana firm that was having trouble contesting the price of Canadian sulfur exports. Probably no one foresaw that the remodeled antidumping regime could create a trade regulator's bazaar, where creative Washington lawyers shopped on behalf of clients who were having problems with their competition. Certainly few legislators seem to have paused over the ramifications of the rules governing "sales below cost." In the months leading up to passage of the 1974 trade bill, most members were distracted by other problems, such as a proposal by Senator Thomas J. McIntyre to freeze tariffs for the benefit of the footwear industry and a renewed attempt by Representative James A. Burke and Senator Vance Hartke to impose rigid import quotas across-the-board. Under the cloud of dust raised by these contentious projects, the reworded antidumping section slipped through.

The Trade Agreements Act of 1979

When legislative approval was needed to implement the results of the Tokyo Round in 1979, Congress again set to work to refine statutory remedies. For example, in the course of ratifying the subsidy code of the GATT, the lawmakers detailed the kinds of export subsidies that might be subject to countervailing duties. The list grew long, including loans or loan guarantees at below-market rates, provision of government services on preferential terms, grants of funds or forgiveness of debt to cover an industry's operating losses, and the assumption by government of any production costs.[7] Although such activities were only off-limits when aimed at "a specific enterprise or industry," regulators interpreted the law to mean that enterprises within delineated geographic regions constituted specific recipients. As required by the GATT, the imposition of any countervails would now be based on an injury test. Tie votes in the U.S. International Trade Commission (ITC) would suffice to establish injury. Proven cases of subsidization (and of dumping) could be suspended without formal duties if the offending party agreed to rectify wrongs through negotiation.[8]

By legalizing negotiated resolutions of cases in lieu of visible penalties, Congress indirectly sanctioned a trend toward voluntary export restraints and orderly marketing arrangements. Parties on both sides increasingly chose to dispose of trade complaints in this politically commodious manner, even though it was economically least efficient. Most important, administration of dumping actions and countervailing duties was transferred from the Department of the Treasury to the Department of Commerce, which now operated under more stringent statutory deadlines and a more intensive system of judicial review.

Tight Schedules

In the ensuing years the changes of the 1979 law had consequences. The Trade Act of 1974 had managed to quadruple the number of petitions for countervailing duties and antidumping relief within a year.[9] Now, with the Commerce Department in charge, the number of investigations multiplied again. The combination of increased caseloads and compressed timetables required administrative shortcuts.

Not everyone had standing to file an antidumping or antisubsidy complaint; a petition had to be "on behalf of an industry." But with fewer days in which to check, it was harder to tell whether an individual firm was really speaking for the rest of its industry.[10] Once questions of standing were dispatched, the Commerce Department was required to reach a preliminary determination in less than four months. Voluminous foreign financial disclosures had to be collected within this period to calculate dumping or subsidy margins. Even cooperative foreign producers would sometimes fail to translate and return in time or in the proper format the extensive questionnaires required by the International Trade Administration (ITA).[11] Under these circumstances, the law authorized substituting "constructed values" and "the best information available" (or BIA), which the ITA often took to mean the information submitted in the domestic petitioner's brief.[12] Predictably, increased use of BIA (and constructed values) in dumping and subsidy investigations led not only to more affirmative determinations but to wider margins of unfair pricing.[13] Larger margins could, in turn, increase the chances of positive injury decisions by the ITC.[14]

Vigilant Courts

A more assertive judiciary would stiffen the spine of the investigative agencies. Prior to 1979 the Treasury Department exercised discretion in pursuing cases. Frivolous complaints were shelved or delayed, but sometimes so were cases that might involve significant economic or diplomatic strains. When the Court of International Trade (CIT) began reviewing many decisions, however, it curtailed administrative leeway, ordering the administering authority to follow up on all but the most patently deficient petitions.[15]

While Congress tightened the ITA's procedural time frames, judicialization added informational requirements. The ITA would be rebuked for revoking antidumping orders or terminating antidumping investigations, for instance, without up-to-date information on whether sales at less than fair value had ceased or, if they had ceased, might resume.[16] In 1984 the Court of Appeals for the Federal Circuit further required the Commerce Department's investigators to verify all information submitted by foreign respondents, not only at the outset but in annual reviews of antidumping orders.[17]

The courts also held the ITC to new standards. The commission had been in the habit of weighing conflicting facts in the earliest stages of its injury assessments. Consequently, petitions were sometimes dismissed after a preliminary inquiry. In a series of cases during the first half of the 1980s, however, the CIT ruled that any evidence of injury, regardless of offsetting facts, would constitute "reasonable indication" that a complete investigation was warranted.[18] The intent of Congress, the court affirmed, was that the trade laws be administered under a very low evidentiary threshold in preliminary hearings to allow almost all cases to run their full course.

Understanding the Reforms

One explanation for the modernization of the trade laws in 1979 was that the antidumping and countervailing duty statutes were still being inadequately enforced in the years following the 1974 act. Suffering industries were getting only slightly more support from the administrative procedures than they had before.[19] This interpretation, however, seems deficient. In the mid-1970s, thanks to a depreciating dollar, the U.S. trade balance in manufactured products shifted from deficit to surplus, a decline in America's portion of world trade in these goods was halted, and foreign commerce supplied a net addition to domestic output and jobs in manufacturing.[20] These conditions were not conducive to widespread calls for protection. Some argued that the protection actually afforded between 1974 and 1979 was considerable in light of the double-digit inflation plaguing the economy.

Numerous countervailing duties were waived during the Ford and Carter administrations, denying successful petitioners the full remedy of the law. But until 1979 the law under which duties could be imposed lacked an injury test, which kept it out of step with the emerging international code on subsidies. A discretionary waiver was temporarily indispensable if American negotiators were to pull other signatories into line. As for antidumping actions, the 1974 legislation had clearly induced an upsurge. A year after enactment, 75 dumping cases were being processed; by mid-1978 the number was 129.[21]

In part, Congress may also have revised the rules in 1979 because the revisions of 1974 had simply invited more. Although earlier attempts by American steel companies to curb imports through antidumping initiatives had failed, a 1977 complaint filed by Gilmore Steel against carbon steel plate from Japan hit pay dirt, thanks to skillful utilization of the law's cost-recovery and BIA criteria.[22] The Gilmore decision helped set off an avalanche of additional dumping charges, covering nearly $1 billion worth of steel shipments from Japan, from all the major European producers, and from India. The breadth of these cases eventually led the Carter administration to trim underpriced imports comprehensively through a so-called trigger price mechanism, which in effect placed a floor under the price of all imported steel. In the first five months of 1978, steel imports fell from 20 percent to 14 percent of the market.[23]

By 1979, however, the effectiveness of the mechanism was being undermined by shifts in exchange rates.[24] Domestic producers and their allies, finding the existing level of protection inadequate, lobbied for additional defenses, such as expedited procedures to offset foreign subsidies through antidumping and countervailing actions. In 1982 the steelmakers again lodged box loads of complaints against foreign (mainly European Community) suppliers. Before the ITC had ruled definitively on many of these cases, the Europeans volunteered to suppress exports in what amounted to a pretrial settlement, and the U.S. industry withdrew its petitions.

Although the 1979 act represented a major overhaul of the trade laws, the final package breezed through Congress (395 to 7 in the House, 90 to 4 in the

Senate). This was not just because the skids had been greased by parliamentary procedures that barred controversial riders on the floor, but also because the would-be hitchhikers had been picked up and placated elsewhere. Late in 1978, for example, Senator Ernest F. Hollings had almost won adoption of a measure that would have disallowed most of the Tokyo Round's negotiated reductions in textile duties. To block that bill from resurfacing in the next session, the Carter administration offered to ration textile imports through adjustments in the Multi-Fiber Arrangement. Likewise, the Senate bill included restrictions on sugar imports that were designed to keep the price of sugar from falling below 17 cents per pound. The provision was removed in conference, but only after the president agreed to raise the domestic price of sugar to 15.8 cents a pound (the world price was about 8.5 cents) by means of higher import fees or, if necessary, quotas on top of an additional half-cent-a-pound subsidy to farmers.[25] In the celebration at having sidetracked outright protectionist amendments, less unease was felt about the side deals that were cut or the potential for elliptical "process protectionism" in the 1979 legislation.

The Trade and Tariff Act of 1984

Despite an explosion of successful trade cases after 1979, vocal groups continued to fault the regulatory statutes. These criticisms gained force in the economic and political conditions of the early 1980s. Several basic industries, wracked by the 1981–82 recession, did not bounce back when the economy recovered. Renewed consumer demand and a high-flying dollar spurred competing imports, which the depressed industries sought to constrict by amending the trade laws.

Access points in Congress abounded. Responsibility for managing trade measures had once been concentrated in the Senate Finance and House Ways and Means committees by virtue of their primary jurisdiction over tariffs. As trade questions moved beyond tariffs and conceptions of foreign malfeasance changed, however, legislative power flowed downward to subcommittees and outward to other panels. At one time the chairmen of the two tax-writing committees could control the contents of trade bills. Now the cast of characters and the agendas they were trying to advance were becoming longer because of new, more complicated policy requirements and because of increased staff support and opportunities for political aggrandizement. Participation spread to include the House Energy and Commerce Committee (domestic content, certification standards), the House Foreign Affairs and Senate For-

Table 5-1. Foreign Trade Measures Referred to Selected House Committees, 1979–88

Number of trade measures having multiple referrals in parentheses

Congress	Years	Total	Agriculture	Banking, Finance and Urban Affairs	Energy and Commerce	Foreign Affairs	Ways and Means
96th	1979–80	565	60 (26)	45 (24)	53 (33)	145 (52)	262 (85)
97th	1981–82	593	57 (28)	51 (34)	58 (33)	155 (65)	272 (56)
98th	1983–84	674	42 (28)	65 (29)	68 (35)	151 (68)	348 (59)
99th	1985–86	866	88 (55)	85 (52)	78 (57)	173 (100)	442 (134)
100th	1987–88	904	49 (32)	108 (71)	83 (57)	199 (133)	465 (137)

Source: Library of Congress SCORPIO legislative files (CG) database.

eign Relations committees (foreign loans, export controls), the Judiciary committees (antitrust reciprocity), the banking committees (financial services, foreign investment, the Export-Import Bank), the agriculture committees (farm trade), the armed services committees (procurement codes), and so forth (see table 5-1). Trade bills had always been potential legislative Christmas trees, but weaker congressional gatekeepers, multiple referrals, and new parliamentary norms that invited changes from the floor meant that more ornaments could be hung on them.

These tendencies would be fully exhibited in drafting the landmark 1988 Trade Act, but hints of what lay ahead appeared in 1984. General trade legislation enacted that year amalgamated more than a hundred measures, many of which purported to fix deficiencies in existing law. Several additions had long-term significance.

Cumulative Dumping and Upstream Subsidies

An industry unable to prove that a country's dumped or subsidized exports caused hardship might still be damaged by the combined shipments of multiple foreign producers, no matter how small individually. The 1984 act, at the behest of domestic textile and steel companies, stepped in to stop such death by a thousand cuts.[26] Now, under a mandatory cumulation proviso, a domestic complainant could persuade the ITC that, say, $250,000 worth of Canadian fresh-cut flowers contributed to material injury. The ITC was required to lump in Canada's minimal flower exports with eight other countries whose annual U.S. sales each totaled more than $10 million.[27] Cumulation would force the Commerce Department to conduct more full investigations of dumping for more countries, even though predatory pricing was least plausible under import competition from many sources (including some with minuscule market shares).[28]

To this extensive task was added another: section 613, which enabled Commerce to impose countervailing duties on subsidized components if they "bestow[ed] competitive benefits" and had a "significant effect" on the manufacturing costs of final products for export. While the department retained discretion in making these judgments, an initial decision under the provision concluded that upstream subsidies accounting for more than 1 percent of the cost of producing the export product had a "significant effect."[29]

Generic Rules for Particular Reasons

At least three additional parts of the Trade and Tariff Act of 1984 were attempts to buttress specific business interests. The act made it harder for the

ITC to reject requests for relief under the standards of section 201. Earlier in the year the commission had turned down a petition from the shoemaking industry on the basis that large manufacturers of footwear were operating more profitably than the manufacturing average.[30] With the welfare of these producers in mind, Congress rewrote the law to ensure that regulators, in assessing injury, would consider factors other than mere profitability.[31]

In January 1984 a coalition of grape growers from New York and California had accused Italian and French winemakers of exporting wine at less than fair value. The ITC decided two months later that the petitioners lacked standing. The complaint had come from grape farmers, not vintners. Grapes could be sold for a variety of purposes—such as table fruit, juices, or raisins—other than making wine. In the commission's judgment, the degree of integration between the growers and the wineries was insufficient to establish the plaintiffs as representative of the winemaking "industry." The Senate balked, however, and rushed to revive the case by adopting a measure that would have broadened the definition of any agricultural industry to include the makers of the principal raw inputs along with the makers of the processed product. The House followed with similar legislation but narrowed its application to encompass only grapes and wine. The House's sui generis approach, along with a sunset clause, eventually prevailed in conference.

Title VIII of the 1984 act was dedicated to the steel industry. The steel lobby, turning up the political heat from one end of Pennsylvania Avenue to the other, had opened the year stoking a three-part strategy: Congress was urged to enact stringent quota legislation (labeled the Fair Trade in Steel Act of 1984); an escape clause petition was timed to force a presidential decision on the eve of the November election; and, as in 1982, the ITA and the ITC were crammed with dumping and subsidy complaints. The White House, hoping to lower the temperature, responded by promising to tighten existing voluntary restraint agreements with the EC and to negotiate similar agreements with the remaining "uncontrolled" suppliers. The stated goal of the administration's plan was to keep import penetration down to a target of 18.5 percent of domestic consumption for finished steel, or approximately 20.2 percent if semifabricated steel was included in the calculation.

The gesture soothed legislators, but not enough to deter them from trying to take matters a few steps farther. House Ways and Means Committee Chairman Dan Rostenkowski pursued a proposal, modeled on presidential candidate Walter Mondale's steel program, to set the import market share at 17 percent rather than 20.2 percent. What finally emerged was a compromise directing the executive to enforce the myriad voluntary restraints over five years, backed by the sense of Congress that imports should be kept within the 17 percent to 20.2 percent range.[32]

As had been true in 1979 and 1974, technicalities like these bored most people and were inserted over few objections. If anything, the insouciance was all the greater this time because the 1984 legislation had started out larded with blunt amendments protecting garments as well as grapes, bromine as well as table wine, copper as well as carbon steel, ferroalloys as well as footwear, and cow's milk as well as concentrated orange juice, but it had emerged from conference a good deal sleeker. The *Washington Post*, which a fortnight earlier had urged President Reagan to veto the bill, hailed the outcome as a "happy ending" in which "most of the bad stuff got thrown out and all of the good stuff stayed in."[33] Perhaps. But what remained perforce seemed tame in comparison with the original extremes. The story of the 1984 trade debate, in short, is not only about how a tall legislative Christmas tree was trimmed down, but also how, in its final rendition, the bill added more decorations to an ornate display of trade regulations already in place.

The Omnibus Trade and Competitiveness Act of 1988

The script was similar for the progress of the 1988 trade bill, except that it was played out over three years in an atmosphere more charged with partisan politics. This pageant's opening scene took place outside the Beltway—in east Texas on August 3, 1985. Running for a vacant House seat, Democratic candidate Jim Chapman fastened on trade as a "real red, white and blue issue." Chapman blamed Reagan administration policies for unilateral economic disarmament in the war on unfair imports and for the closing of a local steel plant, and he won (by a margin of less than 2 percent) in a district that had never sent a Republican to Congress.[34] Gearing up for the 1986 midterm campaign, Democratic strategists took the returns from the special election in Texas to mean that stern trade proposals, which had seemed so unpromising after Mondale's crushing defeat a year earlier, might provide live ammunition in the upcoming congressional contests. In the words of Representative Tony Coelho, chairman of the Democratic Congressional Campaign Committee, trade had become "a Democratic macho issue."[35]

To be sure, the various incarnations of the latest trade bill were born of more than partisan calculations. In 1985, when the House Ways and Means Committee reported out the first of a series of plans to penalize countries that stubbornly sold more merchandise to the United States than they bought, U.S.

external deficits were hitting new heights. The mood on Capitol Hill was that
doing something about these deficits, even something largely ineffectual, was
better than doing nothing, and that so far the administration had done nothing.
The sense of urgency was genuine. Democratic lawmakers felt it, but so did
some Republicans, particularly in the Senate, who had been advocating a
harder line on trade for years and who had left their mark on the 1984 bill.
Eventually the administration also joined the push for new legislation, mainly
to secure reauthorized negotiating powers for the Uruguay Round of multilateral discussions.

Party Favors

Still, the omnibus bill did not signify a concerted effort to fix the nation's
trade imbalance, nor was it plainly an exasperated reaction to a passive president; partisan politics played a notable part. The Reagan administration's record, if not its rhetoric, was hardly laissez-faire. In September 1985, the president announced a coordinated program of currency intervention to devalue
the dollar and reaffirmed his determination not to "stand by and watch American businesses fail because of unfair trading practices abroad."[36] Yet three
years later the legislative wagon continued to roll in spite of these preemptive
steps. Its drivers were principally the Democratic leadership, which perse-
vered in trying to flog a bulging trade package into law even after the October
1987 stock market crash had raised new doubts about its expediency and when
the monthly trade figures began showing a torrid increase in exports.[37] For
when the Democrats took control of the Senate in January 1987, adoption of
the trade bill had become the party's cause célèbre, and on both sides of the
Capitol, a process of political mobilization got under way that could be
slowed but not stopped.

The partisan maneuvering associated with H.R. 3 both delayed the bill's
enactment and freighted it with politically self-serving items. Until the Democrats regained a majority in the Senate, that body was unlikely to rally behind
the militant measures that were simmering in the Democratic House. With
notable exceptions, Republicans tended to distrust the House initiatives as
Democratic ploys to best Reagan's economic policies with a competing economic issue. (In theory, trade policy, like Reaganomics, involved little non-
defense spending and no obvious tax increases.) In the One-hundredth Congress, under unified Democratic control, the two bodies were better able to
act in tandem.

They were also in a stronger position to challenge the president, even strong enough to court a veto fight. That temptation became overwhelming in the spring of 1988 as the parties positioned themselves for the fall election. At the eleventh hour, after months of haggling to reach a compromise acceptable to the administration, the congressional negotiators suddenly dug in their heels over the only remaining insertion the White House had vowed to resist: a requirement that companies give advance notice of plant closings or layoffs. The Democrats, under intense pressure from organized labor to retain the stipulation at all costs, also sensed that they would enjoy a political windfall if the president carried out his threatened veto. He did, and the legislation was shelved for several more months pending resubmission of a twin version. Before recessing in the summer, however, a cloned H.R. 3 minus the plant closure clause finally cleared Congress. Satisfied, the president signed off.

The second result of partisanship was that the early drafts of the 1988 bill teemed with special provisions to please particular constituents and to provide grist for the campaign mills of some Democratic candidates. And because H.R. 3 was to be not just another trade act but something like a Democratic party economic program dealing comprehensively with "competitiveness," nearly two dozen standing committees fed in more than the usual number of controversial contributions. Although, again, most of the red herrings were gutted in conference, the effect was to move the debate's center of gravity toward the bill's widening coalition of support.

Gephardt & Bros.

During the debate, participants eased in a number of items that the conferees regarded as moderate substitutes compared with the lightning rods attracting media attention. An example was the substitution of the Senate's revision of section 301 for the Gephardt amendment.

As an influential member of Ways and Means, Congressman Richard A. Gephardt had managed to include a proposal requiring countries with "excessive and unwarranted" trade surpluses to make specified reductions in their bilateral imbalances with the United States or face the prospect of sanctions.[38] Because Gephardt was also running for president and fighting unfair trade was his main message, the amendment received a thorough inspection; free traders, newspaper editorialists, and political rivals rained derision on it. Having barely squeaked by on the House floor with a vote of 218 to 214, the proposal was generally expected to die in conference. It did, but observers paid less immediate attention to what the conference committee put in its place.

Senators Donald W. Riegle, Jr., and John C. Danforth drafted new language for section 301, requiring the U.S. Trade Representative (USTR) to identify publicly a list of countries having "a consistent pattern of import barriers and market distorting practices."[39] Negotiations with the identified countries would have to eliminate or otherwise compensate for those barriers and unjustifiable practices, with the "expectation" of lifting U.S. exports "as a result." If these talks failed, sanctions would loom.

To its critics "Super 301," much like the Gephardt amendment, conjured up the spectacle of the world's supreme superpower subjecting its trading partners to public humiliation.[40] These fears proved to be exaggerated. The conference agreement set a two-year expiration period for the most indelicate part of the law, the mandatory "identification" of offenders, and the USTR did not repeatedly indict suspected recidivists (like Japan) under the Super 301 process. Nonetheless, the notion of promulgating an "expectation" that exports had to increase incrementally in the course of bilateral consultations was reminiscent of Gephardt's results-oriented approach. Although the Riegle-Danforth plan did not develop into a twin "brother of Gephardt," as one skeptic quipped, it was obviously a relative, one that Congress adopted with comparatively little fuss.[41]

Some significant changes in the administration of section 301 were permanent. Retaliation was made mandatory whenever negotiations did not "obtain the elimination" of unjustifiable foreign trading practices. Although the president could waive action under specified circumstances, conditions were created that would render routine waivers difficult. Under existing law, the USTR could only investigate trade complaints and make a recommendation to the president, who would decide what steps, if any, to take. The new rules transferred to the USTR the power to determine which foreign economies were unfair and what remedial measures to impose. Although the USTR would still be lodged in the Executive Office of the President, where it would remain decidedly a presidential agency, the shift of responsibilities made it harder for the president to refuse retaliation; to do so would give the appearance of blocking the lead trade agency in the conduct of its newly mandated duties.

Dumping Revisited

This transfer of authority and the Riegle-Danforth "World Market Opening Initiative" were relatively prominent elements of the big trade law. Other elements were buried more deeply. Particulars of antidumping and antisubsidy regulation once again were reworked. Several changes originated in specific recommendations from domestic companies that, for one reason or another, had failed to obtain import relief before 1988.[42]

In 1987 the Court of International Trade had overturned a Commerce Department decision to countervail imports of pork products from Canada.[43] The department had erroneously assumed that Canadian subsidies to pig farmers should be fully reflected in final prices for processed pork. Rising to the defense of frustrated local producers in their states, Senators Max Baucus, Charles Grassley, and David Pryor outflanked the CIT: section 1313 of the 1988 act would require that, under conditions like those in the pork case, the entire subsidy on agricultural inputs be passed through in identifying unfair prices for processed foods.

Until 1988, the antidumping statute dealt only with imports to the United States. This limited scope no longer suited certain industries whose products might be undersold in third markets as well as at home. Hence Congress updated the law, coaxing the USTR to prevail on other countries to conduct dumping investigations on behalf of U.S. petitioners.[44]

After 1979 the main obstacle to petitioners seeking protection under the dumping or countervailing duty laws was not the Commerce Department's procedures but the causality test before the ITC. The commission was charged with evaluating not just the existence of material injury but the possible "threat" thereof. To highlight these prospective threats, Congress in 1988 told the commissioners to begin taking into account a suspected foreign producer's behavior in the markets of other GATT members as an indication of how that producer was likely to behave in the U.S. market.[45] This nuance was a response in part to domestic manufacturers of outboard motors, who feared that Japanese competitors were poised to target the United States after they had undercut prices in Australia and Europe.

The lawmakers also widened the reach of antidumping enforcement in the following three respects. Smith Corona Corporation and some other firms had complained bitterly that foreign exporters were evading the law by making small changes in product design or by shipping parts and reassembling products in the United States. In some cases, unfairly priced goods were being diverted to third-country markets, where they would be incorporated into new merchandise for export. In still other cases, there was concern that some offenders, unless rapidly deterred, would follow a chronic pattern of desisting and then resuming their dumping.

To counter the first form of circumvention, the new legislation extended existing antidumping orders to remodeled or reassembled products, even at the risk of discouraging foreign investment in U.S.-based assembly operations and the efforts of U.S. companies to improve their competitiveness by importing components.[46] In addition, procedures were established to monitor downstream products.[47] So if, say, country X dumped brass into country Y, which then exported brass lamps to the United States, the lamps would be subject to investigation even if the lamp producers were consistently selling the lamps at more than 100 percent of cost. Lobbied by the Semiconductor Industry Association, the lawmakers mandated expedited investigations of foreign exporters caught dumping "short life-cycle products" (like Japanese computer chips) more than once in an eight-year period.[48]

Other Corrections

Section 1342 received scant publicity, yet it introduced a fundamental change in the procedures for protecting intellectual property rights (section 337 of the 1930 Tariff Act). Corning Glass, set back by the dispositions of the ITC and the District of Columbia Circuit Court in a complaint about patent violations, prevailed on the legislators to eliminate any need to prove injury in patent-infringement cases.[49] Meanwhile, growing competition for Boeing and McDonnell Douglas from Airbus Industrie resulted in new wording in the countervailing duty law: under section 1314, subsidies to international consortia from an ad hoc group of countries were to be combined in calculating the duties.

For the telecommunications equipment industry, sections 1374 and 1375 instructed the USTR to negotiate suitable "market opportunities" with countries that had denied "mutually advantageous" ones to U.S. manufacturers. Where the negotiations bore no fruit, the president was required to choose from a list of sanctions, including higher tariffs, exclusion from government procurement, and revocation of other bilateral trade agreements.

An extensive array of other industries and individual companies received special consideration. The USTR was ordered to initiate a section 301 action for the benefit of architectural, engineering, construction, and consulting services seeking to do business in Japan (section 1305). The president was ordered to "establish reciprocity" between sales of metallurgical coal to Japan and steel products bought from that nation (section 1933). The ITC was ordered to probe imports of lamb (section 1937). The Department of Commerce was ordered to open "an initiative" to increase the market for U.S.-made auto parts and accessories in Japan (section 2123). The Federal Reserve of New York was prohibited from allowing foreign-owned securities companies to operate as primary dealers of U.S. government debt instruments if the dealers' home country did not extend corresponding privileges to U.S. counterparts (sections 3501 and 3502). The secretary of the treasury was instructed to submit periodic reports to Congress on efforts to overcome foreign discrimination against U.S. banks and securities firms (section 3602). Additional subsidies for a wide range of farm exports were authorized (sections 4301 through 4311), and new price supports were provided for some products (sunflower seeds, for example). Section 4404 directed the Department of Agriculture to "actively use" concessional programs and export credit guarantees for more than food: wood and processed wood products would now qualify. To help one pharmaceutical manufacturer, Warner-Lambert, the Commissioner of Patents and Trademarks was ordered to extend a patent on the cholesterol-reducing drug Lopid beyond its original expiration date (section 9201).[50] Stuffed with all these and other specific instructions and directives, the 1988 trade legislation ran on for hundreds of pages.

Conclusion

Anxious to be a player in the trade policy game, but also apprehensive about reverting to primitive protectionism, Congress has practiced an indirect role: it expresses its preferences without legislating, or it legislates mainly to provide more administrative redress against unfair competitors. This approach has reflected more than the fact that "lots of Democrats want to vote for a protectionist bill, but don't want to appear protectionist."[51] Concern about asymmetrical trading relationships pervaded the legislature, and not only for partisan gain. Much energy was channeled into legislation that tried to liberalize markets abroad, resisting in general a temptation to create excuses for more market closures at home. On the whole, the revamping of section 301 in 1988 turned out to have some of its intended effect, as did some other market-access provisions. By all accounts, for instance, the "primary dealers" sections of the 1988 act, which insisted on the principle of national treatment for dealers of government bonds, were useful in encouraging Japan to accelerate liberalization of the bond market.

Still, frequent amendment of the trade statutes was also a means of serving specific constituents—mostly without the disagreeable fallout of crude, high-handed intervention. Illustrative were the antidumping procedures. Administrative recourse against dumping had been repeatedly reorganized and adjusted to afford more protection than had been possible under the original law of 1916. These incremental adjustments and reorganizations were seldom conspicuous enough to provoke great controversy. The revisions tended to be too arcane to be understood by anyone but cognoscenti, and they often looked modest when juxtaposed with more colorful proposals in legislative debates. The antidumping amendments adopted in 1988, for instance, were mild compared with a bill, rejected by the Senate, that would have given plaintiffs the right to sue for damages in dumping cases.

The cumulative effect of the legislative activity, however, was becoming significant; an extensive patchwork of regulations was being pieced together, with new layers repeatedly stitched to older ones. The massive trade bill of 1988 was touted at the time as a crowning achievement, not to be readily superseded. Three years later, with a presidential election year looming, the retailoring and reinforcing of trade legislation began anew.[52]

CHAPTER SIX

Functions of the Executive

ON MARCH 23, 1981, Foreign Minister Masayoshi Ito of Japan paid a visit to the Oval Office. President Reagan brought up a touchy issue: the administration firmly opposed import restraints, but strong sentiment was building on Capitol Hill to impose them on Japanese automobiles. The president explained that he wasn't sure the congressional moves could be stopped. "But," he told Ito, "I think if you *voluntarily* set a limit on your automobile exports to this country, it would probably head off the bills pending in Congress and there wouldn't be any mandatory quotas."[1] The idea worked; on May 1 the Japanese announced a multiyear plan to control car exports, and a few days later the House and Senate sponsors of quota bills canceled their markups.

It is hard to know what Congress would really have done if the Reagan administration had refused to negotiate protection for the automobile industry. Rounding up enough votes to overcome a veto of legislated quotas would not have been easy in view of the president's extraordinary popularity at the time. Furthermore, such quotas would have been a flagrant breach of American obligations under article 11 of the General Agreement on Tariffs and Trade (GATT) and article 14 of the Treaty of Friendship, Commerce and Navigation between the United States and Japan. But the administration cooperated anyway, and not just because Congress may have been on a credible legislative warpath. Reagan felt the Japanese "weren't playing fair in the trade game."[2] He had vowed during his election campaign to "convince [them that] . . . the deluge of [their] cars into the United States must be slowed."[3] With that pledge plainly on record, a veto ceased to be a live option.

Naturally, in arranging with the Japanese government to rein in exports, the administration found it useful to emphasize that the legislative branch had forced the executive's hand and that a negotiated solution with the good cops downtown would be milder than the alternative contemplated by the bad cops

109

on Capitol Hill.[4] Noting that Congress had compelled the administration to act, the White House could shift some of the onus for the $5 billion the voluntary restraint agreement would cost society.[5] Responsibility could be suspended somewhere between the two institutions, since the legislature had not legislated, and it too would not take all the blame.

Four years later the diplomatic pas de trois became even fancier. The restraint agreement was due to expire at the end of March 1985. At the beginning of that month, the administration announced it would not seek an extension (though the Japanese were also told that "we look[ed] forward to reciprocal treatment").[6] A few weeks later the Ministry of International Trade and Industry (MITI) raised the quota on auto shipments by 25 percent. The prospective increase caused consternation in Congress, where the House and the Senate adopted nonbinding resolutions reproaching Japan. Prime Minister Nakasone, retreating to safer ground, described the higher limit as an "error in judgement."[7] Any thought of eliminating the cap on exports altogether now seemed out of the question. The May 1981 "token agreement" continued in force, with no end in sight.[8]

Evidently, significant programs of trade rectification could develop even when Congress enacted nothing. Some were joint ventures, so to speak, in which the White House played more than a reactive role. This active partnership may have seemed strange with an administration that preferred to let markets take care of themselves. The Reagan administration was only following a longstanding tradition, however: trade determinations had always turned, to an important degree, on presidential politics. From the oil import quotas of the Eisenhower years to the steel regulations of the Carter administration, the major trade-controlling programs of the postwar period seldom sprang directly from acts of Congress (see table 6-1).

Moreover, Reagan was not the first to invoke fairness as the justification for many of these efforts. Considering expansion of the existing quotas on textiles in the early 1970s, Richard M. Nixon contended that wider quotas would rectify "unfair" differences in market access.[9] Jimmy Carter's steel trigger price system was framed, not as simple protection afforded by imposing constraints on quantities of imports, but as a remedy for a trade abuse. The administration drew on accusations of unfair pricing and deployed the antidumping laws to regulate supplies. Indeed, justifying this approach, the president appeared to outdo even the fiercest congressional firebrands: he had harsh words not only for foreign steel manufacturers but for his own Treasury Department, which he charged with "derogation of duty" in enforcement.[10]

Episodes like this were part of a wider phenomenon: the executive could

Table 6-1. *U.S. Industries with a Domestic Market Above $100 Million Protected by Statutory and Administrative Trade Restrictions, 1948–90*

Industry	Year[a]	Industry	Year[a]
Statutory		Sugar	1977
Sugar	1948	CB radio tranceivers	1978
Fish		High-carbon ferrochromium	1978
Nicholson Act	1950	Unalloyed unwrought copper	1978
Maritime Industry		Electric motors	1980
Merchant Marine Act	1950	Leather apparel	1980
Cargo Preference Act	1954	Nonelectric cookingware	1980
Air transport	1958	Pig iron	1980
Book Manufacturing		Automobiles	1981
Copyright Act	1970	Ceramic floor and wall tiles	1982
Fish		Leather apparel	1982
Magnuson Act	1976	Nitrocellulose	1982
Frozen concentrated orange juice	1984	Sugar	1982
		Heavyweight motorcycles	1983
Administrative[b]		Iron construction castings	1985
Dairy products	1953	Oil country tubular goods	1985
Canned tuna	1956	Brass sheet and strip	1986
Textiles		In-shell pistachio nuts	1986
Voluntary restraint agreements	1956	Semiconductors	1986
Lead and zinc	1958	Softwood lumber	1986
Petroleum	1959	Wood shakes and shingles	1986
Textiles		Color picture tubes	1987
Short-term agreement	1961	Fresh-cut flowers	1987
Long-term agreement	1962	Industrial phosphoric acid	1987
Meat	1964	Machine tools	1987
Carbon steel	1968, 1982, 1984	Tapered roller bearings and parts	1987
Ceramic kitchen and table articles	1972	Internal combustion engine forklist trucks	1988
Ball bearings	1974	Nitrile rubber	1988
Bolts, nuts, and screws	1974, 1978	3.5″ microdisks and media	1988
Textiles multifiber agreement	1974, 1978, 1982, 1986	Aluminum sulfate	1989
		Industrial belts	1989
Prepared mushrooms	1976, 1980	Telephone systems and subassemblies	1989
Slide fasteners and parts	1976	Gray Portland cement	1990
Specialty steel	1976, 1983	Sweaters wholly or in chief weight of manmade fibers from Hong Kong	1990
Color TV receivers	1977		
High-carbon ferrochromium	1977		
Nonrubber footwear	1977, 1985		

Sources: I.M. Destler, *American Trade Politics: System under Stress* (Washington: Institute for International Economics, 1986), pp. 238–41; Gary C. Hufbauer, *Trade Protection in the United States: Thirty-One Case Studies* (Washington: Institute for International Economics, 1986), pp. 43–355; Publication 2242 (United States International Trade Commission (December 1989); Pub. 1930 (December 1986); Pub. 2099 (July 1988); Pub. 2046 (December 1987); Pub. 1116 (December 1980); Pub. 2222 (October 1989); Pub. 2314 (September 1990); Pub. 1956 (March 1987); Pub. 1968 (April 1987); Pub. 2154 (February 1989); Pub. 2305 (August 1990); Pub. 2376 (April 1991); Pub. 1988 (June 1987); Pub. 845 (December 1977); Pub. 2194 (May 1989); Pub. 2000 (August 1987); Pub. 1875 (July 1986); Pub. 2082 (May 1988); Pub. 1720 (June 1985); and Pub. 1838 (April 1986); Pub. 1030 (January 1980); Pub. 2170 (March 1989); Pub. 2090 (June 1988); Pub. 1280 (August 1982); Pub. 1694 (May 1985); Pub. 1865 (June 1986); Pub. 1048 (March 1980); Pub. 2383 (May 1991); Pub. 1190 (October 1981); Pub. 2360 (February 1991); Pub. 757 (February 1976); Pub. 807 (March 1977); Pub. 2312 (September 1990); Pub. 1999 (August 1987); Pub. 1983 (June 1987); Pub. 2237 (November 1989); Pub. 905 (August 1978); 50 Fed. Reg. (1985); Department of the Treasury, U.S. Customs Service, *Harmonized Tariff Schedule of the United States* (Washington, 1991), chap 64; *Impact of Mushroom Imports on the U.S. Mushroom Industry,* report prepared for the American Mushroom Institute (Alexandria, Va.: Daft & Earley, September 1990); and Department of Transportation, *Midway-US Air Route Transfer,* Docket no. 47301 (Washington, February 11, 1991).

  a. Year indicates the date restriction was first imposed.

  b. Administrative category includes protection under the following: section 201 (escape clause) and section 301 (unfair trade practices) of the Trade Act of 1974; section 731 (antidumping) and section 701 (countervailing duties) of the 1930 Tariff Act; discretionary protection ordered under the executive's inherent constitutional powers in foreign relations (voluntary restraint agreements); and discretionary protection authorized under numerous trade statutes including section 22 of the 1933 Agricultural Adjustment Act, section 204 of the 1956 Agriculture Act, section 232 of the 1962 Trade Expansion Act, and the discretionary meat and sugar quotas under the Jones-Costigan Act of 1934 and the Meat Import Act of 1965.

check and balance the pressures for measures regulating foreign trade, but it also contributed to them. Sometimes the contribution was contemplated with diplomatic or political considerations in mind; at other times it seemed more like an unintended byproduct of the interplay between governmental branches.

Courting Congress

Executive trade moves have been motivated in large part by the fact that sustaining control of trade policy requires maintaining the confidence of Congress. Presidents have not just coveted for its own sake the power that Congress has delegated to them; they have needed it to keep negotiating new multilateral pacts that have increased national and global welfare and that have helped hold protectionist forces at bay. By continually peddling toward better world trading rules, each administration could cite the higher authority of international law to keep the American commitment to open markets from flagging. Every president has needed to affirm an interest in fair trade regulation to elicit congressional cooperation when it was time to renew negotiating authority. Executive latitude on policy could depend on how keen that interest appeared to be and on how well the regulations preempted the legislative lobbying activity of various trade-sensitive factions. Put another way, executive-legislative interactions resembled a marriage of convenience in which the pragmatic partners periodically endeared themselves, not just by reacting belatedly to each other's demands, but also by anticipating one another's wishes.[11]

But that is not the whole story. Presidential courtship of Congress was sometimes unnecessarily solicitous. Many members of Congress, despite their gripes, did not relish the responsibility of a fully emancipated relationship. Imaginably, presidents less prepared to compromise their preferences for unintrusive trade policies and more willing to call Congress's bluff could hold their own. So many protective concessions were made on behalf of textiles and other industries to win passage of the Trade Expansion Act (the 1962 authorization for the Kennedy Round) that no one was sure how soon the fruits of trade liberalization under the act would offset the specific restrictions.[12] The bartering for votes may have exceeded what was needed to ensure a minimum winning coalition; the bill passed much more comfortably than expected (298 to 125 in the House, 78 to 8 in the Senate).[13] Clearing every subsequent international trade treaty has necessitated numerous side payments, but maybe not the overkill that tacticians in the White House might consider necessary. The Tokyo Round codes and the comprehensive trade agreement with Canada, too, were adopted by margins so lopsided that passage might have been ensured with less vote-buying.[14] When the chips were down in these high-stakes games, most legislators were amply motivated by another incentive: they had little desire to be held responsible for trashing the GATT or spoiling free trade with an important next-door neighbor.

The traditional distinction between a constituent-minded legislature clamoring incessantly for import bars and a globally minded president standing steadfastly for regulatory minimalism is somewhat simplistic. Both dread being burned by protectionism, but neither can always refrain from spilling some fuel on the flames.

Bigger Fish to Fry

Although international economic problems have claimed more presidential attention in recent years, they have seldom ranked at the top of an increasingly congested agenda.[15] The White House, unlike much of the Congress, has traditionally viewed trade tiffs as a sideshow. Even the most salient trade issues could still seem prosaic and picayune in comparison with the momentous questions of war and peace or the big stories in domestic policy. To put matters in perspective, the cost to taxpayers of the savings and loan bailout alone is several times as large as the direct annual cost to consumers of all extant U.S. import restrictions.[16] Many congressmen may have longed for commercial altercations to be the focus of more lengthy cabinet sessions and summit meetings; they would complain when "the President has gone off to Tokyo and he's taken neither the secretary of commerce or the U.S. trade representative."[17] But for better or worse, trade policy has not been the stuff of presidential memoirs.[18] Whether the annals of the Bush administration would look the same was less clear. In January 1992, the president abruptly transformed a long-awaited state visit to Japan into a trade mission, departing with a retinue of corporate executives. The 1992 Tokyo summit included much haggling over items like car sales, auto parts, and paper products.

Trade-Ins

To conserve political horsepower for high-priority initiatives and to help lubricate the legislative pistons, presidents make compromises. Consistency

in trade policy has sometimes been among the luxuries to be selectively sac-
rificed. For all the disagreeable risks, few fatal accidents seemed likely to
result from short-run digressions, and some quick political mileage could
even be recorded: here and there a sputtering firm or industry might be jump-
started, pleasing some representatives in Congress and loosening gridlock.
The sticker prices attached to these measures were hard to read; they rarely
translated into visible tax increases or big lines in the federal budget. When
the potential liabilities threatened to cause discomfiture in the economy or in
foreign relations, they could be finessed to a considerable degree by diplomacy.

Carter's steel import regulations served the dual purpose of saving the administration's 1979 omnibus trade bill by staying one step ahead of the
congressional steel caucus and marshaling support for a more publicized project on which the president had staked his reputation: the National Energy
Plan. When the controversial energy package was teetering in Congress during the summer of 1978, key business leaders were invited to a series of meetings at 1600 Pennsylvania Avenue. By mid-September, the names of scores of
major corporations, financial institutions, and trade associations that had decided to back the energy legislation were being circulated on Capitol Hill.[19]
The legislation soon passed, but corporate interests had wrested various promises in return for their consent; special arrangements for the steel industry
were reportedly among the concessions.[20]

The Reagan White House repeatedly subordinated commercial policy decisions to other, more basic ends such as fiscal experiments. Early in 1981,
the new administration was on record as opposing higher crop supports for
sugar. That summer, however, the president's operatives were wheeling and
dealing to compose a congressional majority for his first budget proposal.
Some conservative Democrats in the House held back their swing votes until
the last moment and then named their price: a new sugar program. With the
help of the Boll Weevils, the Reagan budget was adopted—and by the following spring, so were sugar import quotas. One leader of the sugar state faction,
Representative John Breaux of Louisiana, delicately allowed that his vote had
been "rented, not bought."[21]

Divided government and weak party discipline indeed meant that support
in Congress was never purchased in perpetuity, only rented. A different ad hoc
coalition had to be pieced together a few years later to secure the Tax Reform
Act. With the fate of this historic project riding on a vote of confidence from
the Senate Finance Committee in the spring of 1986, the administration could
ill afford to ignore the desires of influential constituents, particularly those in

the chairman's home state of Oregon. It was not surprising, therefore, to hear U.S. Trade Representative Clayton Yeutter suggest in mid-April that Canadian pricing practices for standing timber were unfair.[22] If Yeutter appeared to pre-judge the outcome of an upcoming Commerce Department investigation, the political timing was just right: Senator Packwood and several other committee members from lumber-producing areas received a signal that relief for the lumber industry was probably on the way.

Marginal inducements like these were not normally decisive in themselves, but cumulatively they almost certainly made a difference. At a White House meeting on September 11, 1985, Republican congressional leaders let it be known that a brawnier trade policy might become a quid pro quo for any plan to revamp the income tax system. "If we don't act on trade before we act on tax reform," one senator explained, "I don't think there will be any tax reform bill."[23] The president declined to cooperate with congressional Democrats on their omnibus trade legislation until two years later, but long before that he and his aides showed some willingness to take more seriously Congress's underlying concerns. The September 11 strategy session featured a number of legislative suggestions from the administration, including proposals to aug-ment the authority of the U.S. Trade Representative, to strengthen intellectual property protection, to sharpen the antidumping laws, and to square off against foreign tied-aid export programs. The administration's hardening line on trade soon became more than a rumor; on September 23, Reagan vowed to "work unceasingly" to defend "those industries that are victims of unfair trade."[24]

Tools of the Trade

Every president has known, of course, that clumsy departures from free trade can be economically and politically damaging, sometimes having direct, nondiffuse impacts at home and causing angry reactions abroad. But thanks to the way potentially explosive cases have generally been handled—through bilateral executive agreements instead of legislated tariffs—the perils often seemed less grave.

At home the political advantages of negotiated export restraints and orderly marketing agreements were considerable.[25] The implicit subsidies and costs were largely hidden. Calling the restraints "voluntary" provided a fig leaf for government intervention and avoided the need to compensate the exporting country (as the GATT requires when a discriminatory tariff or quota is im-posed). The voluntary agreements often appealed to the foreign suppliers. Not only would they enable producers to make higher profits on the mix of merchandise sold to the restricted market, as the Japanese car and semiconductor manufacturers were able to do; they also permitted dominant companies in an industry to form export cartels, shielding these firms from the possible competition of more dynamic newcomers.[26] Under normal circumstances this kind of connivance would be difficult to arrange or, if arranged, hard to uphold. But officially negotiated restraints could create what amounted to government-engineered cartels, enforced by export licenses and safe from legal challenges because the member firms could technically claim immunity under the doctrine of "sovereign" (or governmental) compulsion.

Arrangements that have enabled foreign producers to capture the scarcity profits created by protection (instead of at least allowing the U.S. Customs Service to collect these rents, as a straight tariff would) might appear to make little sense from the standpoint of the national economic interest. In most cases, however, the revenues were willingly forgone because the political and diplomatic expediency of voluntary restraints seemed to outweigh them. In any event, most taxpayers remained unaware of the waste.

Promises

Negotiated restraint agreements and orderly marketing accords have seemed to offer painless solutions to pesky trade disputes. Sometimes they afforded a means of advancing policy initiatives unrelated to trade. In addition, electoral pressures have often driven the executive to act. Indeed, the tug of electoral politics on the trade decisions of presidents (and would-be presidents) has sometimes been at least as strong as the periodic need to co-opt congressional protectionists.

The modern process of presidential selection has ultimately accounted for much of the gravitational force. Contenders in recent decades have had to hustle to obtain (or to retain) nominations and to finance excruciatingly long campaigns. Inevitably, obligations to special interests would accumulate in the course of these marathons. Nixon, laboring to amass support in the South, was an early case in point. During the tight contest of 1968, George Wallace was claiming a sizable conservative base in key southern states. To help retake the base, Nixon assured Senator Strom Thurmond of South Carolina that "necessary" steps would be taken to extend the existing quotas on cotton to wools, synthetic fibers, and blends.[27] This element of the Republican "southern strategy" helped carry the Carolinas and win the election. In due time, it was also responsible for the first multifiber agreement encompassing all textile articles.

In 1976 Gerald Ford confronted first a stiff challenge for the nomination and then the prospect of a rugged general election. When a report from the International Trade Commission (ITC) favoring protection for specialty steel producers landed on his desk amid this turmoil, the recommendation was difficult to turn down. Orderly marketing arrangements with the major supplying countries followed. Unwilling to grant protection to every group seeking similar aid at the time, however, the Ford administration rejected a request for relief by the footwear industry in April.[28] A year later, following a close race that had left the victor in need of solidifying his credentials with key Democratic constituencies, such as organized labor, Jimmy Carter seemed more careful to err on the safe side; he rejected an ITC plan for higher shoe tariffs, but directed his special trade representative, Robert S. Strauss, to negotiate orderly marketing programs with Taiwan and Korea.[29]

In the 1980s Walter Mondale's candidacy was perhaps the most flagrant example of a presidential campaign towing heavy commitments to groups with trade afflictions. Had Mondale won, his many understandings with labor and other factions experiencing troubles ascribed to imports could have forced him to deliver on much of his rhetoric. Although Ronald Reagan was not equally burdened, neither was he wholly unencumbered. As noted in chapter 4, several of the trade plans initiated during his presidency—most notably, curbs on automobile and textile imports—could be traced to the politics of presidential elections.

Even in 1988, when presidential aspirants who talked tough on trade fared poorly, the jockeying in a few pivotal primaries altered some positions. In Iowa and Michigan, caucus states where contestants attempted to pitch highly parochial appeals at tiny bands of voters, the campaign elicited new pledges to negotiate a better shake for the Midwest's long-suffering farmers, workers, and businesses. In preparation for the Michigan primary, Michael Dukakis, the eventual Democratic nominee, suddenly announced support for the stiffest provision in the pending trade legislation, Super 301, cosponsored by Senator Riegle of Michigan, whose endorsement he had just received.[30] Dukakis lost the Michigan caucus but remained on record in favor of Riegle's amendment for the rest of the campaign. George Bush later successfully painted the Massachusetts governor as a foreign policy neophyte with a wobbly understanding of international economics. But while Bush set off on the high road of free trade, he took a few detours of his own to secure key states. In one such state, Pennsylvania, he promised to prolong the comprehensive restraint agreements for the steel industry. When his administration took the reins in 1989, the USTR also duly deployed Super 301 against Japan (albeit more gingerly than Congress had apparently intended).

How many declarations of devotion to fair trade regulation a candidate issued in the course of a campaign turned in part on how close the election appeared to be. Reagan's staff in 1980 felt it necessary to make more binding overtures to particular interest groups than did Bush's staff in 1988. The Bush campaign's promissory note to the steel lobby seemed to reflect the growing influence of cautious political handlers more than the rigors of a closely contested general election. How nearly presidents adhered to their pronouncements, in turn, has depended on a host of factors, including the nature and size of the electoral mandate, the strength of the president's party in Congress, the extent of inflationary pressures in the economy, foreign policy, and the latitude Congress is willing to grant. On the whole, postwar presidents managed to remain nimble enough to modify, if they could not avoid, some regrettable campaign promises.[31] But their flexibility has not been unlimited, no matter how Congress delineated presidential discretion.

Bureaucratic Forces

Compared with the commercial ministries of America's main competitors, the trade agencies in Washington have traditionally lacked independent power. With the exception of the Finance Ministry, Japan's fabled MITI has long enjoyed more autonomy and prestige than any other bureau in the Japanese government, including the Ministry of Foreign Affairs. The U.S. Department of Commerce, by contrast, has always been something of a stepchild in the cabinet, usually upstaged on foreign economic policy by the departments of state, treasury, and defense. The Office of the U.S. Trade Representative is an elite organization, but it, too, is constrained. Its upper ranks are almost entirely staffed by appointive, noncareer officials serving very much at the president's pleasure. At the same time, this agency often has to satisfy two masters: like other units in the executive office, the USTR is an annex of the White House. Unlike the rest of the executive office, it must also report directly and frequently to Congress.

Nevertheless, recent trade representatives and commerce secretaries have been able to discharge their duties imaginatively at a number of critical junctures. In the spring of 1989, for example, Ambassador Carla A. Hills played one overseer off against another during intramural skirmishes (principally staged by the Office of Management and Budget and the Council of Economic Advisers) and managed to turn the Super 301 provision of the 1988 Trade Act to good advantage. Japan, Brazil, and India were promptly cited as "priority" unfair traders (thereby assuaging Congress), but the USTR surgically selected issues that were at once eminently negotiable and emblematic of the administration's broader multilateral objectives under the terms of the GATT.[32]

At about the same time, Commerce Secretary Robert A. Mosbacher, backed by the USTR, the Labor Department, the National Aeronautics and Space Administration, and most of the Congress, called into question an arrangement with Japan to codevelop a new fighter aircraft (the FSX). In the interdepartmental debate that raged during this sensitive affair, the Pentagon, with support from the State Department and the National Security Council, was more worried about the foreign policy negatives of renegotiating an existing agreement with a strategic ally than about the possible hijacking of American aerospace technology. On balance, the Mosbacher faction prevailed: when the infighting was over, a new, "clarified" FSX deal emerged.

Trade administrators had begun to flex more muscle well before these contests. During Reagan's second term, the USTR opened several section 301 investigations that echoed a strong sentiment in Congress to do something about unfair trade but that had not been the subject of formal démarches from private industry. The timing of some of these cases even caught some of their beneficiaries by surprise. U.S. computer and software companies, for example, reportedly regarded as inopportune the onset of an action against Brazil's informatics law in 1985. The companies claimed they had not been consulted.[33]

The Commerce Department, too, was given more rope. Under Malcolm Baldrige, perhaps the most prominent commerce chief in recent memory, the department won some major bureaucratic battles, including a hotly contested decision in 1982 to place steel quotas on several European countries. Later, ferreting out trade offenses became the charge of a special "strike force," which Baldrige headed. Some new scuffles with trading partners, involving issues such as the construction contracts at Osaka's Kansai airport, originated with entrepreneurs in the department, not businessmen, congressmen, or White House policy planners. In addition, some consequential standard operating procedures used by the department in dumping investigations were institutionalized without explicit directives from either the president or the Congress.

In sum, while most of the government's efforts to correct trade were induced by aggrieved interest groups and legislators (and sometimes presidents trying to stay in their good graces), some were informed or reinforced from within, by the bureaucracy.

Mission

Those who administer the trade laws typically describe their tasks not as charting broad commercial strategies, but as responding to disturbances on a day-to-day basis—"putting out fires." For some, this role has been too passive. According to these critics, American economic interests around the world would be better served if policymakers behaved less like firefighters and more like strategic planners, formulating definite trade targets and goals.

Veterans of the grueling negotiations with Japan in the 1980s later suggested that the U.S. government might have been better off to "negotiate a market share or a specific amount of sales," or that the Japanese government should be expected to "set import goals for Japan, established as *objectives*."[34] Officials with these views had grown impatient with the complacency they perceived in the midst of a trade crisis and had urged the government to wake up. To be sure, outspoken revisionists were a minority, sometimes accused of being too inclined toward "managed trade" and "industrial policy." Nevertheless, their main premises—that a minimalist government could no longer ensure an even shake in the world economy and that a more assertive, programmatic approach to trade policy would do better—had gained considerable currency. The theme was embraced by more than a few eccentric functionaries and congressmen; increasingly, it was challenging the federal trade establishment to develop a stronger sense of mission.

Disincentives?

The trade bureaucracy's higher profile might not have amounted to much if other organizational incentives had been holding it back. Employees in the upper tiers of the American trade bureaus, unlike their counterparts in Japan or in the European Community, have been recruited from other agencies, congressional offices, or the private sector. Many pursue entirely different careers after a brief stint in the trade agencies. Deputy USTRs, for example, have tended to exit after an average of two to three years of service.[35] The relatively low salaries of U.S. senior officials have, at least until recently, furthered the comparatively high turnover rates and the allure of greener pastures.[36]

Despite the drawbacks, however, a tour of duty in trade administration was time well spent. Public service in this area was gaining importance. Afterward, the acquired expertise and experience seemed to be in considerable demand in the private sector. Washington law firms, corporate governmental affairs offices, and foreign businesses and governments could make use of former federal employees with inside knowledge of how the trade policy process works. Between 1974 and 1990, some 47 percent of ex-senior officials of the USTR had joined firms representing various commercial interests, including some touched by trade regulations.[37] At least a score of Commerce Department officeholders who left the government between 1980 and 1990 entered firms with major foreign trade clients.[38]

Critics have been quick to assume that the revolving door subverted the implementation of the trade laws: officials with an eye on high-paying jobs as attorneys and lobbyists for regulated interests might be tempted to play regulatory nerfball instead of hardball.[39] But the theory was questionable. If the skills of former administrative personnel were especially worth buying (a debatable matter), they would probably be *more* marketable, not after "pulling punches," but after schooling in the art of enforcing elaborate rules and heavy caseloads.

Currying Congressional Favor

Much of the rigor in fair trade administration, particularly in the Department of Commerce, came from bureaucratic routines. The methodology for determining whether imports were unfairly priced, for instance, increased the probability that alleged dumping would be confirmed with significant margins. In one of the few studies attempting to explain this pattern, Robert E. Baldwin and Michael O. Moore suggest that the expectations in Congress gave the Commerce Department little incentive to alter its decision rules.[40] In one forum or another, lawmakers would signal their interpretation of the department's primary purpose: to champion commercial interests. At confirmation hearings, for example, a congressional committee might remind a nominee that Congress expected the Commerce Department to perform as an "advocate," and assurances would be returned that administration of the antidumping and countervailing duty laws offered opportunities for the agency to play a "pro-active role."[41]

How to be an honest broker, weighing the merits of specific grievances, but also a "pro-active" advocate could present a dilemma. With Congress imagining impartiality but also insisting on advocacy, administrators were likely to follow the path of least resistance, letting the existing procedures stand.

Good Cop, Bad Cop

When the executive branch was impelled to take trade actions, the separation of powers sometimes proved more useful than inconvenient. The system has enabled both branches to syndicate responsibility, thereby affording the twin advantages of political burden-sharing at home and greater bargaining power abroad. Any administration espousing a free market ideology, but deviating from it now and then for tactical, electoral, or bureaucratic reasons, might welcome the chance to point a finger at the legislature, whose militancy presumably left the government no alternative. The shifting of blame could be all the more helpful in the context of international negotiations. A thinly veiled message conveyed across the negotiating table would go something like this: "Come to terms with the president, or face the prospect of drastic punishment from the United States Congress."

Other countries occasionally saw through this gambit, but on the whole they seemed to develop a healthy respect for it. The presidency, after all, is not really the "sole organ of the nation in its external relations"; a large and complex deliberative body shares the honor.[42] The members of Congress have sometimes been sufficiently rambunctious to float "kamikaze legislation" (as President Reagan once characterized the aggressive proposals hatched in the House of Representatives) or even to let such legislation fly out of control (as occurred in 1930 and in a few near misses since then). At a minimum, congressional participation introduces an effective element of uncertainty in the game of global economic diplomacy.[43]

The good cop, bad cop routine could also get confusing. For one thing, it was sometimes nearly impossible to tell who had been responsible for what. When the antidumping and countervailing duty laws were tightened in 1988, it may have looked as though Congress, over steady presidential objections, had simply taken matters into its own hands. But was this entirely true? It could be argued that the White House had all but guaranteed new antidumping and antisubsidy rules by indicating, three years earlier, that the administration was "looking forward" to working with Congress to rework these laws "so that business can have full and rapid protection in receiving help against unfair imports."[44] Maybe this strategy was indispensable in heading off worse protectionism. Nevertheless, what the legislative process lacked in the many months of work on the 1988 trade act was a rigorous public debate, not on marginalia such as the virtues of plant-closing notifications, but on the social net benefits of repeatedly tinkering with import regulations. If the chief executive, a consummate deregulator, was not going to join that debate, it was not clear who would.

The administration, mostly to smooth ruffled relations with Congress in the mid-1980s, intensified its efforts to identify and arrest the practices of more commercial renegades. Much of this activity was politically unavoidable, and perhaps some of it was an essential propellant for the upcoming round of the GATT. But sometimes it came uncomfortably close to creating newly vested interests in import protection. A 1987 section 301 action aimed at Brazil's piracy of computer software patents, for instance, had drawn the attention, not just of software manufacturers, but also of domestic producers of leather shoes, cheap dinner dishes, and ferroalloys, who lined up to lobby for 100 percent retaliatory tariffs on imports of those products. If the protection materialized, who would answer for it? In most instances, the executive could contend it had taken its cues from the industrial hinterlands or from Capitol Hill; indeed, many actions had been preceded by explicit requests. But even then, it was not easy to figure out where the buck really stopped. For example, a widely cited letter to the president in March of 1986, in which the Senate Democratic Working Group on Trade Policy itemized numerous grievances against virtually every major trading partner, was reportedly based on information supplied by the administration, which in turn had reportedly been invited to do so by the senators.[45]

Finally, the kinder, gentler constable's role in policing unfair trade had the potential for another dilemma. What began as an attempt to buy time with Congress and to find ways for parties to save face might also inadvertently raise expectations, feed frustrations, and perhaps remain powerless to prevent another spate of proposals to rewrite the trade laws. Although they were unexceptionable in most respects, the Bush administration's wide-ranging consultations with Japan on structural trade impediments raised this possibility.

The Structural Impediments Initiative

In May 1989, in accordance with the intent of the previous year's act of Congress, Japan was flagged as an egregious culprit of unfair trade. The Japanese government, however, publicly refused to open talks under the terms and timetables of Super 301. Partly to salve Tokyo's bruised sensibilities, the administration proposed a parallel negotiation, outside the 301 framework, that was supposed to address root causes of economic disequilibria on both sides of the Pacific. This formula was thought to offer several advantages.[46] Framed as a two-way conversation, Japan would be invited to answer American criticisms with a critique of its own. The Office of the U.S. Trade Representative would be able to confine its 301 charges to relatively tractable problems (specific complaints about restrictions on imports of supercomputers, satellites, and forest products), while heeding congressional entreaties to address Japan's trading habits generically. The transpacific policy dialogue would be elevated to a high level of sophistication: instead of focusing on narrow sectoral points that scarcely altered general economic imbalances, the two countries would tackle systemic questions such as underinvestment in social infrastructure, faulty tax policies, rigidities in pricing and distribution, and corporate collusion.

Systems Analysis

This agenda had much to commend it. Some items (lagging social overhead expenditures, for example) contributed to Japan's large excess of domestic saving over public investment, hence to its chronic current account surpluses. Other topics pointed clearly to conditions that suppressed competition. Methods of taxation that inflated land prices made it harder for newcomers to set up shop in Japanese metropolitan areas. Restrictions on the establishment of large retail facilities posed barriers for sales of competitively priced goods and hampered consumer access to those goods. Opaque cross-shareholding arrangements and lax enforcement of rules against collusive relationships among firms could allow those firms to allocate markets, fix prices, reap artificial profits, and attract undeserved investment.[47]

Granted, the structural impediments initiative (or SII) strayed far beyond the bounds of traditional trade negotiations. Not all the private sector practices and public sector programs at issue were deliberately designed to exclude foreign participants. Preferential taxation of urban farm land, to take an obvious example, made for expensive real estate in Japanese cities—so expensive, in fact, that it drove even established foreign affiliates to disinvest.[48] The intent of the tax system was not, however, to induce a sell-off by foreign investors. A frontal assault on domestically oriented policies with incidental effects on international commerce might encroach on national sovereignty.

But the changing world economy could not continue to respect supposed sovereign rights at every turn. Modern trading partnerships required deepening mutual integration. Considerable harmonization of incompatible national standards, including many that bore only indirect relation to foreign trade policies, was well under way in Western Europe and could not be indefinitely postponed in a bilateral relationship as important as that between Japan and the United States. Japanese businessmen and government officials could not continue to defend restricted markets as mere indigenous customs, or *Nihon-jinron* ("Japaneseness"). Foreign beef, we were told, was ill-suited to the Japanese because their intestines were longer than those of Westerners.[49] Native ski and tire-chain manufacturers retained their commercial advantage because Japanese snow was unique. Builder bid-rigging was excused as helpful to avoid "confusion," or "to defuse destructive competition."[50] The talks on structural impediments would brush aside such nonsense and come to the point. Much of the exclusionary pattern was neither "cultural" nor uniquely Japanese; in no small part it existed in Japan, as it would anywhere, in the absence of preventive rules and regulations.

Restructuring Japan's antitrust policies, distribution channels, and other antiquated economic institutions *was* likely to yield a decided welfare gain.[51] The majority of Japanese consumers seemed to grasp this possibility.[52] So did a sufficient number of well-placed opinion leaders in Japan, who looked on the SII as a chance to accelerate reforms that were mostly in the country's own best interest.[53] Thus the government eventually committed itself to doubling outlays for social overhead during the 1990s. Prodded by the Finance Ministry, the Diet finally began formulating a proposal to lower land values by levying a national landholding tax and reducing tax breaks for farmland.[54] Modified retail regulations permitted the MITI to approve twice as many applications for large stores in 1990 as in 1988.[55] Likewise, anticartel activity intensified; the Fair Trade Commission more than doubled the number of companies penalized and tripled the amount of fines between 1988 and 1990.[56]

Invitation to Muddle?

But would the top-to-bottom inspection of Japan's economic structure calm jittery nerves in the American political arena? The complicated exercise would take years, not months, to bring about possible changes in trade flows, and even then it was not certain those changes would deliver much in the way of political comfort. Indeed, as some wary lawmakers foresaw, while a fully modernized Japanese economy could improve American business opportunities, it was also likely to enhance the efficiency of that economy's mighty export industries, from which U.S. domestic producers would feel additional competitive heat.[57] Academic economists would consider this good. The protectors of shaky American businesses and workers, on the other hand, might feel considerable nostalgia for the days when Japan, a maker of supercomputers, was still also a place where old ladies whittled toothpicks by hand.

There was no consensus on how to gauge success in the negotiations. In February 1990, the *Economic Report of the President* had cautioned that even a thorough "removal of trade barriers, while desirable in and of itself, would not necessarily change Japan's bilateral trade surplus with the United States."[58] In March, high-level administration witnesses before the trade subcommittee of the Senate Finance Committee reiterated the need for patience: "to measure success in the short term by changes in exports and imports directly," counseled John B. Taylor of the Council of Economic Advisers, "would be a mistake."[59] These assessments were not what the oversight committees wanted to hear. Members told the administration's negotiators that the SII needed to be "results-oriented." They wanted to know how quickly, and by how much, the talks would reduce the bilateral deficit.[60] To no one's surprise, when the U.S. and Japanese negotiating teams issued an interim report a month later, some legislators called it too "soft and fuzzy," while others wanted the administration to predict exactly how much the interim agreement would boost exports.[61]

Administration officials, who had hoped that the SII would contain the perennial firestorms on Capitol Hill, not ignite new ones, found themselves on the defensive, pleading for more time and leeway. Congress seemed in no mood to wait. Disgruntled members suspected that at the end of the day the Japanese economic system, preserving the largest *keiretsu*, many small shopkeepers, and untold "invisible handshakes," would remain pretty much intact. But now, having cemented such issues into the lengthening catalogue of Japanese trade depredations, expectations would also move up to a new base line from which "success" (somehow defined) might have to be reported on many fronts by a date certain.[62]

The second SII report, announced at the end of June 1990 with considerable satisfaction by the negotiators on both sides, drew little applause on Capitol Hill. More typical was the reaction of House Majority Leader Richard Gephardt, who questioned the value of an agreement that would do "little or nothing to address the size of the trade deficit."[63] In the Senate, Finance Committee Chairman Lloyd Bentsen reserved judgment in the absence of "hard trade results." But hard trade results, at least as measured by further reductions in Japan's surplus, were to prove evanescent. In 1991, after a three-year decline, the surplus began moving up again after a shift in exchange rates and as a slower Japanese economy took in somewhat fewer imports.[64] Promptly, bills to renew and redeploy the Super 301 process were back in the legislative hoppers.[65] The USTR did its best to convince observers to look on the bright side. Summing up the status of the various trade parleys with Japan that spring, Deputy U.S. Trade Representative S. Linn Williams conceded that "Reasonable people can differ on the speed of market access," but, he stressed, "I can think of no instance in which we have disappointed an industry that has a problem."[66] Meanwhile, the National Association of Manufacturers had decided that the time had come to call on President Bush for a complete reassessment of U.S.-Japan relations.

Finally, while the structural impediments initiative seemed to sharpen congressional understanding of exotic sources of economic distortion ten thousand miles away, the other part of the bargain—mundane home repairs requiring some unpopular legislation in Washington—was the object of less fascination. So when, in the course of the talks, the idea was floated that Congress reduce the federal budget deficit by, say, levying a serious tax on gasoline, everyone knew the proposal was a nonstarter ("crazy," according to MITI's Makoto Kuroda).[67] Congress concurred. In October 1990, it turned down a mere 9.5-cent gas tax, proposed by the White House as part of a comprehensive deficit reduction package.[68] Despite the instructive colloquy of the SII, the politicians continued to search for a level playing field without putting the government's own fiscal backyard in order.

Conclusion

For the most part, presidents since World War II have striven valiantly to liberalize international commerce and to hold the line against the periodic excesses in trade policy emanating from Congress. But the conventional model of interbranch politics, in which the legislature is forever pushing interventionist projects that the executive indefatigably resists, is an oversimplification. Both institutions set the agenda, typically citing the problems posed by alleged unfair economic competition.

Trade activism on the executive side was multifaceted. Parts of it (various section 301 cases, for example) were aimed at coaxing recalcitrant trading partners into taking their multilateral treaty-making obligations seriously, and at opening individual markets. Parts also reflected other determinants, such as efforts to establish credibility with Congress; decisions to sacrifice lower policy priorities for higher ones; quadrennial electioneering; and the self-propulsion of various bureaucratic wheels.

Legislators would not let commercial policy languish on the back burner. Presidents, when the heat was on, would respond by grappling with unfair trade. Even in the course of trying to preempt or to moderate legislative initiatives, the executive could find itself doing most of Congress's bidding by non-legislative means, sprinkling in a few remedial trade programs of its own and perhaps stirring appetites for more. This complex partnership was not without advantages for both branches, but whether it would ultimately give presidents and lawmakers the political slack they needed to start solving economic problems more fundamental than foreign trading practices remained to be seen.

CHAPTER SEVEN

Whither Trade Policy?

STRENUOUS EFFORTS TO counter the misdeeds of international competitors became a distinctive feature of American foreign economic policy in the 1980s. Much of this tilt in commercial relations remained reasonably congruent with a longstanding U.S. commitment to multilateral free trade. Indeed, from Bretton Woods to Punta del Este, no other country's leaders championed with as much conviction the idea that collective well-being and security would be enhanced by lowering barriers to commerce and investment among nations. The heightened concern about the outside world's trade-distorting conditions, however, was new. Foreign trading practices in previous decades had been ceded a wider margin of error. Now they were held to increasingly fastidious standards of equity, if not symmetry.

New Challenges

An international convergence in technological and industrial capacities lay behind some of this new emphasis. In 1950, when other countries were still digging out of the rubble of the Second World War, the United States accounted for more than 40 percent of the world's gross domestic product and almost 17 percent of the value of the world's exports. Japan represented less than 2 percent of world GDP and about 1.5 percent of world exports. By 1980 the U.S. share of global GDP had slid to approximately 22 percent, while exports had settled at about 11 percent. The figures for Japan had moved up to almost 9 percent and 6.5 percent, respectively. Many American firms were now less comfortably advanced, and the head-to-head competition would only intensify. As other countries narrowed America's commanding technological lead, small differences in institutional environments could make significant differences in the competitive performance of firms.

The U.S. government no longer had the luxury of attaching few caveats to open trade. It could not remain satisfied with a multilateral system that, after seven major rounds of negotiations, still enabled foreigners to do business more freely here than American companies could in many markets abroad. One-sided dispensations that we had granted to our trading partners when their economies were smaller—and when the East-West confrontation required leniency toward allies—seemed anachronistic after those economies had matured and the cold war was winding down. Businesses in many sectors took note of the changed circumstances; for some the changes were critical. As long as the U.S. market was much larger than markets abroad, domestic manufacturers of high-technology products could match the scale efficiencies of foreign firms operating behind trade walls. But as overseas markets developed, these producers needed easier entry for exports and investment. Equitable access was also necessary to avoid the effects of repeated currency devaluations, worsening terms of trade, and an erosion of living standards.

In the early 1980s the challenges of a tougher international economy came home with a vengeance. Large external deficits and a wrenching realignment of American industry came on the heels of a deep recession as many companies found themselves priced out of world markets. Damaged firms and communities implored their elected representatives to arrange relief.

Ambiguities

This turbulent context provides a basis, but not the end point, for understanding recent U.S. trade policy. Although the 1980s were a period of economic flux, prosperity generally overtook hard times and severe sectoral dislocations. If foreign trade had wreaked nothing but havoc and the national economy had shown unrelenting signs of weakness, voters would have clamored for greater government intervention year after year. But by the time presidential candidate Walter Mondale was struggling to warn the electorate about a future of lousy jobs ("a lifetime serving McDonald hamburgers"), America did not seem to be on its way to becoming a nation of hamburger-flippers. Instead, indifferent to gaping trade deficits, the economy reached full employment, with little inflation, and with more new jobs in higher-skilled categories than it had in the 1970s.[1] Contrary to decline theorists who contended that the country's industrial base was contracting, manufacturing output regained the hefty share of GNP recorded in the 1960s. And with re-aligned exchange rates, revitalized U.S. manufacturers reappeared on the global scene; a formidable export boom got under way. Such conditions did not put the public in a funereal mood about the nation's economic health. Nor did the setting clarify for policymakers the economic pathologies that additional trade rules might reliably ameliorate. The national current account imbalance, in particular, was likely to be marginally affected by trade regulations.

Although the international trading system was generating fierce competitive pressures, for the most part the pressures and the system were not less "fair" than in the past. Despite speculation about rising foreign protectionism and a moribund GATT, world trade and welfare grew throughout the 1980s, and by the end of the decade, our robust export sectors were leading the parade. To be sure, adversarial economic practices continued to interfere. Industrial targeting and predatory pricing could endanger strategic U.S. export industries. But most of the complaints about harmful subsidizing and dumping did not involve them. Moreover, many complaints reflected changes in conceptions of fairness rather than increases in pernicious subsidies or pricing strategies.

Amid these ambiguities, trade actions gathered momentum. Between 1980 and 1990 federal regulators confronted more than eleven hundred alleged breaches of commercial rights and administered a widening array of measures to affirm those rights. No other economic regulatory program took on such an increase in caseloads.

The New Regulation

How did this burst of activity compare with others earlier in the century? In the early 1920s, industries that had been shielded from foreign competition during the First World War were abruptly exposed to a rise in competing imports.[2] Congress reacted by tightening restrictions. Similarly, in recent years businesses in an uphill battle for market share received help in the form of import restraints and tougher reciprocity requirements for foreigners. Yet the contemporary reaction has also differed in style and in scope. With no discursive preamble, the Tariff Act of 1922 had simply presented a "dutiable list" of 5,300 items. By contrast, the trade law of 1988 increased no duties but detailed page after page of administrative provisions aimed at curbing offensive international business practices.

The policy stance seventy years ago was unapologetically protectionist, whereas the overarching goal after the Second World War has been to encourage market freedom and multilateralism. A liberal trade orientation increasingly sensitized to market imperfections can engender its own form of regulation, however, whether or not the global marketplace is more flawed than before. Never mind that the economies of major trading partners were no more restrictive in the mid-1980s, when our trade deficit topped $150 billion, than in the mid-1970s, when trade was relatively balanced. The remaining asymmetries, particularly with Japan, were nettlesome enough to provide a rallying cry for advocates of both import remedies and export promotion.

The pursuit of equity has been politically expedient. The days when Congress had the brass to favor constituents by hiking tariff rates were over. (Except as a safeguard action, reversion to that blunt instrument would virtually guarantee retaliation and an uproar in the GATT. Through rampant logrolling the level and coverage of trade interference might be extended uncontrollably. As costs to the economy became unmistakable, legislators would be branded protectionists.) Nevertheless, improving the prospects of particular firms or industries competing with other firms or industries has been a prime motive of commercial policy, old or new. When the going gets rough, and domestic policies fail to provide a cushion, trade programs are pressed into service. Summoned to intervene but conscious of the risks, policymakers repair to the relative safety of regulating unfairness. Here, presumably, government would not spread protection or privileges among special interests, only ensure equality of opportunity for aggrieved groups. And here responsibility for the remedies could be delegated or partitioned so as not to put Congress back in the business of enacting, and being accountable for, "dutiable lists."

An Assessment

Just how self-limiting this regulatory regime has been in practice is a matter of debate. Technically, formal grievances about trade violations peaked in 1982, but our preference for open trade remained sturdy enough to keep the country more hospitable to imports than were various other industrial nations. Fears that the United States was resorting to extraordinary "export protectionism" also proved largely unfounded.[3] Europe's direct agricultural export subsidies and Japan's mixed credit expenditures continued to outpace American efforts. So far the retaliatory provisions in recent U.S. laws have not caused the widespread trade diversion or rigged market allocations that critics had foreseen. American negotiators generally succeeded in steering these new legal devices in a constructive direction, not only winning a number of concessions for U.S. companies but sometimes advancing broader interests. While many foreign governments took umbrage at the "lone ranger" style of our market-access initiatives, other parties abroad occasionally stood to gain from them as much as we did or more. Unilateral U.S. pressure did not derail the latest attempt to reach multilateral accords, and may even have provided some stimulus.

Toward Tranquillity?

But there were unsettling developments in the picture as well. A propensity to complain about commercial inequities had been ratcheted to unprecedented levels in the first half of the 1980s, and the status quo ante was not restored in the second half. The modal complaint—that imports were being sold at less than fair value—was indicative. Not including steel industry petitions, requests for antidumping actions in 1990 exceeded those of all but two of the ten preceding years. The trade remedy laws were meant to mitigate, not to magnify, spasms of commercial restraint and recrimination. But some of this capability had been chipped away after repeated legislative revisions and presidential compromises. At the end of the Reagan administration, some form of remedial restriction covered about 23 percent of the $500 billion a year the United States spent on imports.[4] The figure in 1980 had been 12 percent. In one guise or another, actions against unfair trade had contributed significantly to this upward drift.

Not only was this supposed remediation expensive; it did not seem to buy much satisfaction. The $80 billion a year we spent for import protection might be considered an investment if it ultimately enhanced the nation's industrial prowess, or at least convinced people that a fairer playing field had resulted.[5] Instead, bruised firms and workers often discovered that their distress persisted after years of trade redress. The official groundskeepers, having already worked overtime, would then be asked to reinspect the field for more patches of uneven turf to correct.

The aggressive export program was more promising, but it too did not bring enough peace of mind. More market apertures were being negotiated, but they were often slow to bear fruit for, or to gratify, the intended beneficiaries. A number of bilateral disputes festered inconclusively for years. Ninety percent of the goods and services consumed by Americans were still being produced by Americans. Although expansion into offshore markets improved the terms on which we traded exports for imports, the productivity of the domestic economy remained the overwhelming determinant of our living standards, as it always has been.[6] Moreover, without a major increase in U.S. savings, the gap between exports and imports would remain wide, no matter what tactics were used to remove international commercial obstructions.[7] The 1988 Trade Act may have vindicated the view that foreign markets, in Randolph Churchill's phrase, needed to be opened with a "strong clasp knife," not just "tickled with a feather."[8] In short order, the legislation helped persuade Colombia to be more respectful of certain patents, trademarks, and copyrights; Taiwan, to appreciate its currency; Japan, to stop restricting dealers of government bonds; the Republic of Korea, to cease barring foreign travel agents, advertising firms, and cosmetics wholesalers; and so on.[9] These were not negligible accomplishments, but neither were they the bedrock on which would rest big improvements in American living standards and international competitive strength.

It was not as though lawmakers refused to recognize the fundamentals. Advocates of stronger trade measures often conceded that they were operating on the margins of economic deficiencies rather than at the core. If the purpose of economic policy was to deliver gains in real income, the main problem was to bring productivity growth back to pre–1970 levels. That would call for much more than hacking away at unfair trade; it would require boosting productive investment through higher savings, upgrading the preparation of the work force, and shedding regulatory deadweight and myopic business habits. The political process duly debated these imperatives, but at the end of the day, it was the trade bills, not the rest of the agenda, that repeatedly attracted congressional majorities and became law.

Discomforts of Astroturf

Bearing a disproportionate burden, trade policy has had trouble keeping up with expectations. This has made it the focus of further attention. If existing legislation showed poor results, or if its good results did not suffice, amendments would be added, filling in gaps and extending the reach of regulation. The range of commercial conduct to be enjoined seemed to widen with each major trade bill. Whereas dumping was once defined strictly as predatory pricing (the intent on the part of the dumper being "to injure or destroy" an American industry), the antidumping law would gradually engulf pricing patterns that were common business practice and that were lawful under domestic antitrust doctrine. Illegal subsidies were originally defined as direct "bounties or grants" bestowed by foreign governments on products imported into the United States. By the mid–1980s, however, precedents existed for countervailing duties on everything from regional development programs to industrial adjustment payments.[10] Section 301 of the 1974 Trade Act was meant to be used mainly against countries that breached their international trade agreements with the United States. By 1988 the provision encompassed such novelties as failure to meet standards for minimum wages, hours of work, and occupational health or safety even though the United States had not signed the international agreement that specified those workers' rights.[11]

This trend posed at least two obvious difficulties. One was how to keep the game in bounds. Trade might remain unequal without greater commonality not only in wage scales and working conditions, but also in exchange rates, debt-equity ratios, depreciation, interest rates, accounting techniques, tort law, tax codes, banking regulations, antitrust rules, land use planning, environmental controls, consumer protection, minority hiring procedures, and entitlement programs—indeed, in the entire spectrum of relations between public and private sectors.[12] Where should the line be drawn? The task tested the ingenuity of those responsible for enforcing the trade laws in ways that would undergird multilateral covenants and set reasonable limits on demands for equalization. That the Office of the U.S. Trade Representative was largely able to pull off this feat did not guarantee that some future team would succeed. For there were pressures on and within *both* branches of government to increase the breadth of "remedial action."

The second difficulty was that the United States would not be the only referee. Other countries would make up their own lists of unjustifiable foreign trading methods (including a number of American practices) and write their own rules and regulations to combat them. Fifteen years ago only the United States, Canada, Australia, and the European Community had active antidumping statutes on the books. Today some thirty nations do, with American corporations a frequent target. (Between 1980 and 1988, for instance, the antidumping regulators of Australia, Canada, and Mexico targeted U.S. companies more often than Japanese companies.)[13] The American fair pricing strictures contained biases, but everyone else's procedures did too, and theirs were worse.[14] U.S. officials eventually reacted by calling on others to establish greater transparency and respect for due process in administration.[15] This approach seemed to miss the larger point: increasingly, the rest of the world was likely to take a page or two from our expanding rulebook, and then apply its lessons in perverse ways that would prove difficult to bring under control.

Accountability

Much fair trade administration ultimately unfolded in a fashion that was less explicit and less subject to public reckoning than the legalistic system of trade remedies might suggest. Billions of dollars were added to the cost of purchasing a variety of products, but obliquely, by way of negotiated settlements with foreign producers to restrain their exports voluntarily. Many of these ad hoc solutions evolved without a plan to revitalize the petitioning industries or to neutralize their demands and reduce the expense to other domestic industries. A number of deals effectively transferred enormous revenues in the wrong direction, to the foreign producers rather than to the U.S. Treasury. These policy choices could seldom be traced directly to recorded votes that the nation's elected representatives might be asked to defend. Rather, the decisions often emerged in a muddier mix of congressional ferment and executive accommodation.

When major industries were complaining, the process of trade rectification commonly burst the seams of routine administrative proceedings. The Congress would weigh in. At times, legislative insurgencies seemed possible if the plight of ailing businesses was not adequately relieved. In hopes of keeping the situation in hand, presidents would seize the initiative by driving bilateral bargains. These preemptive moves were said to be more benign than the undiplomatic alternatives circulating on Capitol Hill, but as a practical matter, it was sometimes hard to be sure. The mischief lawmakers were actually prepared to make, if they were left on the hook, was not always what their rhetoric implied. Meanwhile, because every administration came to the deliberations carrying some political baggage of its own (in the form of presidential campaign commitments, for example), the executive could not always practice the economic temperance it preached. In these circumstances a little congressional coercion went a long way—all the more so because lines of responsibility were blurred. Elaborate executive agreements accumulated amid disclaimers that Congress left no choice, while the legislators obtained adjustments in prices or market shares without actually legislating.

These arrangements could be as opaque as they were capacious. The old tariffs had little to recommend them, but at least their price tags and political parentage had been relatively plain for all to see. Indeed, the visibility of tariffs ultimately helped reformers negotiate reductions. The spread of amorphous "voluntary" restraints, informal price undertakings, and agreements to ensure "orderly marketing" would prove harder to discipline.

Alternatives

All this has led commentators to consider three kinds of recommendations. One set of critics proposes an outright suspension of the regulatory campaign against "unfairly traded" goods and services.[16] Another group goes to the opposite extreme, proposing that government manage trading relations on a larger scale. A third would not discharge foreign trade policymakers from active duty, but would encourage them to concentrate on structural sources of competitive erosion in the domestic economy.

The Libertarian Prescription

Arguably, the forces of globalization and interdependence have become so bewildering that government regulators cannot hope to stay abreast, much less ahead, of the curve. Traditional contestations over commercial infractions like dumping and subsidies may have been better suited to a time when the international marketplace was simpler. They are not practical in a world of floating exchange rates, fluid capital markets, and transnational corporations enmeshed in global production strategies and complex interfirm alliances. In this confusing theater of operation, the best advice to trade warriors may be, "Don't just do something. Stand there."

DISENGAGEMENT.   Deregulation might have several advantages. For one, fewer casualties would result from friendly fire, so to speak. With no 20.2 percent quota on steel imports, for example, construction-equipment manufacturers would not resort to airlifting finished steel parts from abroad rather than making them in U.S. plants.[17] Without the recent 62 percent antidumping duty on active-matrix screens, manufacturers would have less reason to move their laptop computer production offshore.[18]

There could also be less worldwide interest in mimicking the U.S. trade arsenal, and thus less incentive to train similar legal weaponry (or "new commercial policy instruments") on American firms.[19] Reversing the spiral of fair trade laws might reaffirm the logic of international trade. Governments have shown signs of equating fairness with uniformity, as if healthy commerce depended on making other economic systems similar to their own. Witness the early drafts of the EC's "Second Banking Directive," which came close to insisting on mirror-image reciprocity for financial services. But trade occurs precisely because national environments *differ*.[20] Just as differences in factor endowments provide a basis for trade, so could differences in saving rates, industrial organization, social conditions, or even regimes. The United States and EC transact with one another (or with Saudi Arabia, for that matter) not because their societies are symmetrical, but because each side gains.

Finally, if microeconomic remedies were downplayed, the macroeconomic foundations of international competitiveness might receive more than lip service. Even without the will to lay those foundations, more people might concede that unregulated market forces could put some building blocks in place. The Japanese population is aging and is likely to save less.[21] Japanese, German, and American costs of capital have been converging.[22] Japanese consumers are unlikely to accept indefinitely a way of life in which many middle-class homes lack central heating.[23] More than interminable trade litigation, basic social transformations could eventually equalize the playing field. There is something to be said for backing off and letting the invisible hand do its work.

THE CATCH. But the hands-off approach is unrealistic. Trade regulation is here to stay. No responsive government can remain oblivious to vocal domestic interests hit hard by foreign competitors. Grievances would be heard, and special protections given. The pragmatic explanation for many of these maneuvers has been that it is better to bend in a storm than to be broken by it. One may ponder the virtues of so much bending: has it reached a stage of diminishing returns? Would further political contortions make the world any safer for liberal trade? Such reflections are often beside the point. Claimants will continue to demand and to receive restitution, whether classical trade theorists like it or not.

The claimants, furthermore, have not just lodged conventional protectionist appeals. Some make an intuitively compelling case: as long as foreigners liberally peddle their wares in the United States, their markets ought to be made comparably free of encumbrances for American firms. Particularly for technology-intensive industries, where scale economies are critical, a relatively protected home market such as Japan's can create an unfair advantage. Firms in such sanctuaries may amass surplus profits with which to accelerate technological improvements, weather losses, and exploit markets abroad.

Some U.S. industries weakened by this kind of competition are important to national security. To let them be run out of business is to countenance military reliance on foreign sources for critical components and technologies. Such dependency is hazardous if the foreign suppliers have a capacity to exert monopoly power.[24] Even when the danger is not imminent, a sacrifice of economic welfare may be necessary to preserve defense capabilities. Adam Smith, too, acknowledged that defense "is of much more importance than opulence."[25]

Foreign commercial practices that are targeted on our most viable exports of merchandise and services or that destroy incentives for technological innovation need to be brought under better international discipline. American countermeasures against European subsidies for wheat flour, sugar, poultry, and oil seeds may have encouraged the European Community to put agricultural export subsidies on the table for the Uruguay Round. A series of section 301 actions involving services and intellectual property rights helped highlight the need for GATT codes in these areas. Well-aimed retaliatory options have a role to play in international economic diplomacy.

Strategic Trade Policy

Libertarians see futility in regulating unfair trade. So, in their own way, do some proponents of bolder interventionism. The case for administered market-sharing programs, for instance, often seems to be framed as follows. Critical industries must be preserved. These industries cannot survive without a sales base comparable to that of the competition. Negotiations, bilateral and multilateral, may peel away layers of discriminatory hindrances in foreign markets without obtaining adequate shares in key sectors. What is needed is greater parity of results, not just nominal equality of opportunity. In plain words, markets must be secured, not merely rendered more "accessible." The way to accomplish this objective is simply to establish and enforce quantitative import-export targets, and then cease begging the rest of the world to play by "fairer" rules.

The notion of managed outcomes can be alluring. Bilateral trade imbalances, at least in some sectors, might be automatically reduced. Producers deemed indispensable to the nation's industrial and technological base would be promoted. The promotion is presumably overt and unvarnished. Detailed critiques and frustrating discussions of other countries' trading tactics would be obviated, thereby avoiding counterclaims about America's own economic vices, past or present.[26] British economic doomsayers at the turn of the century accused America of having "invaded Europe not with armed men, but with manufactured products."[27] Sixty-five years later, French economic nationalists declaimed that Europe would soon "become an annex of the United States."[28] A confident American trade policy, by contrast, would neither envy nor vilify trading partners; it would speak softly while carrying a big stick.

A BIG STICK FOR WHOM? Managed trade means negotiating numerical import goals among nations and enforcing the numbers with nasty sanctions when necessary. Clearly, applying such a policy across the board would be a drastic step; most advocates prefer a lighter touch, zeroing in on strategic industries.[29]

But what is a "strategic" industry? Would-be trade managers do not confine the category to economic activity essential for national defense; they have proposed support for producers that are knowledge-intensive, pay good wages, create high value-added, face rapid product cycles, are subject to high demand elasticity, exhibit scale economies, contribute to economic growth and productivity, and affect many other industries. Almost any industry qualifies under one or more of these crude tests. The criteria for efficient strategic targeting have to be more parsimonious: only firms capable of generating supranormal profits (rents), premium wages, or localized spillover benefits to the economy are to be favored—and only if doing so yields a higher return than would other uses of the same resources.

Under this more exacting standard, however, it is hard to see why government planners would select champions any better than private investors do. Justifying a planned allocation of resources requires more than observing that market forces can cause misallocations. Markets are imperfect, but so are governments. Nor is it sufficient to point in admiration at the industrial policies of international rivals. Where do strategic micromanagers consistently add to, rather than often subtract from, national income? The Europeans have toiled to build an independent domestic capability in advanced technologies only to discover that their heavy investment (in programs like Esprit, Eureka, Jessi) has generally come up short.[30] Even in the more auspicious case of Japan, *welfare-enhancing* bureaucratic guidance may have been the exception rather than the rule.[31]

Even if experts could identify a limited group of suitable candidates to single out for advantage by preallocating markets, politicians would almost certainly insist on widening the pool of applicants. Preferential treatment for high-tech, export-oriented industries that earn above-average profits and pay high wages raises thorny distributional issues. Legislators who wish to nurture these interests will have to bargain with representatives of less glamorous groups such as textile manufacturers, shoemakers, or sugar farmers. How can it be equitable, after all, to increase the returns of profitable companies and to raise further the wages of well-paid workers when resources are thereby diverted from hard-hit firms and workers in industries that are competing with imports? Spokesmen for these constituents will demand compensation, and probably get some. Each year a coalition has enabled the Export-Import Bank to confer trade advantages on Boeing, General Electric, and Westinghouse. Would that coalition be so stable if the government had not also been willing to provide trade benefits (through import quotas) for the steel industry, the automobile industry, the apparel industry, and so on? Commercial preferences extended to strategic producers are likely to carry in their wake plenty of preferences for nonstrategic producers.

LESS "DEAD-END MORALISM"?[32] Management of strategic trade without self-righteous overtones, hence with less abrasiveness than the extant fair trade refrain, seems utopian. Trade flows with particular countries might be realigned if commerce were managed in enough sectors. This correction of bilateral deficits by administrative fiat might quell the political panic those deficits seem to create. But reaching that restful state of affairs requires contentious decisions. Judgments about how markets ought to be apportioned would inevitably deteriorate to politicized requests for "fair shares" by special interests.

Frictions would reach well beyond the reaction of nations served with ultimatums on quantities they must import or export. Unlike market-access negotiations based on most-favored-nation principles, the imposition of "fair shares" for the sole benefit of domestic pressure groups would brazenly defy GATT precepts. It would also ignore the position of third parties who currently sympathize with U.S. complaints about closed markets and anticompetitive practices. If bilaterally arranged quotas diverted actual or potential trade, the international shock waves could be far worse than after the promulgation of Super 301.

On top of this imaginable mess could come a final irony: the officially sponsored cartelization of buyers and of exporters. It is easy to speak in vague generalities about managing trade balances, but in concrete terms, what would the implementation look like? The governments of target countries would have to oversee their volumes of imports and exports. How? Would bureaucracies like Japan's Ministry of International Trade and Industry, reputedly adept at organizing cartels, be invited to tighten control?[33] This scenario would give those who stew over foreign orchestration of corporate collusion more, not less, reason to grumble.

Back to Basics

Somewhere along the continuum of theoretical policy options lies common sense: the United States ought to keep pressing for equitable rules of commerce abroad but also carry out the economic changes needed to make government a better partner of industry at home. Highest priority should go to fostering a robust rate of productivity growth by raising the level of public and private savings, curbing the costs of health care, creating a less adversarial regulatory environment, and equipping the labor force for the work it will have to do.

The argument is straightforward. If Japan saves several times as much of its income as the United States, Japanese industry can invest more in new plants and equipment, Japanese productivity can continue to grow faster, and the chasm in trade between the two countries cannot readily disappear. If schools in other societies are preparing a more competent and adaptive work force than ours, the qualitative edge of certain imported products or the ability of some foreign manufacturers to move more rapidly along the learning curves in some emerging technologies should not be surprising. If American corporations are more burdened by medical insurance expenses, the threat of litigation, and rigid financial regulations, their managers are not as well positioned to plan for the long term.[34]

The reforms these observations imply face long political odds. Consider the problem of saving. A federal budget deficit of $300 billion (the figure is adjusted for the S&L bailout and contributions to Desert Storm) drains about a third of the already meager national savings pool and pumps it into consumption.[35] At these levels, eliminating two-thirds of the deficit could wipe out our current account imbalance.[36] Fiscal retrenchment that great is infeasible, of course, without trimming entitlement programs. But spending for Social Security and Medicare (about $354 billion in 1990) is not likely to be restrained as long as voter turnout among retirees remains higher than in the rest of the electorate.[37]

Just as the bulk of federal spending seems to be off-limits for deficit reduction, so is the use of consumption taxes. A higher user fee on petroleum transport fuels would target a problematic sector. Between 1973 and 1990, U.S. dependency on foreign oil rose from 36 percent to 47 percent of total use.

During the same interval, Japan's oil imports fell almost 25 percent.[38] A 50-cent per gallon excise could collect more than $50 billion, while still leaving prices at the pump lower in real terms than they were at their peak in 1980 and far below the levels of motor fuel prices in virtually every other major industrialized country.[39] After tempestuous debates in 1975, 1977, 1980, 1982, and 1990, Congress succeeded in raising the federal impost on gasoline—by a grand total of 10 cents a gallon.

What about augmenting the private rate of saving and investment? At a minimum, this would seem to require another revolution in national tax policy. A system that allows broad interest payment deductions on loans, exempts most transfer payments, and effectively taxes savings twice (first on earnings then on interest from those earnings) encourages debt and consumption. Moreover, a case can be made that limited taxation of long-term capital gains (as in Japan) stimulates more investment than indiscriminate taxation of those gains at the same rate as ordinary income (as in the United States).[40] The 1986 Tax Reform Act eliminated deductions for interest on consumer loans but continued to shelter multiple home mortgages and interest on home equity lines of credit.[41] Tighter caps on these subsidies are a dim prospect. How to obtain lower rates on capital gains without more dubious revisions in the tax code (like a deficit-inflating middle-class tax cut, for the sake of "fairness"), is far from clear.

U.S. employers may be significantly handicapped by onerous health-care costs, frequent legal scrapes over everything from product liability to personnel decisions, and unusual institutional constraints, including a heavily regulated financial system.[42] Yet inertia persists on each of these problems. Expenditures for health care have been left to escalate uncontrollably. Outlays represented 4.8 percent of gross national product in 1950 but now absorb 13.7 percent, a burden unlike that of any other nation.[43] The corporate workplace, already suffocating in lawsuits, will probably become more litigious as a consequence of recent federal legislation.[44] Proposals to grant banks broader powers to address a wider range of their customers' needs have languished.

The item that seems to have drawn the greatest interest, and a mixed bag of experiments by local governments, is education.[45] A superior system of education helped propel American industry past the competition during the 1800s, and there appears to be broad consensus that overhauling the nation's schools is a key to economic primacy in the next century.[46] Progress toward educational reform is running afoul of at least two societal trends, however. First, it is hard to imagine how significant strides can be made, or even measured, without some form of standardized achievement testing. So far, this essential anchor has proved impossible to embed amid the currents of academic multiculturalism increasingly in vogue. The second impediment is the instability of the American family structure. Family background characteristics have long been recognized as the main determinants of scholastic performance.[47] No school reorganization, however desirable, can fully offset the dysfunctional effects on children of the explosion in divorce, births outside wedlock, single-parent households, and dual wage-earner families—all of which have meant that parents, on average, spend seventeen hours a week with their children, down from thirty hours a week in 1965.[48] Plainly stated, how generations raised with this parenting deficit can be disciplined to study proficiently remains a mystery. Much of the answer may require more than reinventing schools; it does not lie within the easy reach of public policy.

Some Midrange Suggestions

Even though these basic aspects of the nation's competitive vulnerability have mostly eluded our grasp, it remains crucial to keep them in sight. And though there will continue to be a natural tendency to search elsewhere for causes of perceived economic failings, trade decisions can be made to complement, rather than subordinate, the primary agenda.

Dusting Off the Escape Clause

The problem of providing emergency relief to industries that are seriously impaired by trade is a political fact of life and cannot be wished away. When relief is granted, however, more of it should be channeled through the safeguard mechanism (section 201) than through provisions against unfair imports. Section 201 cases are meant to provide firms experiencing substantial dislocation with an opportunity to undertake orderly adjustment over a finite period of time, not an entitlement to indefinite protection (as is possible with antidumping or antisubsidy measures).[49] Section 201 has also been characterized by somewhat less congressional tampering and less administrative arcana than the rules for computing dumping and subsidy margins.[50] Perhaps most important, this avenue of the law, unlike the others, minimizes the distracting polemics about unjust prices and practices. Put another way, section 201 offers a means of responding to economic hardship with less emphasis on blame and odium. The less political energy is dissipated exporting blame, the more may be available to address the domestic economy's larger needs.

As stressed in chapter 3, the political incentives to skirt the escape clause in favor of unfair trade redress are manifold. It is good politics to endorse restrictions when imports are "unfairly traded," dismal politics to call for restrictions when trade is "fair." Furthermore, the injury threshold is higher in section 201 cases; relief is less certain (the president can reverse the ITC); the supplying countries can demand offsetting concessions (article 19 of the GATT); and the action is supposed to be nondiscriminatory (may affect third countries).

But the relative magnetism of the different trade remedies might be rebalanced somewhat if the GATT safeguard code were revised, lowering the norms for compensation and causality. What is the point of maintaining more stringent standards for safeguard cases than for dumping and countervailing duty cases if the latter outnumber the former by a 44-to-1 ratio? Relaxing the antitrust rules when the firms damaged by imports propose to adjust through mergers might add another attractive dimension to section 201 petitions.[51] Depriving the unfair import regulations of their political charm is impossible, but sweetening the alternative is at least a start.

Making Sense of Dumping and Subsidies

Ideally, the injury test for complaints about foreign dumping or subsidies should ask not merely what a corrective trade action can do for the petitioner, but what it can do for the country—that is, the national welfare and security. Countervailing duty regulations make little attempt to distinguish between subsidies that clearly distort international trade and subsidies that do not (or that may even be offsetting some distortions). Neither the antisubsidy nor the antidumping proceedings differentiate between pricing patterns that pose an anticompetitive threat and pricing patterns that favor competition and that may be conferring dynamic net benefits on the economy as a whole. Short of rethinking the question of injury, negotiating an end to "sales below cost" provisions in national antidumping laws would remove the most protectionist element of these laws and bring them closer to the standard prevailing in domestic price discrimination doctrine.[52] Barring that, the Department of Commerce might be asked to modify various operating procedures that are not required by law (most notably, the practice of not comparing averages of both U.S. and foreign prices in computing dumping margins).[53]

The motivation to move in any of these directions is minimal without presidential leadership. The White House, as I suggested in chapter 6, is hardly in an enviable political position to improve the process of remedial import administration. But it is not in a hopeless position either. In trade policy, as in other kinds of economic regulation, the devil typically lurks in the details. Congress has micromanaged a growing number of these details but has also left many to executive discretion. If presidents are prepared to veto legislation over technicalities (like a provision for plant-closing notification in the 1988 Trade Act), they also have the authority to take a harder look at some discretionary administrative methods in their own cabinet departments.

Even these zones of administrative leeway may be informally constrained. Prevailing decision-rules sometimes reflect anticipatory reactions by executive agencies to signals from Congress. One cannot change those rules while ignoring the signals, but there may be ways to heed congressional concerns without reclining into bureaucratic business as usual.

Credibility can be maintained by acting forcefully when the case for decisive trade action is sound. The economic logic of antidumping measures directed at competitive global industries whose only misbehavior is selling at different prices in different markets may be suspect. But when a foreign monopoly or cartel is doing the selling—and driving out U.S. producers, preparing to gauge, or seeking to exercise market power in other ways, such as limiting foreign access to new technologies in other product markets—regulators are on much firmer ground.[54] Indeed, they may be well advised to intervene early, before the domestic industry has been irreparably damaged, particularly when the industry at risk is vital to security. If a domestically based capability to manufacture computer chips is deemed more critical to defense than an ability to produce potato chips, it ought to be safeguarded without hesitation, not as an afterthought. In many such instances, convoluted efforts to set "fair values" for imports may not even be necessary. Under section 232 of the 1962 Trade Act, the president has long possessed ample power to order restrictions on any article "imported in . . . such quantities or under such circumstances as to threaten to impair the national security."[55] This mandate should be used discerningly, but forthrightly, as intended.

Challenging Trade Barriers

Trade negotiators cannot abandon the struggle to improve market opportunities for U.S. exporters and investors, particularly in advanced economies like Japan's. There are economic reasons to persevere. Export growth will help brighten the nation's economic future. Improved terms of trade can, however modestly, raise American living standards. Important high-technology industries, if permitted to attain greater scale economies, could gain additional ground. Equally plausible, on balance, are the political considerations. Differential market access provides today's neoprotectionists with the justification they badly need to press for compensatory import barriers. Stripped of this casus belli, the coalitions that conditionally support these barriers are somewhat more likely to come unglued, not only for lack of a unifying symbol, but also because more U.S. commercial interests will find themselves exposed to the perils of counterretaliation abroad.[56] In any event, no president can expect much congressional forbearance by ducking the question of trade reciprocity.

How to keep the quest for reciprocal access from sliding down the slippery slope to managed trade, or how to discourage supplicants from constantly expecting a government-led sales pitch, is far from certain. Yet the federal trade bureaucracy is not without brakes to control the skid. Trade officials, like barristers, prefer clients they can readily defend and suits they can win. They also prefer a receptive international jury. The U.S. Trade Representative has generally gone to trial, so to speak, with a precise brief, enough friendly witnesses, and a willingness to abide by internationally codified rules of evidence. This helps explain why American negotiators have been able to chalk up a number of victories in recent years.

Underlying respect for the GATT and the existence of reasonably coherent American aims for strengthening it appear to have supported greater tactical selectivity. As long as this scaffolding holds up, it remains possible to set some priorities among trade cases and to work effectively with the most promising ones. In deciding which sectoral disputes to pursue on a bilateral basis, the chances of success are probably improved by hewing closely to issues on which the United States can cite not only a degree of support from constituencies in the target country but a clear violation or deficiency of the GATT that is acknowledged in the international community. Tying section 301 investigations and sanctions, whenever possible, to formal GATT proceedings (for example, by invoking the "nullification or impairment" provisions of article 23) would seem to offer a more cost-effective wedge than resorting to unbridled unilateralism on the theory that the GATT is "dead."[57]

No Pain, No Gain

A track record of well-managed dispute resolutions can quiet some congressional unrest and perhaps lessen the frustration that fuels demands for additional regulation. Yet the fact is, none of the proposed administrative solutions, no matter how nuanced, can really cool down the overheated politics of trade if expectations are not realistic.

The president has principal responsibility for setting sensible expectations for commercial policy. No one else has the same authority to speak for the *national* economic interest, and no one else commands the same bully pulpit. Politicians know what a majority of the American public suspects: the country's ability to compete economically depends more on maintaining internal fitness than on protesting external conditions.[58] Moreover, people suspect that the politicians know this. When presidents imply that the key to "jobs, jobs, jobs" for Americans lies in foreign commercial concessions (or when presidential candidates warn of the "pulverization" of American industry if the concessions are too "small"),[59] voters may consider the message simplistic or escapist. For all the political pain associated with keeping the nation in firm competitive shape, there may also be a penalty for leaving an impression that a hamstrung government really expects to squeeze bigger gains from trade confrontations than from dealing with domestic structural priorities.[60]

The terms of national debate about the potentialities and limitations of trade intervention are best defined by balanced rhetoric. If it is useful to sit up and take notice of the "massive unfair trade practices" of trading partners, it is also essential to add emphatically that those practices account for a relatively small part of our industrial infirmities. Further, it is helpful to be reminded that the regulatory analgesics often prescribed can be iatrogenic. President Reagan was at his best when he vowed not just to aid the victims of unfair trade but also to oppose "any trade law that we wouldn't want another nation to pass in just the same form."[61]

Raising the Stakes

To strike a better balance between trade regulation and other important tasks, it may be necessary to go a step farther: the political stakes may have to be raised and institutional responsibilities clarified. The customary good cop, bad cop roles played by the president and Congress can have some advantages in international bargaining, but may also be furnishing both institutions with too much cover. The role playing has been a factor in a number of voluntary restraint agreements and other negotiated arrangements in which the executive, claiming duress, cuts the deals while the legislature postures. "Voluntary" trade restraints ought to be banned under the GATT and converted to tariffs. The imposition of tariffs, like other taxes, ought to require a vote of the Congress, as the framers of the Constitution clearly intended. And the revenues from the protection ought to be used to reduce the federal deficit rather than to line the pockets of overpaid corporate executives or of foreign exporting cartels (as voluntary restraint agreements and orderly marketing arrangements have sometimes done). These new rules of the game would flush dubious decisions on segmenting or restricting markets into the open, subjecting those decisions to the same political rigors (like highly visible roll calls) as other difficult choices about economic policy. The merits of some of these features have been of more than theoretical interest; tariffication of nontariff restraints, particularly in agriculture, was embraced as an integral part of U.S. strategy for the Uruguay Round and has been applied in some bilateral settlements.[62]

The assumption that the American trade policy process suffers whenever Congress is presented with a polarizing choice is questionable. An administration defending a regime of liberal trade may wind up better off debating its dissidents than trying too hard to co-opt them. The reason is quite simple: most lawmakers are not anxious to restore outmoded protectionism. They remain conscious that a reprise of the Smoot-Hawley syndrome would constitute, in the words of Senator John C. Danforth, "an act of gross stupidity."[63] And their prudence grows stronger when the members are made to stand up and be counted on decisions of high saliency.[64]

Viewed this way, it becomes easier to understand how, within weeks, the same legislators who in 1988 added fine points to the art of import administration were also willing to endorse overwhelmingly a historic opening of the commercial border with Canada. Amid the technical minutiae of dumping and subsidy regulations or negotiated quotas with "arrangement countries" for specific industries, a majority of legislators found it irresistible to tighten the regulatory screws.[65] But when it was time to vote up or down, either for open trade with Canada or for killing the accord, only one congressman in nine found it expedient to look like a spoilsport.[66] Likewise, in the spring of 1991, Congress dutifully went along with an extension of negotiating authority for the GATT round and simultaneously authorized talks on enlarging the North American free trade zone to include Mexico.[67] Again, as one chastened opponent of this initiative found, voting against free trade was scorned as "not looking out for this country's interest."[68] It is "almost a shameful thing," he concluded, "to be labeled a protectionist."

That agreeable generalization may not last forever, but neither should it be dismissed prematurely as passé.

Notes

Author's Preface

1. See Robert E. Baldwin, "U.S. Trade Policy, 1945–1988: From Foreign Policy to Domestic Policy," in Charles S. Pearson and James Riedel, eds., *The Directions of Trade Policy* (Basil Blackwell, 1990); James Bovard, *The Fair Trade Fraud* (St. Martin's, 1991); Jagdish Bhagwati, *The World Trading System at Risk* (Princeton University Press, 1991), chap. 2; I. M. Destler, *American Trade Policy* (Washington: Institute for International Economics, 1992); Charles S. Pearson, *Free Trade, Fair Trade? The Reagan Record* (The Johns Hopkins Foreign Policy Institute, 1989); J. David Richardson, "U.S. Trade Policy in the 1980s: Turns—and Roads Not Taken," Working Paper 3725 (Cambridge, Mass.: National Bureau of Economic Research, June 1991).

2. "Can America Compete?" *Economist*, January 18, 1992, p. 66.

3. The phrase is from Jagdish Bhagwati, *Protectionism* (MIT Press, 1988), p. 62.

4. The bottom fifth experienced a real net decline in family income between 1979 and 1990. See Alice M. Rivlin, *Reviving the American Dream* (Brookings, 1992), p. 47.

5. See Sylvia Nasar, "Why International Statistical Comparisons Don't Work," *New York Times*, March 8, 1992, p. E5. According to the OECD, U.S. gross domestic product per person, adjusted for purchasing power parity, was $21,449 in 1990—17 percent higher than the level in Germany and 22 percent ahead of Japan. German factory workers now earn more than American factory workers, but the difference is trivial when adjusted for Germany's higher living costs. What enables Americans as a whole to enjoy a higher living standard (while working about 260 hours a year less than Japanese workers) is the overall economy's comparatively high output per employee (40 percent higher than Japan's). International comparisons of living standards, moreover, do not adequately measure qualitative differences—such as the fact that the average floor area of American dwelling units is 136 square meters, compared with 94 square meters in Germany, 86 in France, and 81 in Japan.

6. Recently, the United States threatened retaliation on $1 billion worth of European exports after the European Community refused to comply with a GATT panel that had issued an adverse ruling on soybean subsidies and another panel had ruled that German subsidies to its partner in Airbus Industrie (compensating for currency fluctuations) violated international rules. Stuart Auerbach, "U.S. Vows Duties on EC Imports," *Washington Post*, May 1, 1992, pp. B1, B4.

7. International Monetary Fund, *International Financial Statistics* (Washington, August 1985), p. 488, and *International Financial Statistics* (Washington, July 1992), p. 540.

Chapter 1

1. Paula Stern, "Promoting Competitiveness in the Trade Laws," statement for the Subcommittee on Economic Stabilization of the House Committee on Banking, Finance, and Urban Af-

fairs, March 10, 1987, p. 10. The voluntary export restraint on Japanese automobiles, instituted in 1981, accounted for a large part of the increased protection. Technically, the auto restraint agreement did not arise from an unfair trade suit. Proponents of relief for the automobile industry, however, repeatedly invoked fairness as a basis for trade restrictions. The congressional debates leading up to the voluntary restraint agreement are laced with references to Japanese discriminatory barriers, inequitable practices, closed markets, and subsidies that put U.S. producers at a disadvantage. See, for instance, *Congressional Record - Senate*, June 11, 1980, pp. 14131–32; *Congressional Record - House*, June 24, 1980, pp. 16566– 67; *Congressional Record - House*, December 2, 1980, pp. 31514–15.

2. Reports of the Twentieth Century Fund Task Force on the Future of American Trade Policy, *The Free Trade Debate* (New York: Priority Press, 1989), p. 77. (The Tokyo Round is estimated to have expanded world exports between 1 and 2 percent.) See Alan V. Deardorff and Robert M. Stern, *The Michigan Model of World Production and Trade* (MIT Press, 1986), p. 53.

3. In 1986, for example, Democratic congressional candidates labored especially hard to arouse interest in the trade issue. In the exit polls taken by CBS and the *New York Times* in fifteen key states, however, merely 10 percent or less of the voters in thirteen of these states indicated that trade had been the most important issue affecting their vote. In the two states where the percentages were higher, North Carolina and Pennsylvania, the results were 15 percent and 11 percent. Karlyn H. Keene, "What the Polls Tell Us," in Claude E. Barfield and John H. Makin, eds., *Trade Policy and U.S. Competitiveness* (Washington: American Enterprise Institute for Public Policy Research, 1987), p. 129. In general, the population continued to show relatively little interest in the issue of trade imbalances. A Gallup poll conducted at the beginning of 1989, for example, found that 36 percent of the sample paid "a great deal of attention" to the U.S. trade deficit, 41 percent to the federal savings and loan crisis, 45 percent to the budget deficit, 48 percent to environmental pollution, 55 percent to U.S. relations with the Soviet Union, 73 percent to the drug problem, and 74 percent to the problem of crime. Gallup Organization, *The People, Press and Economics: A Times Mirror Multi-National Study of Attitudes Toward U.S. Economic Issues* (Washington: Times Mirror, May 1989), p. 24.

4. Warwick J. McKibbin and Jeffrey D. Sachs, *Global Linkages: Macroeconomic Interdependence and Cooperation in the World Economy* (Brookings, 1991), p. 129. The 1991 recession inevitably darkened the debt picture.

5. The Daniel Yankelovich Group, Inc., *Americans Talk Security: A Series of Surveys of American Voters—Attitudes Concerning National Security Issues*, National Surveys nos. 10 and 11 (Boston: Marttila and Kiley, December 1988), pp. 46, 96.

6. By 1990, forty American states had set up offices in Tokyo to attract Japanese investment. Clearly many state governors and legislatures cultivated foreign investment sensing that the payoff exceeded the political risks. "America and Japan: The Unhappy Alliance," *Economist*, February 17, 1990, p. 24.

7. As recently as September 1991, in a poll commissioned by the Council on Competitiveness, 73 percent said the most difficult challenge facing the United States lay ahead, whereas 18 percent believed it was already behind us. Thirty-eight percent of the respondents suspected that America's ability to compete economically had deteriorated. But 37 percent felt that American competitiveness had remained about the same, and 21 percent believed it had improved. See Peter D. Hart Associates, Inc., *American Viewpoint* (Bossier City, La., September 1991).

8. Gallup, *The People, Press and Economics*, pp. 15, 17. Even though only 33 percent felt the United States would be the leading economic power in the year 2000, Americans were evidently far more likely to foresee competitiveness improving than to believe it would get worse: 46 percent versus 17 percent. More generally, the trend in public satisfaction with the country's economic fortunes (at least until the 1991 recession) had been indisputably upward over the past ten years. In 1979 fewer than 20 percent expressed satisfaction "with the way things are going in the

U.S. at this time." By February 1990 the level was up to 55 percent. Gallup polls reported in Peter Passell, "America's Position in the Economic Race: What the Numbers Show and Conceal," *New York Times*, March 4, 1990, p. 4E.

9. Keene, "What the Polls Tell Us," p. 127.

10. Gallup, *The People, Press and Economics*, p. 15; Keene, "What the Polls Tell Us," p. 128. See CBS/*New York Times* and Matthew Greenwald & Associates, discussed in William Schneider, "Americans Don't See Japan as a Threat," *National Journal*, January 24, 1987, pp. 218–19, and Ronald Brownstein, "Tangling over Trade," *National Journal*, September 19, 1987, p. 2331.

11. In a sample of government officials, Gallup discovered that fully 86 percent believed Japanese trade policies were unfair to the United States. Sixty-nine percent and 57 percent felt similarly about the policies respectively of the European Community and South Korea. The corresponding percentages for the general public were noticeably lower: 63 percent with respect to Japan, 39 percent, South Korea, and 26 percent, EC. Gallup, *The People, Press and Economics*, p. 15. See also, William Schneider, "Protectionist Push Is Coming from the Top," *National Journal*, April 27, 1985, pp. 932–33.

12. Public opinion does not always drive the adoption of new regulatory policies, but historically most seem to require rather broad coalitions, hence considerable public support. James Q. Wilson, "The Politics of Regulation," in James Q. Wilson, ed., *The Politics of Regulation* (Basic Books, 1980), p. 365.

13. Samuel P. Huntington, "The U.S.—Decline or Renewal?" *Foreign Affairs* (Winter 1988/89), p. 81. More generally, see Joseph S. Nye, Jr., *Bound to Lead: The Changing Nature of American Power* (Basic Books, 1990), pp. 5–9.

14. Robert Z. Lawrence, *Can America Compete?* (Brookings, 1984), p. 18. There was some debate whether this estimate, based on industry output data in national income and products accounts, accurately represents manufacturing's share of national output. Some economists have argued that the prevailing computations have seriously overstated manufacturing output growth and that they mask an erosion of the U.S. industrial base after 1973. See Lawrence R. Mishel, *Manufacturing Numbers: How Inaccurate Statistics Conceal U.S. Industrial Decline* (Washington: Economic Policy Institute, April 1988). Subsequent reanalysis of the data, however, corroborated the original estimates.

15. Barry P. Bosworth and Robert Z. Lawrence, "America's Global Role: From Dominance to Interdependence," in John D. Steinbruner, ed., *Restructuring American Foreign Policy* (Brookings, 1989), pp. 30–31.

16. On the theory of strategic trade management, see: James A. Brander, "Rationales for Strategic Trade and Industrial Policy," in Paul R. Krugman, ed., *Strategic Trade Policy and the New International Economics* (MIT Press, 1987), pp. 23–46; Barbara J. Spencer, "What Should Trade Policy Target?" in Krugman, *Strategic Trade Policy*, pp. 69–89; and Paul R. Krugman, "Import Protection as Export Promotion: International Competition in the Presence of Oligopoly and Economics of Scale," in Henry Kierzkowski, ed., *Monopolistic Competition and International Trade* (Oxford, Clarendon Press, 1984), pp. 180–93.

17. Cited in Michael L. Dertouzos and others, *Made in America: Regaining the Productive Edge* (MIT Press, 1989), p. 249.

18. Robert Hof and Neil Gross, "Silicon Valley Is Watching Its Worst Nightmare Unfold," *Business Week*, September 4, 1989, p. 63.

19. By 1990 the GATT reported that world trade reached $3.1 trillion in 1989, after eight straight years of expansion. Between 1983 and 1989, world trade expanded nearly 50 percent faster than world economic growth, and it was expected to expand another 5 percent to 6 percent in 1990. "World Trade Grew in 1989," *New York Times*, March 22, 1990, p. D2, and Bruce Stokes, "Après Gatt le Déluge?" *National Journal*, January 12, 1991, p. 75.

20. Rachel McCulloch, "The Challenge to U.S. Leadership in High-Technology Industries (Can the United States Maintain Its Lead? Should It Try?)" Working Paper 2513 (Cambridge, Mass.: National Bureau of Economic Research, February 1988), table 2.

21. Twentieth Century Fund Task Force, *The Free Trade Debate*, p. 62. Exports of high-technology manufactures rose from 35 percent of all U.S. exports of manufactured goods to 42 percent.

22. See Kenneth Flamm, *Targeting the Computer: Government Support and International Competition* (Brookings, 1987), p. 4. Gallup's 1989 international survey of opinion leaders found that fully 96 percent of Japanese investors said the United States was still the leading economic power in the world. Gallup, *The People, Press and Economics*, p. 15.

23. The rough ranking here is derived from the following sources: Technology Administration, *Emerging Technologies: A Survey of Technical and Economic Opportunities* (U.S. Department of Commerce, Spring 1990), p. xi; U.S. Department of Commerce, *U.S. Industrial Outlook 1990* (Washington, 1990), pp. 20-2–20-10; Office of Technology Assessment, *Technology and the American Economic Transition: Choices for the Future* (Washington, May 1988), pp. 323–25, 328; "Electronics," *Standard and Poor's Industry Surveys*, January 12, 1989, section 3; Peter Morici, *Reassessing American Competitiveness* (Washington: National Planning Association, 1988); Daniel I. Okimoto, "The Japanese Challenge in High Technology," in Ralph Landau and Nathan Rosenberg, eds., *The Positive Sum Strategy: Harnessing Technology for Economic Growth* (Washington: National Academy Press, 1986), p. 554; Gene Bylinsky and Alicia Hills Moore, "Special Report: The High Tech Race—Who's Ahead?" *Fortune*, October 13, 1986, pp. 26–37; International Trade Administration, *Biotechnology* (U.S. Department of Commerce, July 1984), p. 15; and Office of Technology Assessment, *International Competitiveness in Electronics* (November 1983), p. 5.

24. This at least is the general verdict of the MIT case studies on industrial productivity in these industries. Dertouzos and others, *Made in America*.

25. Martin Neil Baily and Alok K. Chakrabarti, *Innovation and the Productivity Crisis* (Brookings, 1988), pp. 3–5. Measured in annual rates of growth in GDP per worker, U.S. productivity growth between 1980 and 1987 did lag behind the rates not only of Japan but also of Canada, France, West Germany, Italy, and the United Kingdom. Bosworth and Lawrence, "America's Global Role," in Steinbruner, *Restructuring American Foreign Policy*, p. 32. Much of the (narrowing) gap, however, reflects inevitable economic convergence as other countries catch up with the United States. See William J. Baumol, Anne Batey Blackman, and Edward N. Wolff, *Productivity and American Leadership* (MIT Press, 1989). For various reasons, comparative measurements of productivity are problematic. See Edward N. Wolff, "The Magnitude and Causes of the Recent Productivity Slowdown in the United States: A Survey of Recent Studies," in William J. Baumol and Kenneth McLennan, eds., *Productivity Growth and U.S. Competitiveness* (Oxford University Press, 1985), pp. 29–57.

26. Bosworth and Lawrence, "America's Global Role," in Steinbruner, *Restructuring American Foreign Policy*, pp. 32–33.

27. James Fallows, "Getting Along with Japan," *Atlantic Monthly*, December 1989, p. 62; Lee Price, "Trade Problems and Policy from a U.S. Labor Perspective," in Robert E. Baldwin and J. David Richardson, eds., *Current U.S. Trade Policy: Analysis, Agenda, and Administration*, NBER Conference Report (Cambridge, Mass.: National Bureau of Economic Research, 1986), p. 82.

28. For alternative explanations of rigidity in the trade deficit and delays in the "pass-through" of dollar devaluation, see Paul R. Krugman and Richard E. Baldwin, "The Persistence of the U.S. Trade Deficit," *Brookings Papers on Economic Activity 1: 1987*, p. 41; and "Passing the Buck," *Economist*, February 11, 1989, p. 63.

29. C. Fred Bergsten, *America in the World Economy: A Strategy for the 1990s* (Washington: Institute for International Economics, 1988), p. 85.

30. See, for example, Herbert Stein, "A Primer on the Other Deficit," *AEI Economist* (March 1987), pp. 5, 8; Stein, "Problems and Non-Problems in the American Economy," *Public Interest* (Fall 1989), pp. 57–64; and Richard B. McKenzie, "American Competitiveness—Do We Really Need to Worry?" *Public Interest* (Winter 1988), pp. 73–74.

31. For example, Robert Kuttner, *Managed Trade and Economic Sovereignty* (Washington: Economic Policy Institute, 1989), p. 38.

32. Council of Economic Advisers, *Economic Report of the President, February 1988*, pp. 284–85; and OECD Department of Economics and Statistics, *Report of Main Economic Indicators* (Paris, March 1984), p. 18, and *Report of Main Economic Indicators* (June 1989), p. 22.

33. Robert E. Hudec, "Thinking about the New Section 301: Beyond Good and Evil," in Jagdish Bhagwati and Hugh T. Patrick, eds., *Aggressive Unilateralism: America's 301 Trade Policy and the World Trading System* (University of Michigan Press, 1990), p. 149.

34. S. Con. Res. 15, *Congressional Record*, March 28, 1985, pp. 6664–65; and H. Con. Res. 106, *Congressional Record*, April 2, 1985, pp. 7104–05.

35. Richard A. Gephardt, "The Carrot and Stick in Foreign Trade Relations," *New York Times*, July 15, 1987, p. A27. Right after the 1988 election, during a trip to Japan, Congressman Gephardt would add, "We are way behind in getting serious about selling in this market. It's as much America's fault as Japan's." David E. Sanger, "How Japan Does What It's Doing to Keep Its Economy in Top Gear," *New York Times*, November 27, 1988, p. 24.

36. *Congressional Record*, July 10, 1987, p. S9639.

37. Quoted in Paul Magnusson and others, "Will We Ever Close the Trade Gap?" *Business Week*, February 27, 1989, p. 88.

38. Twentieth Century Fund, *Free Trade Debate*, p. 12.

39. Robert Z. Lawrence, "The International Dimension," in Robert E. Litan, Robert Z. Lawrence, and Charles L. Schultze, eds., *American Living Standards: Threats and Challenges* (Brookings, 1988), pp. 52–55.

40. Rachel McCulloch, "United States-Japan Economic Relations," in Robert E. Baldwin, ed., *Trade Policy Issues and Empirical Analysis* (University of Chicago Press, 1988), p. 318.

41. James Fallows, "Containing Japan," *Atlantic Monthly*, May 1989, p. 42. For a sanguine analysis of what pressure on Japan can accomplish, see also Edward J. Lincoln, *Japan's Unequal Trade* (Brookings, 1990), pp. 156–58.

42. Robert Samuelson, "Japan: Fears and Fantasies," *Washington Post*, March 28, 1990, p. A23.

43. See Martha Derthick and Paul J. Quirk, *The Politics of Deregulation* (Brookings, 1985).

44. D. T. Armentano, *Antitrust Policy: The Case for Repeal* (Washington: Cato Institute, 1986), pp. 45–48; Robert H. Bork, *The Antitrust Paradox: A Policy at War with Itself* (Basic Books, 1978), chap. 20; Robert A. Katzmann, "The Attenuation of Antitrust," *Brookings Review* (Summer 1984), pp. 23–27. Between 1981 and 1984, the FTC did not bring a single price discrimination case. *FTC Review (1977–84): A Report Prepared by a Member of the Federal Trade Commission Together with Comments from Other Members of the Commission*, prepared for the House Committee on Energy and Commerce, Subcommittee on Oversight and Investigations, 98 Cong. 2 sess. (Government Printing Office, September 1984), p. 58.

45. Remarks by Secretary of the Treasury James A. Baker III before a conference sponsored by the Institute for International Economics, September 14, 1987, published in *Treasury News*, no. B1118, p. 4.

Chapter 2

1. American Iron and Steel Institute, *Annual Statistical Report 1986* (Washington: AISI, 1987), tables 15 and 19.

2. General Agreement on Tariffs and Trade, Article 23.

3. The extraordinary volume of steel cases conflates the raw data on trade complaints, especially in 1982. The scores of steel cases that year mainly involved a single, generalized grievance—against subsidized imports from Europe. The masses of petitions for countervailing duties were meant to document the extent of the problem, forcing a comprehensive negotiated settlement. I.M. Destler, *American Trade Politics: System Under Stress* (Washington: Institute for International Economics, 1986), pp. 127–30.

4. Cited in Robert E. Baldwin, *Nontariff Distortions of International Trade* (Brookings, 1970), p. 2.

5. See, for instance, Rudiger W. Dornbush, "Policy Options for Freer Trade: The Case for Bilateralism," in Robert Z. Lawrence and Charles L. Schultze, eds., *An American Trade Strategy: Options for the 1990s* (Brookings, 1990), p. 118.

6. Julio J. Nogues, Andrzej Olechowski, and L. Alan Winters, "The Extent of Nontariff Barriers to Industrial Countries' Imports," *World Bank Economic Review*, vol. 1 (September 1986), p. 197. The markets surveyed were the United States, Australia, Austria, Finland, Japan, Norway, Switzerland, and the nine members of the EC in 1983.

7. Notorious examples were the South Korean and Taiwanese shoe manufacturers, who successfully skirted the U.S. orderly marketing agreement on nonrubber footwear. See David B. Yoffie, *Power and Protectionism: Strategies of the Newly Industrializing Countries* (Columbia University Press, 1983), p. 195.

8. World Bank, *World Development Report, 1987* (New York: Oxford University Press, 1987), p. 146.

9. See Joel Kotkin and Yorito Kishimoto, *The Third Century: America's Resurgence in the Asian Era* (Crown, 1988), p. 4. By late 1988 Commerce Secretary C. William Verity's assessment was that Asian markets had become "far, far more open today." David E. Sanger, "The Asians Have Given In and Still Prevailed on Trade," *New York Times*, September 18, 1988, p. E3.

10. See Rudiger Dornbush and Yung Chul Park, "Korean Growth Policy," *Brookings Papers on Economic Activity*, 2:1987, p. 443 (hereafter *BPEA*); Bruce Stokes, "New Rivals in Asia," *National Journal*, May 9, 1987, p. 1117; "Korea: Pre-Olympic Hoopla and Miraculous Economic Growth Mask Deep Social and Political Problems That Must Soon Be Faced," *Business Week*, September 5, 1988, p. 46.

11. Total U.S. exports to Japan grew from $21.2 billion in 1985 to $48.6 billion in 1990. Exports of manufactured products to Japan rose from $11.9 billion in 1985 to $30.9 billion over the five-year period, while agricultural and primary products increased from $10.3 billion to $17.7 billion. Peter L. Gold and Dick K. Nanto, "Japanese-U.S. Trade: U.S. Exports of Negotiated Products, 1985–1990," *CRS Report for Congress* (Washington, November 26, 1991). The United States also sent a larger percentage of its manufactured exports to Japan in 1986 (10 percent) than in 1981 (6 percent). Robert Z. Lawrence and Robert E. Litan, "The Protectionist Prescription: Errors in Diagnosis and Cure," *BPEA*, 1:1987, p. 293.

12. Kan Ito, "Trans-Pacific Anger," *Foreign Policy*, vol. 78 (Spring 1990), p. 134.

13. For a discussion of these developments, see Brian Hindley and Martin Wolf, "The Future of the International Trading System: Blocs, Bilateralism, Reciprocity, and the GATT." Paper presented at the Conference on the United States and Europe in the 1990s, American Enterprise Institute for Public Policy Research, Washington, March 5–8, 1990, pp. 36–51; also Brian Hin-

dley, "Dumping and the Far East Trade of the European Community," *World Economy*, vol. 11 (December 1988), pp. 445–63.

14. Gary Clyde Hufbauer, "An Overview," in Gary Clyde Hufbauer, ed., *Europe 1992: An American Perspective* (Brookings, 1990), pp. 21–23.

15. William E. Brock, "Canadian-U.S. Trade Negotiations: A Status Report," in Edward R. Fried and Philip H. Trezise, eds., *U.S.-Canadian Economic Relations: Next Steps?* (Brookings, 1984), p. 65.

16. Sidney Weintraub, *Free Trade between Mexico and the United States?* (Brookings, 1984), pp. 56, 61.

17. On the danger of "unequal" trade with low-wage suppliers, see John M. Culbertson, "The Folly of Free Trade," *Harvard Business Review*, vol. 64 (September–October, 1986), p. 123, and more generally, Culbertson, *The Dangers of "Free Trade"* (Madison, Wis.: 21st Century Press, 1985), chaps. 2 and 3.

18. Robert Z. Lawrence and Robert E. Litan, "The Protectionist Prescription: Errors in Diagnosis and Cure," *BPEA*, *1:1987*, p. 291.

19. In recent years, the developing countries' share of U.S. exports has risen impressively. American companies sold $146.79 billion of goods and services to nonindustrialized nations in 1991. Keith Bradsher, "American Exports to Poor Countries Are Rapidly Rising," *New York Times*, May 10, 1992, pp. 1, 14.

20. Bela and Carol Balassa, "Industrial Protection in the Developed Countries," *World Economy*, vol. 7 (June 1984), p. 186.

21. Some economists have postulated that levels of protection have become roughly comparable among the leading industrial nations. William Cline surmised as early as 1984 that "the U.S. market is no more open than markets of other major countries." William R. Cline, *Exports of Manufactures from Developing Countries* (Brookings, 1984), pp. 60, 62.

22. Judith Hippler Bello and Alan F. Holmer, *The Antidumping and Countervailing Duty Laws: Key Legal and Policy Issues* (Washington: American Bar Association, 1987), p. v.

23. Revenue Act of 1916, P.L. 64–271, section 801, 39 Stat. 798.

24. From 1921 to 1954, the enforcing authority (at that time, the Secretary of the Treasury) followed the practice of considering the issue of injury first, delaying a full inquiry into the allegation of dumping until a harmful effect—that is, the existence of a real problem—was proven. William A. Wares, *The Theory of Dumping and American Commercial Policy* (Lexington Books, 1977), pp. 95–96, and pp. 19–20, on the history of the 1921 act.

25. Wares, *Theory of Dumping*, pp. 100–101. The legislative history of the 1921 antidumping act clearly indicates that a comparison of foreign-market values with domestic purchase prices was to be the main yardstick in determining the existence of dumping and the dumping margin. Indeed, the House version offered *only* this standard.

26. Section 205(b), Antidumping Act of 1921, as amended by the Trade Act of 1974, Section 321[d]; P.L. 93–618. Technically, under the 1974 amendment, dumping may even be found where U.S. prices are higher than cost and actually *higher than average prices in the country of origin*.

27. Horlick estimates that about 60 percent of all U.S. antidumping cases since 1980 have been based at least in part on allegations of sales below cost. Gary N. Horlick, "The United States Antidumping System," in John H. Jackson and Edwin A. Vermulst, eds., *Antidumping Law and Practice* (University of Michigan Press, 1989), p. 136. The ITA finds in the negative on only 11 percent of its dumping and subsidy determinations. J. M. Finger, "The Meaning of 'Unfair' in U.S. Import Policy," Policy, Research, and External Affairs Working Paper (Washington: World Bank, August 1991), p. 2. This high rate seems intuitively inevitable. As Thurow colorfully observes, "Dumping now legally occurs if a firm sells its products at less than cost plus a 10 percent margin for overhead expenses plus an 8 percent margin for profits. By that definition most

firms dump. Few make an 8 percent profit margin on sales. If the law were applied to domestic firms, eighteen out of the top twenty firms in the *Fortune 500* would have been found guilty of dumping in 1982." Lester C. Thurow, *The Zero Sum Solution: Building a World-Class American Economy* (Simon and Schuster, 1985), p. 359.

28. N. David Palmeter, "The Capture of the Antidumping Law," *Yale Journal of International Laws*, vol. 14 (Winter 1989), p. 185.

29. See Richard Dale, *Anti-dumping Law in a Liberal Trade Order* (St. Martin's Press, 1980), pp. 16, 31; and Klaus Stegemann, "Anti-Dumping Policy and the Consumer," *Journal of World Trade*, vol. 19 (September–October 1985), p. 466.

30. See the critique of domestic price discrimination law by Robert H. Bork, *The Antitrust Paradox: A Policy at War with Itself* (Basic Books, 1978), pp. 149–60. The argument here applies with much the same force to discriminatory pricing in international markets.

31. It is true that the short product cycles in some high-technology industries can act as entry barrier. New firms may have only brief windows through which to enter the markets in which incumbent producers are rapidly developing new, technologically advanced generations of products. More generally, though, dumping seems more likely to occur among producers in competitive industries than in oligopolistic or monopolistic ones. David Weinstein, "Competition and Unilateral Dumping," *Journal of International Economics*, vol. 32 (May 1992), p. 387.

32. Kenneth Flamm and Thomas L. McNaugher, "Rationalizing Technology Investments," in John D. Steinbruner, ed., *Restructuring American Foreign Policy* (Brookings, 1989), p. 140.

33. For instance, there were no fewer than thirteen companies employing 14,000 workers to produce more than 13.5 million TV sets *inside the United States* in 1988. *Wall Street Journal*, March 26, 1990, p. A14.

34. By late 1988, Japan's six largest semiconductor makers were poised to spend nearly $3 billion in new chip fabrication lines, not only for 1-megabit chips but also for 4-megabit devices and custom-designed chips known as ASICs. David E. Sanger, "A New Japanese Push on Chips," *New York Times*, November 9, 1988, pp. D1, D11.

35. Evidence suggests that the STA helped spawn a chip cartel led by MITI. After a careful review, Flamm concludes, "Two key points emerge from the historical record of MITI's interventions through November of 1987. First, whether or not it was issuing orders in the formal, legal sense, MITI clearly had organized a de facto cartel among Japanese manufacturers in 1987. Second, at least in the initial stages, this was encouraged by some within the U.S. government." Kenneth Flamm, "Policy and Politics in the International Semiconductor Industry," paper presented to the SEMI ISS seminar, Newport Beach, California, January 16, 1989, p. 11. Clyde Prestowitz states plainly that the chip pact "amounted to getting the Japanese government to force its companies to make a profit and even to impose controls to avoid excess production—in short, a government-led cartel." Clyde V. Prestowitz, *Trading Places: How We Allowed Japan to Take the Lead* (Basic Books, 1988), p. 62.

36. See George Gilder, "How the Computer Companies Lost Their Memories," *Forbes*, June 13, 1988, pp. 81–82.

37. The run-up in microchip prices helped increase the cost of personal computers by as much as 25 percent between 1987 and 1988. Geoff Lewis, "When the Chips Are Down: The Memory Crunch Is Scrambling Strategies in the Computer Industry," *Business Week*, June 27, 1988, p. 29. Japanese computer manufacturers, enjoying access to homemade chips at prices less inflated by MITI export licensing, began moving toward a cost advantage.

38. John Rawls, "Justice is Fairness," *Philosophical Review*, vol. 67 (1958), pp. 164–94.

39. Richard H. Snape, "Export-Promoting Subsidies and What to Do About Them," Working Paper 97 (Washington: World Bank, September 1988), pp. 3–4.

40. See estimates for selected OECD countries, 1980–86, in *Economic Report of the President, January 1989*, p. 162, and Robert Z. Lawrence, "Structural Adjustment Policies in Devel-

oped Countries," paper prepared for United Nations Conference on Trade and Development, December 20, 1988, pp. 20–21. Industrial subsidies (at least in the form of direct grants or tax expenditures) have never been a particularly prominent instrument of Japanese industrial targeting. Philip H. Trezise, "Industrial Policy is Not the Major Reason for Japan's Success," *Brookings Review*, vol. 1 (Spring 1983), p. 18; and Robert S. Ozaki, "How Japanese Industrial Policy Works," in Chalmers Johnson, ed., *The Industrial Policy Debate* (San Francisco: Institute for Contemporary Studies, 1984), p. 61.

41. Ernest H. Preeg, *The Tied Aid Credit Issue: U.S. Export Competitiveness in Developing Countries* (Washington: Center for Strategic and International Studies, 1989), p. 6.

42. See International Trade Administration, *International Financing Programs and U.S. International Economic Competitiveness* (U.S. Department of Commerce, September 1990), pp. 26–27, and also pp. 31–36. The ITA's data include multilateral disbursements, but the general trends are the same when only bilateral assistance is considered. See Organization for Economic Cooperation and Development, *Development Co-operation in the 1990s: Efforts and Policies of the Members of the Development Assistance Committee* (Paris, December 1989), p. 217.

43. *Economic Report of the President, January 1991*, p. 247.

44. *Economic Report of the President, February 1988*, p. 143. As of 1982–84, the weighted average PSE of the United States was roughly on a par with that of Canada and New Zealand, for example. See Robert L. Paarlberg, *Fixing Farm Trade: Policy Options for the United States* (Ballinger, 1988), pp. 62–63.

45. The cost of agricultural intervention by the U.S. government increased from $3 billion in 1980–81 to $11.9 billion in 1984 and an estimated $20 billion a year for 1986–88. World Bank, *World Development Report, 1986* (New York: Oxford University Press, 1986), p. 122.

46. Brian Hindley and Martin Wolf, "The Future of the International Trading System: Blocs, Bilateralism, Reciprocity, and the GATT," paper presented at the Conference on the United States and Europe in the 1990s, American Enterprise Institute for Public Policy Research, Washington, March 5–8, 1990, p. 5. *Economic Report of the President, January 1989*, p. 175.

47. Organization for Economic Co-operation and Development, *Agricultural Policies, Markets and Trade: Monitoring and Outlook, 1991* (Paris, 1991), pp. 157, 181.

48. "Trade Talks on 'Verge of a Breakthrough'" *Financial Times*, February 1, 1991, p. 7. David Garner, "Record Rise Forecast in the EC's Agricultural Budget," *Financial Times*, February 12, 1991, p. 24; and David Garner, "Alarm Grows in Brussels over Deepening Farm Budget Crisis," *Financial Times*, February 12, 1991, p. 36.

49. Paul R. Krugman, "The U.S. Response to Foreign Industrial Targeting," *BPEA, 1:1984*, pp. 114–15.

50. Robert W. Crandall, "The EC-US Steel Trade Crisis," in Loukas Tsoukalis, ed., *Europe, America and the World Economy* (Oxford: Basil Blackwell, 1986), p. 28. A number of aging plants, however, were replaced by new ones.

51. Patrick A. Messerlin, "Export-Credit Mercantilism à la Française," *World Economy*, vol. 9 (December 1986), p. 386; and Karl H. Jüttemeier, "Subsidizing the Federal German Economy—Figures and Facts, 1973–1984," Working Paper 279 (Kiel, Germany: Institute of World Economics, January 1987), p. 21.

52. Respectively, Chalmers Johnson, *MITI and the Japanese Miracle: The Growth of Industrial Policy, 1925–1975* (Stanford University Press, 1982), p. 17; T. J. Pempel, *Policy and Politics in Japan: Creative Conservatism* (Temple University Press, 1982); Ezra Vogel, "Guided Free Enterprise in Japan," *Harvard Business Review*, vol. 56 (May–June 1978); Ezra Vogel, *Japan as Number One* (Harvard University Press, 1979); and Karel van Wolferen, *The Enigma of Japanese Power: People and Politics in a Stateless Nation* (Alfred A. Knopf, 1989).

53. Karel G. van Wolferen, "The Japan Problem," *Foreign Affairs*, vol. 65 (Winter 1986/87), p. 289.

54. In contrast to Johnson and others, see, for instance, Hugh Patrick and Henry Rosovsky, "Japan's Economic Performance: An Overview," in Hugh Patrick and Henry Rosovsky, eds., *Asia's New Giant: How the Japanese Economy Works* (Brookings, 1976), pp. 1–61; Philip H. Trezise, "Industrial Policy Is Not the Major Reason for Japan's Success," *Brookings Review*, vol. 1 (Spring 1983), pp. 13–18; Gary R. Saxonhouse, "The Micro- and Macro-economics of Foreign Sales in Japan," in William R. Cline, ed., *Trade Policy in the 1980's* (MIT Press, 1983), pp. 259–304.

55. Hiromichi Mutoh, "The Automotive Industry," in Ryutaro Komiya, Masahiro Okuno, and Kotaro Suzumura, eds., *Industrial Policy of Japan* (San Diego: Academic Press, 1988), p. 330; Hideki Yamawaki, "The Steel Industry," in Komiya and others, *Industrial Policy*, pp. 302–03; David J. Collis, "The Machine Tool Industry and Industrial Policy 1955–82," Graduate School of Business Administration, Harvard University, February 1987; Koji Shinjo, "The Computer Industry," in Komiya and others, *Industrial Policy*, pp. 354–61; Michael Borrus, James E. Millstein, and John Zysman, "Trade and Development in the Semiconductor Industry: Japanese Challenge and American Response," in John Zysman and Laura Tyson, eds., *American Industry in International Competition: Government Policies and Corporate Strategies* (Cornell University Press, 1983).

56. See David Friedman, *The Misunderstood Miracle: Industrial Development and Political Change in Japan* (Cornell University Press, 1988), pp. 202–03; Michael E. Porter, *The Competitive Advantage of Nations* (Free Press, 1990), p. 238; and Richard J. Samuels, *The Business of the Japanese State: Energy Markets in Comparative and Historical Perspective* (Cornell University Press, 1987), p. 260.

57. One of MITI's most notorious blunders was the attempt to consolidate Japanese automotive production and eliminate Honda Motors. Daniel F. Burton, Jr., "Markets in Motion: U.S.-Japan Trade in the Fast Lane," *New York University Journal of International Law and Politics*, vol. 18 (Summer 1986), pp. 1139–40. In the early postwar years MITI had tried to discourage Sony from investing in transistor technology. Robert S. Ozaki, "How Japanese Industrial Policy Works," in Chalmers Johnson, ed., *The Industrial Policy Debate* (San Francisco: Institute for Contemporary Studies, 1984), p. 63. See also Hugh Patrick, "Japanese High Technology Industrial Policy in Comparative Context," in Hugh Patrick and Larry Meissner, eds., *Japan's High Technology Industries: Lessons and Limitations of Industrial Policy* (University of Washington Press, 1986), p. 18.

58. See Richard R. Nelson, Merton J. Peck, and Edward D. Kalachek, *Technology, Economic Growth and Public Policy* (Brookings, 1967), chap. 8, pp. 151–70; Richard R. Nelson, ed., *Government and Technical Progress: A Cross-Country Analysis* (Pergamon, 1982), Richard R. Nelson, *High-Technology Policies: A Five-Nation Comparison* (Washington: American Enterprise Institute for Public Policy Research, 1984), pp. 51–52, and pp. 56–57. In aerospace, the Japanese government has experienced a series of false starts, the latest of which was a 30 percent stake in a consortium building the VT–2500 jet engine. ANA, Japan's second-largest airline, passed it up in favor of a competing engine built by General Electric. David E. Sanger, "Mighty MITI Loses Its Grip," *New York Times*, July 9, 1989, p. F9. On disappointments in the Fifth Generation project, see David E. Sanger, "Japan Sets Sights on Winning Lead in New Computers," *New York Times*, April 30, 1990, p. A1.

59. Cray Research, Inc., has remained the world leader in supercomputers and in 1991 looked as though it would overtake Fujitsu as the leading seller in Japan. Recently, Intel Corporation has also shown an ability to beat Japanese supercomputer firms on their home turf. T.R. Reid, "Intel Cracks Japanese Supercomputer Market," *Washington Post*, January 29, 1991, pp. D1, D6.

60. William J. Broad, "U.S. Counts on Computer Edge in the Race for Advanced TV," *New York Times*, November 28, 1989, pp. C1, C13.

61. See, for example, Kozo Yamamura, "Caveat Emptor: The Industrial Policy of Japan," in Paul R. Krugman, ed., *Strategic Trade Policy and the New International Economics* (MIT Press, 1987), pp. 190–92. In his perceptive study of Japanese industrial policy, Daniel Okimoto underscores the continuing function of MITI in providing "a framework for communication and consensus building between government and business." Yet he too acknowledges that the maturation of the Japanese economy has altered the government's role: "If industrial policy once functioned to compensate for market imperfections, the need to rely on it as a compensating mechanism is now significantly reduced; and if the government once derived its capacity to implement industrial policy from the allocation of substantial financial resources, that capacity has been significantly diminished." Daniel I. Okimoto, *Between MITI and the Market: Japanese Industrial Policy for High Technology* (Stanford University Press, 1989), p. 232.

62. Japan has lagged behind the United States in basic research. See Bela Balassa and Marcus Noland, *Japan in the World Economy* (Washington: Institute for International Economics, 1988), pp. 44–45.

63. Saxonhouse may be correct in stressing that U.S. funding of private sector research and development has eclipsed that of Japan through most of the postwar period and that tax credits and special depreciation allowances to stimulate high-tech sectors have been less generous in Japan. Gary R. Saxonhouse, "What's All This about 'Industrial Targeting' in Japan?" *World Economy*, vol. 6 (September 1983), pp. 255, 258, 268. But Saxonhouse miscalculates the role of trade protection (in myriad guises) in subsidizing various Japanese industries. See comments by Laura D'Andrea Tyson on a paper by Gary R. Saxonhouse, "Differentiated Products, Economies of Scale, and Access to the Japanese Market," in Robert C. Feenstra, ed., *Trade Policies for International Competitiveness* (University of Chicago, 1989), pp. 175–80. The genius of Japanese industrial policy, at least in some sectors, lies in shielding the local market while encouraging firms to compete fiercely in international markets, thereby maintaining efficiency. This subtle mix of protection and competition may be *sui generis* among major industrial nations. On how protection can act as an export subsidy, see Paul R. Krugman, "Import Protection as Export Promotion: International Competition in the Presence of Oligopoly and Economics of Scale," in Henryk Kierzkowski, ed., *Monopolistic Competition and International Trade* (Clarendon Press, 1984), pp. 180–93.

64. See, among others, Okimoto, *Between MITI and the Market*, pp. 103–05.

65. Recent scholarly analysis of Japan's commercial advantage no longer stresses the role of "conscious" official protectionism, but rather a mixture of less tangible forces ("the very nature of Japan's political economy") and the residuum of "the past system of formal closure." See, for instance, Stephen D. Krasner, *Asymmetries in Japanese-American Trade* (University of California, Institute of International Studies, Berkeley, 1987), pp. 4, 40, 41, 66. On the dynamic effects of past protection in the semiconductor industry, see Kenneth Flamm, "Making New Rules: High-Tech Trade Friction and the Semiconductor Industry," *Brookings Review*, vol. 9 (Spring 1991), pp. 22–29.

66. I owe this civil rights metaphor to Clyde V. Prestowitz, Jr., who described the U.S.-Japan semiconductor negotiations during the early 1980s in these terms: "In effect, like disadvantaged U.S. minorities, we wanted an affirmative-action program that would offset the effects of past discrimination by actively working to increase imported chips." Clyde V. Prestowitz, Jr., *Trading Places: How We Are Giving Our Future to Japan and How to Reclaim It* (Basic Books, 1988), p. 153.

67. An emphasis on righting old wrongs could be used to justify claims of all kinds: what was to prevent, say, the LDCs and NICs from insisting that they, more than anyone, continued to deserve reparations on the basis that their fully industrialized competitors had acquired long-range (dynamic) advantages from prior infant-industry protection? Or how would we answer the subsi-

dizers of Europe's Airbus Industrie, who kept excusing their current contributions on the grounds that Boeing and McDonnell Douglas had at one time been heavily cross-subsidized through defense contracts?

68. The figures are from Peter Truell, "Why Reactions Differ to Japan and Germany," *Wall Street Journal*, February 26, 1990, p. A1. On import penetration and intraindustry trade patterns, see Bela Balassa and Marcus Noland, *Japan in the World Economy* (Washington: Institute for International Economics, 1988), pp. 62–71; and Edward J. Lincoln, *Japan's Unequal Trade* (Brookings, 1990), chaps. 2, 3.

69. The comparison with Germany is complicated by the fact that Germany is located in the middle of Europe, trades heavily inside a customs union, and is somewhat less dependent than Japan for energy imports. Japan imports 86.7 percent of its coal, 94.8 percent of its natural gas, and almost 100 percent of its oil; Germany is self-sufficient in coal and produces more than a quarter of the natural gas it consumes, though it imports 95.4 percent of its oil. Edward J. Lincoln, *Japan's Unequal Trade* (Brookings, 1990), pp. 66–67.

70. Investment in majority U.S.-owned subsidiaries has long been the main source of foreign sales by American multinationals everywhere except in Japan. There, minority affiliates have accounted for the dominant share of their sales (62 percent, compared to 24 percent in Germany). The fact that most American investment in Japan has remained limited to minority affiliates, evidently unable to create sufficient distribution channels for exports, may well act as an impediment to balanced trade in manufactures. See the interesting analysis of this point by Dennis J. Encarnation, *Rivals Beyond Trade: America Versus Japan in Global Competition* (Cornell University Press, 1992), pp. 89–96, 187.

71. Lincoln, *Japan's Unequal Trade*, pp. 13–18. See also Advisory Committee for Trade Policy and Negotiations, *Analysis of the U.S.-Japan Trade Problem* (Washington: ACTPN, February 1989).

72. Amy Borrus, "Tokyo Unveils This Year's 'Buy American' Plan," *Business Week*, January 15, 1990, pp. 38, 39. Elisabeth Rubinfien, "Tokyo Is Leaning on Companies to Import More and Assuage U.S.," *Wall Street Journal*, December 27, 1989, p. A4.

73. Recently, Japan's Fair Trade Commission was reported to be moving more aggressively against the *dango* system. See Paul Blustein, "Trustbusters Take On the Dango," *Washington Post*, May 14, 1991, pp. C1, C4.

74. Japanese direct investment in the United States almost doubled between 1987 and 1989. U.S. Department of Commerce, Bureau of Economic Analysis, *Survey of Current Business*, vol. 70 (August 1990), p. 41. According to Commerce Department surveys, capital outlays by U.S. companies in Japan jumped 64 percent in 1988 and an estimated 51 percent in 1989. Amy Borrus, "Slowly but Surely, the U.S. Is Buying into Japan," *Business Week*, December 19, 1988, p. 44. Sales by majority subsidiaries as a share of sales by American multinationals in Japan reached 38 percent by 1988, up from 25 percent a decade earlier. Encarnation, *Rivals Beyond Trade*, p. 90.

75. In 1986, 58.4 percent of U.S. manufactured exports to Japan was shipped by Japanese affiliates. By 1987, the share had dropped to 40.5 percent, and by 1988, to 38.4 percent. See Robert Z. Lawrence, "How Open Is Japan?" *Tokyo Club Papers*, no. 4, pt. 2 (Tokyo Club Foundation for Global Studies, 1991), p. 34.

76. Douglas Ostrom, "Statistics, Lies and Computer Tape: Untangling Aggregate U.S. and Japanese Trade Data," *JEI Report*, no. 15A (Washington: Japan Economic Institute, April 19, 1991), p. 8. Japan's overall current account surplus declined by a third between 1987 and 1989, from $87 billion to $57 billion. *Business Week*, April 9, 1990, p. 16.

77. Robert Z. Lawrence, "U.S. Current Account Adjustment: An Appraisal," *BPEA*, *2:1990*, pp. 371–73.

78. ACTPN, *U.S.-Japan Trade Problem*, p. 97. U.S. exports to Japan in all categories of manufactured products subject to negotiations between 1985 and 1990 rose 275 percent. U.S.

exports to Japan of negotiated GATT agricultural products rose 165 percent. Gold and Nanto, "Japanese-U.S. Trade."

79. Stuart Auerbach, "'Unfair' Tag Unlikely for Japan: Hills," *Washington Post*, April 26, 1990, p. E1; and Stuart Auerbach, "Lawmakers Criticize Trade Pact with Japan," *Washington Post*, April 20, 1990, p. A8.

80. Clyde H. Farnsworth, "Japan Criticized on Trade Progress," *New York Times*, June 13, 1990, p. D7.

81. Jay Peterzell, "When 'Friends' Become Moles: American Companies Wake Up to a New Spy Threat: U.S. Allies," *Time*, May 28, 1990, p. 50.

82. ITC estimate cited *Economic Report of the President, February 1988*, p. 140.

83. Geza Feketekuty, *International Trade in Services: An Overview and Blueprint for Negotiation* (Ballinger, 1988), p. 192.

84. This is not to say that every decision in the U.S. telecommunications system is based on free market criteria. When the laying of a fiber optic cable from New York to Washington, D.C., was put up for competitive bidding, the lowest bid—50 percent below the others—came from a foreign firm. It was rejected on national security grounds. Lester Thurow, "The Other Deficit," *Resources*, vol. 80 (Spring 1985), p. 9.

85. Allied Signal, a producer of amorphous metals, waited almost twelve years to get a patent in Japan. Texas Instruments tried for thirty years before obtaining a Japanese patent for its semiconductors.

86. Robert E. Hudec, "Thinking about the New Section 301: Beyond Good and Evil," in Jagdish Bhagwati and Hugh T. Patrick, eds., *Aggressive Unilateralism: America's 301 Trade Policy and the World Trading System* (University of Michigan Press, 1990), pp. 113–59.

87. *Economic Report of the President, February 1991*, p. 249.

88. Robert E. Litan and Peter O. Suchman, "U.S. Trade Policy at a Crossroad," *Science*, vol. 247 (January 5, 1990), p. 33. For figures, see U.S. International Trade Commission, *Review of the Effectiveness of Trade Dispute Settlement Under the GATT and Tokyo Round Agreements*, Pub. 1793 (Washington, 1985).

89. For example, it took seven years for Congress to comply with a GATT ruling that Domestic International Sales Corporations (DISCs) contravened U.S. international obligations.

90. *Hearings on the Trade Reform Act of 1973*, Senate Finance Committee, 93 Cong. 2 sess. (GPO, 1974), pt. 1, p. 2.

91. See "Those Bad Fourth-Quarter Numbers May Be Mostly Sound and Fury," *Business Week*, January 8, 1990, p. 29. Between 1986 and 1990, exports of small manufactures were up 145.9 percent; electrical machinery, 133.1 percent; aircraft, 99.4 percent; computers and office machines, 69.5 percent; and cars and trucks, 61.4 percent. Sylvia Nasar, "Boom in Manufactured Exports Provides Hope for U.S. Economy," *New York Times*, April 21, 1991, p. A1.

Chapter 3

1. Expenditures for trade adjustment assistance in fiscal 1982 fell to less than one-tenth the levels of 1980–81 and then continued to drop in each of the next three fiscal years. The program was revived by Congress in 1986, but only two firms managed to receive direct assistance or loans in 1985–86. Whereas $10.5 million had been spent in 1978 on technical assistance to firms hurt by trade, less than half that amount was spent in 1986. Similarly, while the number of dislocated workers certified for assistance reached 165,866 in 1978, only 93,132 petitions were approved in 1986. Office of Technology Assessment, *Trade Adjustment Assistance: New Ideas for an Old Program* (Washington, June 1987), pp. 26–35.

2. David G. Tarr and Morris E. Morkre, *Aggregate Costs to the United States of Tariffs and Quotas on Imports: General Tariff Cuts and Removal of Quotas on Automobiles, Steel, Sugar, and Textiles* (Federal Trade Commission, December 1984), cited in Gary Clyde Hufbauer, Diane T. Berliner, and Kimberly Ann Elliott, *Trade Protection in the United States: 31 Case Studies* (Washington: Institute for International Economics, 1986), pp. 179, 183. William R. Cline has calculated conservatively that restraints on textile and apparel imports cost American consumers $20.3 billion in 1986, or an average of $238 per household. Inevitably, this implicit excise tax amounts to a regressive income transfer. William R. Cline, *The Future of World Trade in Textiles and Apparel* (Washington: Institute for International Economics, 1987), p. 193.

3. "Récul des Douze: Les Rélations Economiques Entre L'Europe et Les Etats-Unis," *Le Monde*, July 4, 1986, p. 1.

4. See, among others, Clyde H. Farnsworth, "Reagan Threatens Curb on Goods from Europe," *New York Times*, April 1, 1986, p. D1.

5. Jagdish Bhagwati, *Protectionism* (MIT Press, 1988), p. 84.

6. Maggie Ford, "South Korea Unveils Dollars 2.6 Bn Plan to Cut Trade Surplus with U.S.," *Financial Times*, April 27, 1987, p. 6.

7. For example, deregulation of the telecommunications industry intensified competition and increased the importance of access to foreign markets for purposes of securing scale economies. See David B. Yoffie and Helen V. Milner, "An Alternative to Free Trade or Protectionism: Why Corporations Seek Strategic Trade Policy," *California Management Review*, vol. 31 (Summer 1989), p. 122.

8. In recent years, the benefits to producers of the sugar program, as measured by the difference between the value of production at actual prices and at prices that would prevail if the commodity were unprotected, have been estimated at $1 billion to $1.5 billion annually. Large producers have the most to gain, as benefits accrue according to the size of output. In Hawaii, a major producing state, only five corporations produce 90 percent of the sugarcane. In Florida, just two corporations produce more than half the crop. Rekha Mehra, "Winners and Losers in the U.S. Sugar Program," *Resources*, vol. 94 (Winter 1989), p. 7.

9. See I. M. Destler and John S. Odell, *Anti-Protection: Changing Forces in United States Trade Politics* (Washington: Institute for International Economics, September 1987), p. 14.

10. Representative Sam Gejdenson (D-Connecticut), quoted in Clyde H. Farnsworth, "U.S. Will Tie Aid to Exports in Bid to Curb the Practice," *New York Times*, May 16, 1990, pp. D1, D21.

11. Bruce Stokes, "Getting Religion on Farm Exports," *National Journal*, May 25, 1985, p. 1260. On the 1985 farm export program, see William A. Galston, *A Tough Row to Hoe: The 1985 Farm Bill and Beyond* (Lanham, Maryland: Hamilton Press, 1985), pp. 120–21.

12. International Trade Administration, *International Financing Programs and U.S. International Economic Competitiveness* (U.S. Department of Commerce, September 1990), pp. 22–23.

13. *International Financing Programs*, pp. 17–18; and statement of Howard L. Hills, vice president and general counsel, Overseas Private Investment Corporation, statement on the *Role of U.S. Small Business in Rebuilding Kuwait*, before the Subcommittee on Foreign Operations of the Senate Appropriations Committee, March 11, 1991, 102 Cong. 1 sess. (GPO, 1991), pp. 6, 19.

14. Export-Import Bank of the United States, *Report to the U.S. Congress on Tied Aid Credit Practices* (Washington, April 1989), p. 25.

15. Clyde H. Farnsworth, "U.S. Move On Canada Doubted," *New York Times*, June 4, 1986, pp. D1, D2.

16. David B. Yoffie, "American Trade Policy: An Obsolete Bargain?" in John E. Chubb and Paul E. Peterson, eds., *Can the Government Govern?* (Brookings, 1989), p. 125. See also Helen V. Milner, *Resisting Protectionism: Global Industries and the Politics of International Trade* (Princeton University Press, 1988), chap. 7.

17. It was not inconceivable for Japan to swing billions in food imports away from the United States in favor of Europe, where farmers were frantically scrambling to shed their subsidized surpluses and where Japanese manufacturers needed a wedge to widen their European market shares. See Peter Drucker, "U.S.-Japan Trade Needs a Reality Check," *Wall Street Journal*, January 10, 1989, p. A18.

18. U.S. financial authorities worry that restraints on foreign participation in U.S. financial markets, particularly U.S. government debt markets, would make it more expensive to finance the federal deficit.

19. Quoted in "Talking Tough on Trade," *Newsweek*, March 14, 1988, p. 18.

20. Quoted in Steven Schlossstein, *Trade War: Greed, Power, and Industrial Policy on Opposite Sides of the Pacific* (Chicago, Ill.: Congdon and Weed, 1984), p. 3. After the Mondale debacle, a number of Democratic party operatives and pollsters took stock of what had gone wrong with the trade issue. Robert G. Beckel, a Mondale campaign manager, concluded, "As a national issue, I think the trade issue is a potential trap. You can get far out on that limb and it will get sawed off fast." The poll-taker Harrison Hickman observed: "The Democrats have to walk a very careful line. They can't fall prey to the charge that their policies are the protectionism of the past. And the American public does not want to think that American industry is incapable of competing internationally. If the message is one of malaise in the American workplace, then the American people are going to reject it." Ann Cooper and Bruce Stokes, "Buying Time on Trade," *National Journal*, November 9, 1985, pp. 2526–27.

21. It is true that the campaigns of each of these candidates labored under other, more basic handicaps, but the limited appeal of trade militancy was evident throughout the 1988 contests. In the South Carolina primary, Senator Dole campaigned in support of a pending textile quota bill that Vice President Bush opposed. Dole was soundly defeated. The Democratic nominee, Governor Michael S. Dukakis, eventually adopted some of Representative Gephardt's rhetoric, enabling Bush to accuse him of "protectionist demagoguery." Dukakis failed to carry a single Rust Belt state—not even Gephardt's Missouri. Stuart Auerbach, "Dukakis' Tough Trade Stance Moves Him Far from GOP Line," *Washington Post*, October 9, 1988, pp. H1, H10; and "Meet Militant Mike, the Tough Talker on Trade," *Business Week*, October 24, 1988, p. 37.

22. R.W. Apple, Jr., "Trade Warriors: Jobs and Protectionism Test Candidates' Creativity," *New York Times*, March 15, 1992, p. E1.

23. Quoted in Charles Krauthammer, "Bush's Spent Presidency," *Washington Post*, March 6, 1992, p. A23.

24. Catherine Pritchard, "Durkin Charges PAC Trying to Buy Smith Election," *Keene Sentinel*, October 27, 1990, p. 35.

25. Congressman Ed Jenkins, Democrat of Georgia, quoted in Harrison Donnelly, "New Doubts, Reagan Plan Slow Trade Bill Push," *Congressional Quarterly Weekly Report*, September 28, 1985, p. 1910.

26. In a fiscal 1988 omnibus highway reauthorization, Senator Riegle sided with a motion to table an amendment by Senator Thad Cochran to restrict use of imported cement in federal highway projects. Richard J. Whalen and R. Christopher Whalen, *Trade Warriors: The Guide to the Politics of Trade and Investment* (Washington: Whalen Company, 1990), pp. 191–95, 416.

27. In a fiscal 1989 defense authorization, Senator Heinz sought to table an amendment by Senator Phil Gramm of Texas to repeal a current law requiring the Department of Defense to purchase U.S. coal for shipment to European military bases. But during deliberations on the 1988 Omnibus Trade Act, Heinz joined all other Senate Republicans (July 17, 1987) in tabling the Harkin amendment on foreign investment. Whalen and Whalen, *Trade Warriors*, pp. 146–50, 417.

28. For an excellent general analysis of the shift-the-responsibility rationale for delegation, see Morris P. Fiorina, "Group Concentration and the Delegation of Legislative Authority," in

Roger G. Noll, ed., *Regulatory Policy and the Social Sciences* (University of California Press, 1985), especially pp. 186–87. For the definitive theoretical analysis of blame-avoidance politics, see R. Kent Weaver, "The Politics of Blame Avoidance," *Journal of Public Policy*, vol. 6 (October-December 1986), pp. 371–98.

29. President Reagan's remarks on U.S. trade, as delivered to business leaders and members of the president's Export Council and Advisory Committee for Trade Negotiations, September 23, 1985. *Congressional Quarterly Weekly Report*, September 28, 1985, p. 1948.

30. I. M. Destler, *American Trade Politics: System under Stress* (Washington: Institute for International Economics, 1986), p. 134, and Raymond J. Ahearn and Alfred Reifman, "U.S. Trade Policy: Congress Sends a Message," in Robert E. Baldwin and J. David Richardson, eds., *Current U.S. Trade Policy: Analysis, Agenda, and Administration* (Cambridge, Mass.: National Bureau of Economic Research, 1986), p. 109.

31. The administration was persuaded by end users that "the number of copper fabricators' jobs that would have been placed at risk [by import protection] was six times the number of copper miners' jobs that would have been saved." Alan F. Holmer, "Congress and the President—The Issues," in Claude E. Barfield and John H. Makin, eds., *Trade Policy and U.S. Competitiveness* (Washington: American Enterprise Institute for Public Policy Research, 1987), p. 15.

32. After the Supreme Court's decision in *Immigration and Naturalization Service* v. *Chadha* (1982), Congress simply substituted a joint resolution (that could be vetoed by the president) for the newly unconstitutional concurrent resolution to override presidential determinations in section 201 cases. The change was introduced in the Trade and Tariff Act of 1984.

33. E. E. Schattschneider, *Politics, Pressures and the Tariff* (Prentice-Hall, 1935), pp. 86, 88.

34. The term "bargaining tariff" is credited to Joseph M. Jones, Jr., *Tariff Retaliation: Repercussions of the Hawley-Smoot Bill* (University of Pennsylvania Press, 1934), pp. 303.

35. Quoted in Jagdish N. Bhagwati and Douglas A. Irwin, "The Return of the Reciprocitarians—US Trade Policy Today," *World Economy*, vol. 10 (June 1987), p. 113.

36. See, for example, Pat Choate, *Agents of Influence* (Alfred A. Knopf, 1990), especially, chaps. 1–3. The subsidiaries of foreign firms in the United States may also be wielding some clout. As foreign investment increased sharply in states like Kentucky and Tennessee, for example, the orientations of their congressional delegations began to change. Bruce Stokes, "Foreign Owners," *National Journal*, September 19, 1987, pp. 2333, 2335.

37. Robert E. Baldwin, *The Political Economy of U.S. Import Policy* (MIT Press, 1985), p. 50.

38. Helen V. Milner and David B. Yoffie, "Between Free Trade and Protectionism: Strategic Trade Policy and a Theory of Corporate Trade Demands," *International Organization*, vol. 43 (Spring 1989), pp. 239–72.

39. I. M. Destler, *America Trade Politics: System under Stress* (Washington: Institute for International Economics, 1986), p. 47.

40. Daniel P. Kaplan, *Has Trade Protection Revitalized Domestic Industries?* (Congressional Budget Office, November 1986), p. 101.

41. Gary Clyde Hufbauer and Howard F. Rosen, *Trade Policy for Troubled Industries* (Washington: Institute for International Economics, 1986), p. 47.

42. Cited in Paula Stern, "A Burdensome Legacy for the 1990s: The Reagan Administration's Trade Policy," *Brookings Review*, vol. 9 (Fall 1991), p. 43.

43. Some analysts have concluded that the decline in employment was substantially abetted by the voluntary restraint agreement, which raised prices and reduced the U.S. automakers' output. Fred Mannering and Clifford Winston, "Economic Effects of Voluntary Export Restrictions," in Clifford Winston, ed., *Blind Intersection? Policy and the Automobile Industry* (Brookings, 1987), p. 66.

44. By 1985 more than sixty industry groups had filed repeat petitions for relief. David B. Yoffie, "American Trade Policy: An Obsolete Bargain?" in John E. Chubb and Paul E. Peterson, eds., *Can the Government Govern?* (Brookings, 1989), p. 122.

45. Quoted in David E. Sanger, "Corporations Criticized on Trading with Japan," *New York Times*, September 12, 1988, p. D2.

46. Michael B. Smith, "U.S.-Japan Economic Relations in the 1990s: A Crossroads?" in William Brock and Robert Hormats, eds., *The Global Economy: America's Role in the Decade Ahead* (W. W. Norton, 1990), p. 88.

47. Even if Thai farmers did not make off with most of the business, only 28 percent of U.S. rice production is the medium- and short-grained, fully milled variety preferred by the Japanese. Currently, about half of this American rice is sold to Turkey, but if every last grain were to go to Japan, the annual sales volume would represent about $130 million—neither a trivial sum, nor an amount capable of restoring "bilateral harmony" with the United States. See Jim Powell, "Why Trade Retaliation Closes Markets and Impoverishes People," *Policy Analysis*, no. 43 (Cato Institute, November 1990), pp. 7, 11.

48. Export-Import Bank, *Report to the U.S. Congress*, p. 18.

49. Between 1986 and 1990, however, the Japanese market share of U.S. chipmakers rose from 9 percent to 12.4 percent. Jacob M. Schlesinger, "Affirmative Action: U.S. Chip Makers Find 'Quotas' Help Them Crack Japan's Market," *Wall Street Journal*, December 20, 1990, p. A1.

50. The National Corn Growers Association denounced the settlement: "At a time when our U.S. corn farmers are under severe economic pressure, it is inconceivable that our government would accept such an agreement. . . . They should have walked away from the agreement." See John Odell and Margit Matzinger-Tchakerian, *European Community Enlargement and the United States, Part B: Conclusion*, case 130 (Georgetown University, Institute for the Study of Diplomacy, Pew Case Studies Center, 1988), pp. 2–3.

51. Bruce Stokes, "Coping with Glut," *National Journal*, November 1, 1986, p. 2614.

52. See Joseph Grunwald and Kenneth Flamm, eds., *The Global Factory* (Brookings, 1985), pp. 2–9.

53. Robert B. Reich, "Who Is Us?" *Harvard Business Review*, vol. 90 (January-February, 1990), p. 54.

54. For example, AGIE, a Swiss machine maker, won an ITC patent infringement case against Japan's Sodick. Yamazaki Mazak, a Japanese machine-tool manufacturer operating a large plant in Kentucky, recently complained to the Commerce Department that offshore rivals, including some in Japan, were skirting U.S. restraints on machine-tool imports. Zachary Schiller and Roger Schreffler, "Look Who's Taking Japan to Task," *Business Week*, June 4, 1990, p. 64.

55. Robert Z. Lawrence, "Innovation and Trade: Meeting the Foreign Challenge," in Henry J. Aaron, ed., *Setting National Priorities: Policy for the Nineties* (Brookings, 1990), p. 173.

Chapter 4

1. From President Woodrow Wilson's request to Congress in February 1916 to establish a Tariff Commission (the precursor of the modern ITC), quoted in John M. Dobson, *Two Centuries of Tariffs: The Background and Emergence of the United States International Trade Commission* (Government Printing Office, 1976), p. 87.

2. See, for instance, Judith Goldstein, "The Political Economy of Trade: Institutions of Protection," *American Political Science Review*, vol. 80 (March 1986), p. 167.

3. Robert Pastor, "The Cry-and-Sigh Syndrome: Congress and Trade Policy," in Allen Schick, ed., *Making Economic Policy in Congress* (Washington: American Enterprise Institute for Public Policy Research, 1983), pp. 158–95.

4. J. Michael Finger and Andrzej Olechowski, eds., *The Uruguay Round: A Handbook on the Multilateral Trade Negotiations* (World Bank, 1987), pp. 264–65; and Office of the United States Trade Representative, tabulation of section 301 cases (Washington, January 1988).

5. By some estimates the volume of imports actually subject to punitive duties amounted to less than 0.5 percent of total imports over the 1982–85 period. David B. Yoffie, "American Trade Policy: An Obsolete Bargain?" in John E. Chubb and Paul E. Peterson, eds., *Can the Government Govern?* (Brookings, 1989), pp. 117–18.

6. The terms were those used by Representative Charles D. Vanik (D-Ohio), *Trade with Japan*, Hearings before the Subcommittee on Trade of the House Ways and Means Committee, September 18, 1980, 96 Cong. 2 sess. (GPO, 1980), p. 140.

7. Paula Stern, "Stop the Trade Bill Hysteria," *New York Times*, December 15, 1987, p. A31.

8. Philip H. Trezise, "At Last, Free Trade with Canada?" *The Brookings Review*, vol. 6 (Winter 1988), p. 20.

9. Sidney Weinraub, *Free Trade between Mexico and the United States* (Brookings, 1984), p. 54.

10. "E.C. Issues Updated List of U.S. Trade Barriers," *European Community News*, no. 9/87 (April 2, 1987), p. 1.

11. On the asymmetric implications of market closure between the United States and Canada, see Alan M. Rugman and Andrew D. M. Anderson, *Administered Protection in America* (Croom Helm, 1987), p. 49.

12. The deficit in U.S. textile and apparel trade rose to $21 billion, or 12.5 percent of the nation's overall merchandise trade deficit, by 1986. *Textile and Apparel Trade Act*, Hearings before the Subcommittee on Trade of the House Ways and Means Committee, 100 Cong. 1 sess. (GPO, 1987), pp. 549, 587.

13. Executives of the American Textile Manufacturers Institute, for example, would assert that there was "obviously" an essential need for a tighter system of import controls and that various efforts to establish the controls amounted only to "asking for a moratorium" on imports. See Pamela G. Hollie, "Clothing Retailers Now Expect Stable Prices," *New York Times*, August 2, 1983, p. D2; and Mary Ann Huser, "Despite Some Growing Pains, Trade Blossoms," *Congressional Quarterly Weekly Report*, April 14, 1984, p. 864.

14. Christopher Madison, "Chinese Textile Dispute Entangled in Sensitive National Security Issues," *National Journal*, December 3, 1983, p. 2527.

15. Philip M. Boffey, "Textile Producers in America Assail Pact with Chinese," *New York Times*, August 1, 1983, p. A1.

16. Tracking the antidumping and countervailing duty cases of the 1980s, J. Michael Finger and Tracy Murray found that the Commerce Department detected dumping or subsidization in about nine out of every ten complaints. J. Michael Finger and Tracy Murray, "Policing Unfair Imports: The U.S. Example." Working Paper, Policy, Research and External Affairs (Washington: World Bank, March 1990), p. 13.

17. Dated September 3, 1980. Cited in Steven Pressman, "Pressure Mounts on Protectionist Trade Bills," *Congressional Quarterly Weekly Report*, August 4, 1984, p. 1898.

18. Vinod K. Aggarwal, *Liberal Protectionism: The International Politics of Organized Textile Trade* (University of California Press, 1985), p. 179. The pledge was made in spite of the fact that textile imports, in square-yard equivalent, were actually lower in 1981 than in 1971. See Martin Wolf, "Managed Trade in Practice: Implications of the Textile Arrangements," in William R. Cline, ed., *Trade Policy in the 1980s* (MIT Press, 1983), p. 466.

19. This account of the political settlement draws heavily on Art Pine, "How President Came to Favor Concessions for U.S. Textile Makers," *Wall Street Journal*, January 6, 1984, pp. 1, 12. See also Jonathan Fuerbringer, "Negotiations in Textile Fight," *New York Times*, December 12, 1983, p. D2.

20. Under the new criteria, controls could be imposed if total growth in imports of a particular category of textiles exceeded 30 percent of the previous year's total, or if the ratio of total imports to domestic production of that product was 20 percent or more. Controls could also be set if imports from individual suppliers equaled 1 percent or more of the total domestic production of that product. Clyde H. Farnsworth, "Reagan Decides to Tighten Controls on Textile Imports," *New York Times*, December 17, 1983, pp. 1, 32.

21. Farnsworth, "Reagan Decides to Tighten Controls on Textile Imports," p. 32.

22. William R. Cline, *The Future of World Trade in Textiles and Apparel* (Washington: Institute for International Economics, 1987), pp. 214–15.

23. William R. Cline's estimates cited in Peter Passell, "Apparel Makers' Last Stand?" *New York Times*, September 26, 1990, p. D2.

24. The consensus on this point is far from complete. See, for instance, Joseph P. Kalt, "The Political Economy of Protectionism: Tariffs and Retaliation in the Timber Industry," in Robert E. Baldwin, ed., *Trade Policy Issue and Empirical Analysis* (University of Chicago Press, 1988), pp. 339–68.

25. Officials in British Columbia stated publicly that "B.C. stumpage is too low." Quoted in Peter Foster, "Stumped," *Saturday Night*, July 1987, p. 15. On the whole, however, the Canadians felt they had a reasonable legal and economic case that little or no subsidy existed. In particular, they challenged the ITA's premise that a fair value for forest products ought to incorporate "indirect costs" in the form of the "intrinsic values of the trees and land." The Canadians argued that introducing these "costs" contradicted the fundamental principle of economic rent—that natural resources have no value independent of the price of their end products in the marketplace. Charles F. Doran and Timothy J. Naftali, *U.S.-Canadian Softwood Lumber: Trade Dispute Negotiations* (Johns Hopkins Foreign Policy Institute, September 1987), pp. 12, 29.

26. See data in Michael B. Percy and Christian Yoder, *The Softwood Lumber Dispute and Canada-U.S. Trade in Natural Resources* (Halifax, Nova Scotia: Institute for Research on Public Policy, 1987), pp. 35–38.

27. Based on estimates by Wharton Econometric Forecasting Associates, cited in Percy and Yoder, *The Softwood Lumber Dispute*, pp. 113–14. Specifically, according to a 1985 Wharton Econometrics study, a 15 percent increase in the price of softwood imports (full tariff incidence borne by U.S. consumers) would save or maintain about 5,500 jobs in the U.S. lumber sector; it would cost 16,600 jobs in industries dependent on lumber inputs.

28. *Carlisle Tire & Rubber Co.* v. *United States*, 564 F. Supp. 834 (Center for International Trade, 1983). Here the court argued emphatically that "adoption of Carlisle's literal view that generally available benefits are a bounty or grant would, if taken to its logical extreme, lead to an absurd result. Thus, included in Carlisle's category of countervailable benefits would be such things as public highways and bridges, as well as a tax credit for expenditures on capital investment even if available to all industries and sectors. . . . To suggest, as Carlisle implicitly does here, that almost every import entering the stream of American commerce be countervailed simply defies reason." What the court did not mention, however, was that there could be a large gray area between general availability and specificity, particularly since section 771(5)(B) of the Trade Agreements Act of 1979 is sketchy on what constitutes a specific "industry" for purposes of identifying illegal national subsidies.

29. *Bethlehem Steel Corp.* v. *United States*, 590 F. Supp. 1237, 1239 (Center for International Trade, 1984).

30. *Cabot Corp.* v. *United States*, 620 F. Supp. 722 (Center for International Trade, 1985).

31. *Carbon Black from Mexico*, 51 Fed. Reg. 13,271 (Department of Commerce, 1986).

32. Respectively, letter from the U.S. Trade Representative, Clayton Yeutter, to Senator David Pryor (D-Arkansas), April 17, 1986, cited in Percy and Yoder, *The Softwood Lumber Dispute*, p. 146; and reported pledge from President Reagan to Senator Steven D. Symms (R-Idaho), cited

in Steven Pressman, "Larger Issues Almost Derail Canada Trade Talks," *Congressional Quarterly Weekly Report*, April 26, 1986, p. 906.

33. According to van Wolferen, in order for a construction firm to be allowed even to bid on a public works project, it must typically first bribe a powerful politician. Karel van Wolferen, *The Enigma of Japanese Power* (Alfred A. Knopf, 1989) p. 117.

34. Ellis S. Krauss, *Under Construction: U.S.-Japan Negotiations to Open Japan's Construction Markets to American Firms, 1985–1988*, case 145 (Georgetown University, Institute for the Study of Diplomacy, Pew Case Studies Center, 1988), p. 17.

35. See Elisabeth Rubinfien, "Trade Tangle: In Construction Talks, U.S. Showed Japanese It Is Often Confused," *Wall Street Journal*, March 31, 1988, pp. 1, 12.

36. Isobel Derouet Coles, "The Public Works Access Dispute: Case Study of a Japan-U.S. Trade Conflict," master's thesis, Oxford University, April 24, 1989, p. 74.

37. Krauss, "Under Construction," pp. 21, 39.

38. Krauss, "Under Construction," p. 31.

39. David E. Sanger, "Corporations Criticized On Trading with Japan," *New York Times*, September 12, 1988, p. D2.

40. In terms of the size of the import sector and the effect on domestic prices, the lumber fee was the largest countervail action the United States has ever taken against a single trading partner under the terms of the GATT. Joseph P. Kalt, "The Political Economy of Protectionism: Tariffs and Retaliation in the Timber Industry," in Robert E. Baldwin, ed., *Trade Policy Issues and Empirical Analysis* (University of Chicago Press, 1988), p. 340.

41. Art Pine, "How President Came to Favor Concessions for U.S. Textile Makers," p. 12.

42. The Canadian lumber dispute was reopened in the fall of 1991, after Canada decided to terminate the 15 percent export tax. Stuart Auerbach, "U.S. Imposes Interim Duties on Some Canadian Lumber," *Washington Post*, October 5, 1991, p. B1.

43. Quotation from Sam Gibbons (D-Florida), chairman of the House Ways and Means trade subcommittee, announcing hearings and a legislative agenda in April 1983, in Shannon Stock Shuman and Charles Owen Verrill, Jr., "Recent Developments in Countervailing Duty Law and Policy," in Robert E. Baldwin, ed., *NBER Conference Report: Recent Issues and Initiatives in U.S. Trade Policy* (Cambridge, Mass.: National Bureau of Economic Research), p. 121.

44. Quoted in Raymond J. Ahearn and Alfred Reifman, "U.S. Trade Policy: Congress Sends a Message," in Robert E. Baldwin and J. David Richardson, eds., *Current U.S. Trade Policy: Analysis, Agenda, and Administration* (Cambridge, Mass.: National Bureau of Economic Research, 1986), p. 123.

45. Quoted in Stephen D. Cohen and Ronald I. Meltzer, *United States International Economic Policy in Action* (Praeger, 1982), p. 75.

46. Elizabeth Wehr, "Administration Dairy, Sugar Plans Draw Fire," *Congressional Quarterly Weekly Report*, May 8, 1982, p. 1071.

47. I. M. Destler, *American Trade Politics: System under Stress* (Washington: International Institute for Economics, 1986), p. 130.

48. Sally Jacobsen, "Tariffs Raised on Imported Cycles: Attempt to Help Harley-Davidson, The Last U.S. Producer," *Washington Post*, April 2, 1983, p. C7.

49. Why the Democratic gain in 1982 was interpreted this way may be hard to understand. The average midterm loss of House seats by the president's party was 41.2 percent from 1902 to 1946. Since then it has dropped to 27.5 percent. One could observe that the twenty-six-seat loss by the Republicans in 1982 was appreciably below the century-long average. When President Reagan made this point, however, he received a less-than-sympathetic reaction from most pundits, who decided that 1982 was a vote of no confidence in the administration. See Erwin C. Hargrove and Michael Nelson, *Presidents, Politics, and Policy* (Johns Hopkins University Press, 1984), p. 224.

50. Quoted in Steven Scholossstein, *Trade War: Greed, Power, and Industrial Policy on Opposite Sides of the Pacific* (Congdon and Weed, 1984), pp. 3–4.

51. *United States-Japan Trade: Semiconductors*, Hearing before the Subcommittee on Trade, Productivity, and Economic Growth of the Joint Economic Committee, 99 Cong. 1 sess. (GPO, 1985).

52. Harold Hongju Koh, "A Legal Perspective," in Robert M. Stern, Philip H. Trezise, and John Whalley, eds., *Perspectives on a U.S. Canadian Free Trade Agreement* (Brookings, 1987), p. 98.

53. Andy Plattner, "Democrats See Political Gold in Trade Issue," *Congressional Quarterly Weekly Report*, September 21, 1985, p. 1856.

Chapter 5

1. From title of Trade Act of 1974, 88 Stat. 1978.

2. Senate Finance Committee, *Summary and Analysis of H.R. 10710—The Trade Reform Act of 1973*, 93 Cong. 2 sess (Government Printing Office, 1974), p. 45.

3. "The President is authorized to retaliate against foreign countries which impose unjustifiable or unreasonable restrictions against U.S. commerce, including the withholding of supplies. The section also provides the President with explicit authority to retaliate against countries which maintain such restrictions against U.S. services as well as U.S. trade in goods." Senate Committee on Finance, *United States International Trade Policy and the Trade Act of 1974*, 94 Cong. 2 sess. (GPO, 1976), pp. 25–26.

4. See, for example, Robert A. Pastor, *Congress and the Politics of U.S. Foreign Economic Policy: 1929–1976* (University of California Press, 1980), chap. 5.

5. Antidumping Act of 1921, sec. 205(b), as amended by Trade Act of 1974, sec. 321[d] (88 Stat. 2046–48).

6. For a detailed analysis of the antidumping procedure, see Richard Boltuck and Robert E. Litan, eds., *Down in the Dumps: Administration of the Unfair Trade Laws* (Brookings, 1991), chaps. 2, 3, 4, 5, and 7.

7. See Robert E. Baldwin, *The Political Economy of U.S. Import Policy* (MIT Press, 1985), p. 76.

8. *Trade Agreements Act of 1979*, H. Rept. 96–317, 96 Cong. 1 sess. (GPO, 1979), p. 54.

9. Pastor, *Congress and the Politics of U.S. Foreign Economic Policy*, p. 174.

10. Ronald A. Cass and Stephen J. Narkin, "Antidumping and Countervailing Duty Law: The United States and the GATT," in Boltuck and Litan, *Down in the Dumps*, pp. 229–32.

11. Small foreign exporters face the greatest difficulty with DOC questionnaires, which often run to fifty pages or more and demand detailed financial data in English. Joseph F. Francois, N. David Palmeter, and Jeffrey C. Anspacher, "Conceptual and Procedural Biases in the Administration of the Countervailing Duty Law," in Boltuck and Litan, *Down in the Dumps*, p. 126. Sometimes Commerce's informational requirements stretch the capabilities of even the most efficient and well-organized foreign firms. For example, in 1989 the major Japanese trading company, Mitsui & Co., was evidently requested to provide detailed information concerning transactions that had occurred as much as fifteen years earlier. N. David Palmeter, "The Antidumping Law: A Legal and Administrative Nontariff Barrier," in Boltuck and Litan, *Down in the Dumps*, p. 70.

12. Trade Agreements Act of 1979, sec. 733(b)(1). Commerce Regulation, sec. 353.51(b).

13. Baldwin and Moore found that the use of BIA is a powerful predictor of the size of DOC's computed dumping margins. Robert E. Baldwin and Michael O. Moore, "Political Aspects

of the Administration of the Trade Remedy Laws," in Boltuck and Litan, *Down in the Dumps*, pp. 276–78.

14. Cass and Narkin, "Antidumping," p. 207.

15. Shannon Stock Shuman and Charles Owen Verrill, Jr., "Recent Developments in Countervailing Duty Law and Policy," in Robert E. Baldwin, ed., *NBER Conference Report: Recent Issues and Initiatives in U.S. Trade Policy* (Cambridge, Mass.: National Bureau of Economic Research, 1984), p. 108.

16. See, for example, *Freeport Minerals Co.* v. *United States*, 776 F.2d 1029 (Fed. Cir. 1985). Eugene L. Stewart, "Existing Remedies and the Trade Deficit: The Promise of Reform Through Judicial Review," *New York University Journal of International Law and Politics*, vol. 18 (Summer 1986), pp. 1182–83.

17. See *Al Tech Specialty Steel Corp.* v. *United States*, 745 F.2d 632 (Fed. Cir. 1984).

18. See, for instance, *Republic Steel Corporation* v. *United States*, 591 F. Supp. 640 (CIT, 1984); *Jeannette Sheet Glass Corporation* v. *United States*, 607 F. Supp. 123 (CIT, 1985); and *American Lamb Company* v. *United States*, 785 F. 2d 994 (CIT, 1986).

19. *Trade Agreements Act of 1979*, H. Rep. 96–317, p. 48; and I. M. Destler, *American Trade Politics: System under Stress* (Washington: Institute for International Economics, 1986), p. 120.

20. Robert Z. Lawrence, *Can America Compete?* (Brookings, 1984), pp. 7, 94.

21. *Administration of the Antidumping Act of 1921*, Hearing before the Subcommittee on Trade of the House Committee on Ways and Means, 95 Cong. 2 sess. (GPO, 1978), p. 8.

22. Richard Dale, *Anti-Dumping Law in a Liberal Trade Order* (St. Martin's, 1980), pp. 61, 160, 200.

23. Walter Adams and Joel B. Dirlam, "Unfair Competition in International Trade," in Walter Adams and others, eds., *Tariffs, Quotas, and Trade: The Politics of Protectionism* (San Francisco: Institute for Contemporary Studies, 1979), pp. 103–04; and Baldwin, *Political Economy*, pp. 138, 140.

24. Barry Eichengreen and Hans van der Ven, "U.S. Antidumping Policies: The Case of Steel," in Robert E. Baldwin and Anne O. Krueger, eds., *The Structure and Evolution of Recent U.S. Trade Policy* (University of Chicago Press for the National Bureau of Economic Research, 1984), pp. 74–77.

25. Baldwin, *Political Economy*, p. 73.

26. Gary N. Horlick and Geoffrey D. Oliver, "Antidumping and Countervailing Duty Law Provisions of the Omnibus Trade and Competitiveness Act of 1988," *Journal of World Trade*, vol. 23 (June 1989), p. 35.

27. Comments by Gary N. Horlick on Murray G. Smith, "Negotiating Trade Laws: Possible Approaches," in Murray G. Smith, *Bridging the Gap: Trade Laws in the Canadian-U.S. Negotiations* (Toronto: C. D. Howe Institute; Washington: National Planning Association, 1987), p. 54.

28. Who, after all, is the predator-monopolist in a market characterized by multiple sellers with small sales volumes? Section 1330(b) of the Omnibus Trade and Competitiveness Act of 1988 amended the cumulation rule by allowing the ITC a de minimis exception. The legislative history of the 1988 act, however, makes clear that Congress intended "the ITC to . . . apply the exception narrowly," so as not to "subvert the purpose and general application of the [cumulation] requirement." Horlick and Oliver, "Antidumping and Countervailing Duty Law Provisions," p. 37.

29. Michael Sandler, "Primer on United States Trade Remedies," *International Lawyer*, vol. 19 (Summer 1985), p. 772.

30. U.S. International Trade Commission, *1984 Annual Report*, p. 5.

31. Trade and Tariff Act of 1984, sec. 612(a)(2)(B) (98 Stat. 3033–34). As a result of the change, the ITC reversed its decision, recommending import restrictions for the shoe industry in

1985. See Vinod K. Aggarwal, Robert O. Keohane, and David B. Yoffie, "The Dynamics of Negotiated Protectionism," *American Political Science Review*, vol. 81 (June 1987), pp. 358–59.

32. For a complete account of the steel provisions, see Stephen L. Lande and Craig Van-Grasstek, *The Trade and Tariff Act of 1984: Trade Policy in the Reagan Administration* (Lexington Books, 1986), pp. 143–49.

33. "On Trade, a Happy Ending," *Washington Post*, October 12, 1984, p. A22.

34. "The Bill That Came to Dinner," *Wall Street Journal*, April 26, 1988, p. 38; and *Congressional Quarterly Almanac, 1985*, p. 253.

35. Quoted in *Congressional Quarterly Almanac, 1985*, p. 253.

36. *Weekly Compilation of Presidential Documents*, vol. 21 (September 20, 1985), p. 1129.

37. Rose Gutfeld, "Trade Deficit for March Narrowed to $9.75 Billion, Lowest Level in Three Years, on a Surge in Exports," *Wall Street Journal*, May 18, 1988, p. 3.

38. *Congressional Record*, daily ed., April 29, 1987, pp. H2755–2757.

39. *Omnibus Trade and Competitiveness Act of 1988*, Conference Report to accompany H.R. 3, H. Rept. 100–576, 100 Cong. 2 sess. (GPO, 1988), p. 576.

40. "Creature Feature," *Wall Street Journal*, April 6, 1988, p. 24.

41. See Claude E. Barfield, "Brother of Gephardt," *Washington Post*, March 9, 1988, p. A25.

42. On this and subsequent points, see the thorough analysis by Gary N. Horlick and Geoffrey D. Oliver, "Antidumping and Countervailing Duty Law Provisions of the Omnibus Trade and Competitiveness Act of 1988," *Journal of World Trade*, vol. 23, no. 3 (1989), pp. 5–49.

43. *Canadian Meat Council v. United States*, 661 F. Supp. 622 (CIT, 1987).

44. The statutory language seemed to imply that the USTR should lean on the third parties if they did not cooperate. "If the appropriate authority of the [foreign] country refuses to undertake antidumping measures in response to a request made therefor by the Trade Representative . . . , the Trade Representative shall promptly consult with the domestic industry on whether action under any other law of the United States is appropriate." House of Representatives, *Omnibus Trade and Competitiveness Act of 1988*, 100 Cong. 2 sess. (GPO, April 20, 1988), p. 88. [Omnibus Trade and Competitiveness Act of 1988, P. L. No. 100–418, 102 Stat. 1188 (1988).]

45. Section 1329. See also S. Rept. No. 71, 100 Cong. 1 sess. (GPO, 1987).

46. Section 1321. In the first serious test of the new rule's impact, domestic makers of forklift trucks seemed intent on forcing Japanese competitors to abandon forklift assembly plants in the United States. Peter Passell, "Trade Law's Tangled Web," *New York Times*, November 8, 1989, p. D2.

47. Section 1320.

48. Section 1323.

49. The requirement that a petitioner be a domestic industry producing in the United States was also removed. The new law gives licensees of an intellectual property owner legal grounds to bar imports through a section 337 proceeding, even if the licensee does not produce domestically. As one former commissioner of the ITC observed, "This could force the ITC to arbitrate among importers jockeying for market share in the United States, with no appreciable impact on production capability or workers' jobs in the United States. Conceivably, this could hurt American companies that are ordered to stop importing a product subject to a section–337 dispute, even though no one is actually producing that product in the United States." Paula Stern, "Level Playing Field or Mine Field?" *Across the Board*, October 1988, p. 10.

50. See Clyde H. Farnsworth, "Trade Bill Has Special Favors for Companies," *New York Times*, April 11, 1988, pp. A1, D10.

51. Representative Charles E. Schumer, Democrat of New York, quoted in John Cranford, "House Passes Comprehensive Trade Measure," *Congressional Quarterly Weekly Report*, May 2, 1987, p. 814.

52. Eduardo Lachica, "Gephardt Plans Tougher Bill on Unfair Trade," *Wall Street Journal*,

September 11, 1991, p. A7. Helen Dewar, "Sanctions Proposed for Japanese Cars: Democrat's Bill Driven by Trade Imbalance," *Washington Post*, December 21, 1991, pp. C1, C6.

Chapter 6

1. Ronald Reagan, *An American Life* (Simon and Schuster, 1990), p. 255.

2. Reagan, *An American Life*, p. 253. This general theme—"the Japanese are not treating us fairly if they believe in free trade," "we have never had free trade with Japan on autos," and so on—crisscrossed the political debate over auto import relief from the start, even though the automakers had petitioned for protection under section 201, not under the unfair trade statutes. *Congressional Record—Senate*, December 12, 1980, pp. 33761, 33765. The remedies considered by Congress to alleviate Detroit's plight in 1980–81—measures like an auto import "equalization tax"—were sometimes framed emphatically as a response to "unfair competition," the effects of which were said to be so severe for domestic production and employment that "unusual measures are necessary to prevent serious and lasting damages to the United States automotive industry." Section 1 of S. 2808, *Congressional Record—Senate*, June 11, 1980, p. 14136.

3. Quoted in Stephen D. Cohen and Ronald I. Meltzer, *United States International Economic Policy in Action* (Praeger, 1982), p. 75.

4. See Dale Tate, "Congress Prepared to Slow Influx of Japanese Autos If Negotiations Founder," *Congressional Quarterly Weekly Report*, March 28, 1981, p. 551.

5. By 1984 the import restrictions were binding tightly. The welfare loss to household vehicle owners was estimated at $14 billion, while the automakers increased their profits nearly $9 billion. Thus the dead-weight loss to society approached $5 billion. Clifford Winston and Associates, *Blind Intersection? Policy and the Automobile Industry* (Brookings, 1987), pp. 65–66.

6. Quoted in Nancy Green, "Senate Urges U.S. Retaliation Against Japan," *Congressional Quarterly Weekly Report*, March 30, 1985, p. 609.

7. "Nakasone Offers Trade Concessions," *Congressional Quarterly Weekly Report*, April 13, 1985, p. 671.

8. See William A. Niskanen, *Reaganomics: An Insider's Account of the Policies and the People* (Oxford University Press, 1988), pp. 139–41. Representative Bob Traxler, Democrat of Michigan, who had introduced the House's mandatory quota measure, dismissed the negotiated voluntary restraint agreement as a "token agreement" that diffused Congress's efforts to pass "meaningful legislation." Judy Sarasohn, "Auto Import Curb Shelved As Japan Agrees on Limits," *Congressional Quarterly Weekly Report*, May 9, 1981, p. 798.

9. I. M. Destler, Haruhiro Fukui, and Hideo Sato, *The Textile Wrangle: Conflict in Japanese-American Relations, 1969–1971* (Cornell University Press, 1979), pp. 69–70.

10. Carl J. Green, "The New Protectionism," *Northwestern Journal of International Law and Business*, vol. 3 (Spring 1981), p. 13.

11. For a comprehensive treatment of this strategic interplay in presidential program-making, see Mark A. Peterson, *Legislating Together: The White House and Capitol Hill from Eisenhower to Reagan* (Harvard University Press, 1990), especially pp. 60–67.

12. Raymond A. Bauer, Ithiel de Sola Pool, and Lewis Anthony Dexter, *American Business and Public Policy: The Politics of Foreign Trade* (New York: Atherton Press, 1963), p. 426.

13. See Theodore C. Sorensen, *Kennedy* (Bantam Books, 1965), p. 461.

14. The Trade Agreements Act of 1979, implementing the Tokyo Round accords, was adopted 395 to 7 in the House and 90 to 4 in the Senate. The U.S.-Canada free trade agreement was adopted 366 to 40 in the House, 83 to 9 in the Senate.

15. For an interesting exposition of this point, see Richard Rose, *The Postmodern President: The White House Meets the World* (Chatham House, 1988), pp. 258–60.

16. Paul Krugman, *The Age of Diminished Expectations: U.S. Economic Policy in the 1990s* (MIT Press, 1990), p. 104.

17. Representative Sam Gibbons, chairman of the House Ways and Means trade subcommittee, quoted in Steven Pressman, "House Panel Completes Work on Trade Bill," *Congressional Quarterly Weekly Report*, May 3, 1986, p. 994.

18. For example, in his memoirs, Richard M. Nixon scarcely mentions trade issues. The historic Trade Act of 1974 is referred to here and there, but chiefly in connection with foreign policy implications (for example, the Jackson-Vanik amendment's stipulations on Soviet emigration). Richard M. Nixon, *The Memoirs of Richard Nixon* (Grosset and Dunlap, 1978). The same is true of Gerald Ford's autobiography. Gerald R. Ford, *A Time to Heal: The Autobiography of Gerald R. Ford* (Harper and Row, 1979). Ditto for Jimmy Carter. Jimmy Carter, *Keeping Faith: Memoirs of a President* (Bantam Books, 1982). Ronald Reagan devoted more space to trade problems, referring to them briefly at five points in his 726-page book. Ronald Reagan, *An American Life* (Simon and Schuster, 1990), pp. 241–42, 253–55, 273–74, 247, 355–56.

19. See Pietro S. Nivola, *The Politics of Energy Conservation* (Brookings, 1986), p. 120.

20. Robert G. Kaiser and J. P. Smith, "Political Dealing Prompts Big Steel's Flip-Flop on Gas Bill," *Washington Post*, September 7, 1978, p. A2.

21. David A. Stockman, *The Triumph of Politics: Why the Reagan Revolution Failed* (Harper and Row, 1986), p. 222.

22. Douglas Martin, "The Great Lumber Dispute: U.S. Interests Cite Canada," *New York Times*, May 8, 1986, p. D6.

23. Senator John Heinz (R-Pennsylvania), quoted in Bernard Weinraub, "White House Maps Bills to Stem Tide of Protectionism," *New York Times*, September 12, 1985, p. A1.

24. "Text of President Reagan's Remarks on Trade," September 23, 1985, *Congressional Quarterly Weekly Report*, September 28, 1985, p. 1948.

25. This discussion draws substantially on Jan Tumlir, *Protectionism: Trade Policy in Democratic Societies* (Washington: American Enterprise Institute for Public Policy Research, 1985), pp. 39–43. Approximately half of all antidumping and antisubsidy cases in the 1980s led to negotiated export restraints rather than duties. J. Michael Finger and Tracy Murray, *Policing Unfair Imports: The U.S. Example*, Working Paper (Washington: World Bank, April 11, 1989), p. 3.

26. Crandall estimated that the voluntary restraint agreement on Japanese autos "benefitted Japanese producers and their dealers by at least $2 billion per year in price enhancement." Robert W. Crandall, "Import Quotas and the Automobile Industry: The Costs of Protectionism," *Brookings Review*, vol. 2 (Summer 1984), p. 13.

27. Destler, Fukui, and Sato, *Textile Wrangle*, pp. 69–70.

28. See Roger B. Porter, *Presidential Decision Making: The Economic Policy Board* (Cambridge University Press, 1980), pp. 163–65.

29. See Charles O. Jones, *The Trusteeship Presidency: Jimmy Carter and the United States Congress* (Louisiana State University Press, 1988), p. 41. The footwear issue had obviously mattered to the AFL-CIO. The previous year, President Ford had come under considerable pressure from George Meany to impose shoe import quotas. Edwin L. Dale, Jr., "Ford Bars Curbs on Shoe Imports; Fears Price Rise," *New York Times*, April 17, 1976, p. 29.

30. Robin Toner, "Dukakis Takes New Trade Message to North and Gephardt Cries Foul," *New York Times*, March 23, 1988, p. A21.

31. It is often assumed that presidential campaign vows have little staying power. One of the few studies of this question, however, concluded that "When presidential candidates make reasonably specific promises . . . , take those promises seriously!" Jeff Fishel, *Presidents and Promises:*

From Campaign Pledge to Presidential Performance (Congressional Quarterly Press, 1985), p. 18.

32. See Elizabeth Wehr, "Japan, India, Brazil Cited for Import Barriers," *Congressional Quarterly Weekly Report*, May 27, 1989, p. 1242. Reportedly, the OMB and the CEA argued that the president should simply ignore Congress and take no action under Super 301. Clyde H. Farnsworth, "U.S. Citing of Japan Seen on Supercomputers," *New York Times*, May 19, 1989, p. D4. There is some question whether the display of bureaucratic infighting was partly contrived. According to one account, "The Cabinet fight over citing Japan by name . . . was given wide publicity through artful news leaks leading to splashy stories in the *New York Times* and the *Los Angeles Times*. Fearing that Japan would get off scot-free, there was an audible sigh of relief on Capitol Hill when Japan's name appeared." Bruce Stokes, "Off and Running," *National Journal*, June 17, 1989, p. 1563.

33. John Odell and Anne Dibble, *Brazilian Informatics and the United States: Defending Infant Industry versus Opening Foreign Markets*, case 128 (Georgetown University, Institute for the Study of Diplomacy, Pew Case Studies Center, 1988), p. 15. For the most part, however, it is hard to believe that firms benefiting from the USTR's initiatives were unhappy. As one business executive observed about self-initiated actions in a different context, "Government-initiated cases are every corporation's dream. If we file them against a country and lose, we can never do business there again. So it's great to have government carry the ball." "At a Glance: Trade," *National Journal*, September 14, 1985, p. 2103.

34. Clyde V. Prestowitz, Jr., *Trading Places: How We Are Giving Our Future to Japan and How to Reclaim It* (Basic Books, 1988), p. 512; and Michael B. Smith, "U.S.-Japan Economic Relations in the 1990s: A Crossroads?" in William E. Brock and Robert D. Hormats, eds., *The Global Economy: America's Role in the Decade Ahead* (W. W. Norton, 1990), p. 78. (Emphasis in the original.)

35. See Bruce L. R. Smith, "Career Patterns in the Trade Agencies of the U.S. and Other Countries," a report submitted to the Office of Management, Office of the U.S. Trade Representative (Washington, September 30, 1985), p. 10.

36. In the early 1980s, salaries of comparable posts in the international trade bureaucracy of the EC, for example, were reportedly twice as high as in the U.S. government for directors, first secretaries, and mid-level staff. Smith, "Career Patterns in the Trade Agencies," p. 9a.

37. "Trading Places," *Washington Post*, December 14, 1990, p. A25. The numbers in the *Post* article were based on a study by the Center for Public Integrity, Washington.

38. Pat Choate, *Agents of Influence* (Alfred A. Knopf, 1990), app. A.

39. "Trading Places," *Washington Post*, December 14, 1990, p. A25.

40. Robert E. Baldwin and Michael O. Moore, "Political Aspects of the Administration of the Trade Remedy Laws," in Richard Boltuck and Robert E. Litan, eds., *Down in the Dumps: Administration of the Unfair Trade Laws* (Brookings, 1991), pp. 253–80. See, in particular, the authors' analysis of price-averaging techniques and the treatment of indirect selling expenses in the antidumping calculus. See also Gary N. Horlick, "The United States Antidumping System," in John H. Jackson and Edwin A. Vermulst, eds., *Antidumping Law and Practice: A Comparative Study* (University of Michigan Press, 1989), pp. 99–166, especially pp. 124–25, 145–46, 165.

41. See *Nomination of Kenneth W. Gideon, Bryce L. Harlow, Gerald L. Olson, and John Michael Farren*, Hearing before the Senate Finance Committee, 101 Cong. 1 sess. (GPO, 1990), pp. 23–24.

42. The famous phrase is from the Supreme Court's dictum in *United States* v. *Curtiss Export Corporation*, 299 U.S. 304, 319 (1936).

43. See Thomas C. Schelling, *The Strategy of Conflict* (Oxford University Press, 1960), chap. 8.

44. "Text of President Reagan's Remarks on Trade," *Congressional Quarterly Weekly Report*, September 28, 1985, p. 1949.

45. See Clyde H. Farnsworth, "Senate Democrats Complain on Trade," *New York Times*, March 11, 1986, p. D6.

46. See Bruce Stokes, "The Free-Trade Team," *National Journal*, June 9, 1990, p. 1433. SII was originally proposed by the Treasury Department as a necessary complement to naming Japan under Super 301. Fred Barnes, "Patriots and Traders," *New Republic*, September 4, 1989, p. 10. See also, "America-Japan Trade: Dialogue of the Deaf," *Economist*, June 10, 1989, pp. 64–65.

47. Then, pricing their exports at marginal cost, these firms can generate sufficient volume to drive down average unit costs below those of overseas competitors. Whether this leads ineluctably to a monopolistic pricing regime in the export market is another matter. As the discussion of dumping in chap. 2 points out, such an outcome is unusual.

48. The sky-high value of land in Japan raised costs of establishment, sometimes making the sale of assets or stakes in Japanese joint ventures irresistible. Companies like Chrysler, General Motors, CBS, Honeywell, and Avon were pulling back. David E. Sanger, "Even as U.S. Fights for Entry, Some Companies Quit Japan," *New York Times*, March 22, 1990, pp. A1, D5.

49. Edward J. Lincoln, *Japan's Unequal Trade* (Brookings, 1990), p. 86.

50. Ellis S. Krauss and Isobel Coles, "Built-in Impediments: The Political Economy of the U.S. Japan Construction Dispute," in Kozo Yamamura, ed., *Japan's Economic Structure: Should It Change?* (University of Washington Society for Japanese Studies, 1990), p. 341.

51. See, for instance, Robert Z. Lawrence, "Efficient or Exclusionist? The Import Behavior of Japanese Corporate Groups," *Brookings Papers on Economic Activity, 1:1991*, pp. 311–30.

52. In April 1990, a survey by the *Nihon Keizai Shimbun* found four out of five Japanese responding favorably to U.S. requests that structural trade barriers be removed. See Roger A. Brooks, "Japan and America Must Not Flinch," *International Herald Tribune*, May 10, 1990.

53. See Office of the United States Trade Representative, *Interim Report and Assessment of the U.S.-Japan Working Group on the Structural Impediments Initiative*, (Washington, April 5, 1990), pp. 1–32.

54. Karen Lowry Miller, "Bringing Land Back to Earth," *Business Week*, November 26, 1990, p. 72; and Paul Blustein, "Taking Steps to Rein in the High Cost of Land in Japan: Government Targets Prices," *Washington Post*, October 21, 1990, pp. H1, H6.

55. MITI projected more than 1,300 approved applications in 1990, up from 700 in 1988 and 400 in 1982. As of November 1990, one particularly aggressive foreign chain, Toys 'R Us, had announced plans to open more than a hundred stores in Japan. David E. Sanger, "Japanese Give In Grudgingly on a New Way of Shopping," *New York Times*, November 12, 1990, p. D4. See also Christopher J. Chipello, "Toys 'R Us Inc. Plans for Japan Trigger a Tizzy," *Wall Street Journal*, September 10, 1990, p. A7C.

56. Anticartel penalties imposed by the Fair Trade Commission jumped from 84 companies (totaling 419 million yen in fines) in 1988 to 175 companies (totaling 12,560 million yen) in 1990. The FTC's investigative staff also increased from 129 to 154 employees. Robert Thomson, "Japan's Cartel Busters Get Tough," *Financial Times*, April 3, 1991, sec. 1, p. 6.

57. The late Senator John Heinz of Pennsylvania, for instance, pursued this line of questioning when Carla Hills appeared before the Senate Finance Committee on February 7, 1990. *Oversight of 1988 Trade Act—1990*, Hearing before the Senate Committee on Finance, 101 Cong. 2 sess. (GPO, 1990), pp. 12–13. On how efficiency improvements in the Japanese economy would enhance its competitiveness, see Rachel McCulloch, "United States-Japan Economic Relations," in Robert E. Baldwin, ed., *Trade Policy Issue and Empirical Analysis* (University of Chicago Press, 1988), pp. 318–21. See also Anne O. Krueger, "Free Trade Is the Best Policy," in Robert Z. Lawrence and Charles L. Schultze, eds., *An American Trade Strategy: Options for the 1990s* (Brookings, 1990), pp. 86–87.

58. *Economic Report of the President, February 1990*, p. 249.

59. *United States-Japan Structural Impediments Initiative (SII)*, Hearing before the Subcommittee on International Trade of the Senate Finance Committee, 101 Cong. 2 Sess. (GPO, 1990), p. 23.

60. *United States-Japan Structural Impediments Initiative*, pp. 23, 28–29.

61. Stuart Auerbach, "Lawmakers Criticize Trade Pact with Japan," *Washington Post*, April 20, 1990, p. A8; and Clyde H. Farnsworth, "Japan Trade Pact Brings Skepticism in Congress," *New York Times*, April 20, 1990, p. D2.

62. See "Trade Worries Grow as Japan, U.S. Talk," *Wall Street Journal*, November 20, 1989, p. A1. In April 1990 legislation introduced in the Senate Finance trade subcommittee would have placed under Super 301 deadlines a number of the complex issues addressed by the structural impediments initiative. Six months earlier, the subcommittee chairman had called SII "the most important trade negotiations that the U.S. has ever entered into." Quoted in Clyde H. Farnsworth, "'Revisionist' Influence Seen in Japan Talks," *New York Times*, November 6, 1989, p. D2.

63. Quoted in *Japan Economic Institute*, Report No. 41A (Washington, October 26, 1990), p. 6.

64. C. Fred Bergsten, "Taming Japan's Trade Surplus," *New York Times*, November 28, 1991, p. 19.

65. Democratic Senator Carl Levin of Michigan reintroduced a measure, called the Fair Trade and Export Expansion Act, requiring action against countries that accounted for 15 percent or more of the total U.S. trade deficit. Representatives Gephardt and Sander Levin (Democrat of Michigan) moved to revive a version of Super 301 in the House the following September. Eduardo Lachica, "Gephardt Plans Tougher Bill on Unfair Trade," *Wall Street Journal*, September 11, 1991, p. A7.

66. Clyde H. Farnsworth, "U.S. Is Asked to Review Japan Trade," *New York Times*, March 25, 1991, pp. D1, D2.

67. David E. Sanger, "Japan to U.S.: Tighten Up. U.S. to Japan: Loosen Up," *New York Times* March 27, 1990, p. D10.

68. In the eventual budget agreement, a five-cent gas tax increase was reluctantly adopted.

Chapter 7

1. Critics of the Reagan years emphasize that family incomes stagnated. Yet even with rising divorce rates and the growth of single-parent households, median family income rose by 8.1 percent between 1980 and 1989, compared with 6.1 percent between 1970 and 1979 (in 1989 dollars). *Economic Report of the President, February 1991*, p. 320. On the distribution of employment by skill levels, see *Employment-Unemployment*, Hearings before the Joint Economic Committee, 100 Cong. 1 sess. (Government Printing Office, 1989), pp. 117, 186, 198–99, and 231. Part of the reason for the bulge in higher-skilled jobs relative to employment in lower-skilled categories, however, was that "many workers with very low skills . . . either left the labor force completely or spent long periods without jobs." Chinhui Juhn, Kevin M. Murphy, and Robert H. Topel, "Why Has the Natural Rate of Unemployment Increased over Time?" *Brookings Papers on Economic Activity, 2:1991*, p. 125. (Hereafter *BPEA*.)

2. F. W. Taussig, *The Tariff History of the United States* (G. P. Putnam's Sons, 1923), p. 451.

3. On export protectionism, see Jagdish Bhagwati, *Protectionism* (MIT Press, 1988), pp. 124–25.

4. Gary Clyde Hufbauer, "Introduction: Two Challenges," in *The Free Trade Debate: Report*

of the Twentieth Century Fund Task Force on the Future of American Trade Policy (Priority Press, 1989), p. 42.

5. Updated estimate from Gary Clyde Hufbauer, Diane T. Berliner, and Kimberly Ann Elliott, *Trade Protection in the United States: 31 Case Studies* (Washington: Institute for International Economics, 1986), tables 1.1–1.4.

6. See Robert Z. Lawrence, "The International Dimension," in Robert E. Litan, Robert Z. Lawrence, and Charles L. Schultze, eds., *American Living Standards: Threats and Challenges* (Brookings, 1988), p. 53.

7. See Warwick J. McKibbin and Jeffrey D. Sachs, *Global Linkages: Macroeconomic Interdependence and Cooperation in the World Economy* (Brookings, 1991), pp. 2–6.

8. Quoted in Jagdish N. Bhagwati and Douglas A. Irwin, "The Return of the Reciprocitarians—US Trade Policy Today," *World Economy*, vol. 10 (June 1987), p. 113.

9. See Bruce Stokes, "Off and Running," *National Journal*, June 17, 1989, p. 1565.

10. *ASG Industries, Inc.* v. *United States* (1979), discussed in Peter D. Ehrenhaft, "The 'Judicialization' of Trade Law," *Notre Dame Lawyer*, vol. 56 (April 1981), p. 600; and *British Steel Corp.* v. *United States* (1985), discussed in Michael Sandler, "Primer on United States Trade Remedies," *International Lawyer*, vol. 19 (Summer 1985), p. 770.

11. See William A. Niskanen, "Should the New Trade Bill Become Law?" *Business Week*, May 23, 1988, p. 57.

12. See Andreas F. Lowenfeld, "Fair or Unfair Trade: Does it Matter?" *Cornell International Law Journal*, vol. 13 (Summer 1980), p. 219; and more generally, Bruce R. Scott, "National Strategies: Key to International Competition," in Bruce R. Scott and George C. Lodge, *U.S. Competitiveness in the World Economy* (Harvard Business School Press, 1985), pp. 71–143.

13. Eduardo Lachica, "Some Big U.S. Companies Favor Loosening Anti-Dumping Laws," *Wall Street Journal*, August 31, 1990, p. A2.

14. See Christopher Norall, "New Trends in Anti-dumping Practice in Brussels," *World Economy*, vol. 9 (March 1986), pp. 97–111. Foreign antidumping administration in Canada was more comparable to the U.S. system, though evidently more inclined to find injury. Between 1980 and 1985, for example, the Canadian Import Tribunal affirmed injury in twenty-seven out of thirty-one cases in which antidumping actions had been brought against U.S. products. Murray G. Smith, "Negotiating Trade Laws: Possible Approaches," Murray G. Smith with C. Michael Aho and Gary N. Horlick, *Bridging the Gap: Trade Laws in the Canadian U.S. Negotiations* (Washington: National Planning Association, January 1987), pp. 7–9.

15. Eduardo Lachica, "U.S. Proposes Stronger Rules On Dumping," *Wall Street Journal*, November 22, 1989, p. A7.

16. James Bovard, *The Fair Trade Fraud* (St. Martin's Press, 1991), pp. 321–24; and James Powell, "Why Trade Retaliation Closes Markets and Impoverishes People," *Policy Analysis*, no. 143 (Cato Institute, November 30, 1990), pp. 54–60.

17. See Gregory L. Miles and Kathleen Deveny, "The Quotas That Saved Steel Are Backfiring on Buyers," *Business Week*, September 26, 1988, p. 49.

18. See Paul Magnusson, "Did Washington Lose Sight of the Big Picture?" *Business Week*, December 2, 1991, p. 38–39.

19. Consider, for instance, the European Community's new weapon: "On the Strengthening of the Common Commercial Policy with Regard in Particular to Protection against Illicit Commercial Practices," *Council Regulation* (EEC), no. 2641/84 (September 17, 1984).

20. See Robert Z. Lawrence, comment on paper by Paul R. Krugman, *BPEA, 1:1984*, p. 128.

21. Bill Emmott, *The Sun Also Sets: Why Japan Will Not Be Number One* (Simon and Schuster, 1989), pp. 236–38.

22. Low real interest rates and a booming stock market through most of the 1980s translated

into a huge increase in Japanese business investment. For example, between 1987 and 1990, investment rose by 51 percent compared with only 15 percent in the United States. But capital costs began converging sharply after 1988. By 1991 the gap between Japan and the United States had closed. Christopher Farrell, "The U.S. Has a New Weapon: Low-Cost Capital," *Business Week*, July 29, 1991, pp. 72–73.

23. See, more generally, Jonathan Rauch, "Letter from Japan: Gloom among the Riches," *National Journal*, June 23, 1990, p. 1541.

24. See Theodore H. Moran, "The Globalization of America's Defense Industries: Managing the Threat of Foreign Dependence," *International Security*, vol. 15 (Summer 1990), p. 85.

25. Adam Smith, *An Inquiry Into the Nature and Causes of the Wealth of Nations*, R. H. Cambell and A. S. Skinner, eds. (Oxford: Clarendon Press, 1976), pp. 464–65.

26. In trade history, free traders in one era are often the protectionists of another. Under the Fordney-McCumber Tariff Act, for instance, the United States declared its tariff levels to be autonomous, meaning nonnegotiable. At the same time, the act expected most-favored-nation (MFN) treatment of U.S. exports, so as to benefit from the tariff conventions of other nations. Trade retaliations were authorized for refusal to grant such MFN status. "The elements of the ideal predatory trade policy of a large power," writes one critic, "have rarely been stated in policy with such brazen clarity." John A. C. Conybeare, *Trade Wars: The Theory and Practice of International Commercial Rivalry* (Columbia University Press, 1987), pp. 239–40.

27. F. A. McKenzie, *The American Invaders* (Arno Press, 1976), p. 1 (originally published in 1902).

28. J.-J. Servan-Schreiber, *The American Challenge* (Atheneum, 1968), p. 189.

29. For a closely argued exposition of the case for strategically managed trade, see Laura D'Andrea Tyson, "Managed Trade: Making the Best of Second Best," in Robert Z. Lawrence and Charles L. Schultze, eds., *An American Trade Strategy for the 1990s* (Brookings, 1990), pp. 142–94, especially p. 161. For a much broader proposal to manage trade, see Rudiger W. Dornbusch, "Policy Options for Freer Trade: The Case for Bilateralism," in *An American Trade Strategy*, pp. 106–41.

30. See, for instance, Cynthia A. Beltz, *High-Tech Maneuvers: Industrial Policy Lessons of HDTV* (Washington: AEI Press, 1991), pp. 28–29, 100.

31. Marcus Noland, "The Impact of Industrial Policy on Japan's Trade Specialization," Department of Economics, University of Southern California, and Institute for International Economics, Washington, November 1991.

32. The phrase is from Clyde V. Prestowitz, Jr., *Trading Places: How We Are Giving Our Future to Japan and How to Reclaim It* (Basic Books, 1988), p. 62.

33. See Edward J. Lincoln, *Japan's Unequal Trade* (Brookings, 1990), pp. 158–59.

34. It has been estimated that gross U.S. liability expenditures alone reached $117 billion in 1987. See Peter W. Huber and Robert E. Litan, "Overview," in Peter W. Huber and Robert E. Litan, eds., *The Liability Maze: The Impact of Liability Law on Safety and Innovation* (Brookings, 1991), p. 2.

35. The Congressional Budget Office has estimated the adjusted 1992 federal deficit at $307 billion. Congressional Budget Office, *An Analysis of the President's Budgetary Proposals for Fiscal Year 1993* (Washington, March 1992), p. 141.

36. In general, there is a correlation between fiscal deficits and current account deficits: countries with the former tend to have the latter. McKibbin and Sachs, *Global Linkages*, table 1-2, p. 4. Each $100 billion reduction in U.S. government spending could lead, over three years, to a reduction of $35 billion in the current account deficit. Ralph C. Bryant, John F. Helliwell, and Peter Hooper, "Domestic and Cross-Border Consequences of U.S. Macroeconomic Policies," in Ralph C. Bryant and others, eds., *Macroeconomic Policies in an Interdependent World* (Washington: International Monetary Fund, 1989), p. 66. Some estimates of the effects of budget balancing

on external deficits run considerably higher. See, for instance, John F. Helliwell, "Fiscal Policy and the External Deficit: Siblings, but not Twins," Working Paper no. 3313 (Cambridge, Mass.: National Bureau of Economic Research, April 1990) p. 20.

37. In the 1986 election, for instance, 60.9 percent of people 65 and older voted, while turn-out among people between 18 and 24 was merely 21.9 percent and among people aged 25 to 44, 41.4 percent. Steven Mufson, "Older Voters Drive Budget," *Washington Post*, October 15, 1990, pp. A1, A6.

38. The United States ran overall trade deficits in eighteen of the years between 1970 and 1990. In eleven of those years, trade would have been either in surplus or virtually balanced but for the rate of oil importation. In 1990, subtracting oil imports, the U.S. merchandise trade deficit would have been $39.5 billion instead of $101.7 billion. Department of Treasury, *Statistical Abstract of the United States* (Washington, 1980, 1991), sec. 30, 31 and sec. 28, 29, respectively.

39. At 1989 rates of consumption, a 50-cent tax on petroleum transport fuels as a whole would have raised an estimated $80 billion, according to the Atlantic Council of the United States, *Energy Imperatives for the 1990s* (Washington: Atlantic Council, March 1990), p. 15. On comparative gasoline prices and tax rates, see Pietro S. Nivola, "Déjà Vu All Over Again: Revisiting the Politics of Gasoline Taxation," *Brookings Review*, vol. 9 (Winter 1990/91), pp. 29–35.

40. In Japan, capital gains from the sale of securities have not been taxed, except for gains of continuous traders. Other types of gains are taxable, but at lower long-term rates than in the United States. See M. Homma, T. Maeda, and K. Hashimoto, "Japan," in Joseph A. Pechman, ed., *Comparative Tax Systems: Europe, Canada, and Japan* (Arlington, Va.: Tax Analysts, 1987), pp. 406, 408. The Japanese tax system underwent major changes in 1988. Economists are now more divided on how much the difference between rates of saving in the United States and Japan are *directly* attributable to differing tax incentives. Even skeptics concede, however, that the subsidization of home mortgages and the tax deductibility of interest in the United States have helped create "a nation of spenders." See B. Douglas Bernheim, *The Vanishing Nest Egg: Reflections on Saving in America* (Priority Press Publications, 1991), pp. 86–87, 91.

41. Joseph Pechman, *Federal Tax Policy*, 5th ed. (Brookings, 1987), p. 95. Tax deductibility for interest on second homes encourages households in high tax brackets to build more and larger homes than they otherwise might. The effect, again, is to skew resources toward consumption.

42. As one analyst has written recently, "Banks cannot underwrite securities or own stocks. A simple loan agreement that is two pages in Japan requires hundreds of pages in the United States. Investors cannot talk to each other about companies they own without disclosing their discussions to federal regulators. Stockholders cannot vote the shares they own if they accumulate a significant percentage of certain companies' stock. Institutions that should be long-term investors are prohibited from owning a meaningful stake in any individual company or trying to influence its behavior." Michael T. Jacobs, *Short-Term America: The Causes and Cures of Our Business Myopia* (Harvard Business School Press, 1991), p. 214. See also pp. 231–41.

43. Henry J. Aaron, *Serious and Unstable Condition: Financing America's Health Care* (Brookings, 1991), pp. 1, 39.

44. Timothy Noah, "Lawsuits by Women, Disabled Are Likely to Be the Main Result of Compromise Civil Rights Bill," *Wall Street Journal*, October 28, 1991, p. A18; and Carolyn Weaver, "Disabilities Act Cripples through Ambiguity," *Wall Street Journal*, January 31, 1991, p. A16.

45. For a survey of recent developments, see Denis P. Doyle, Bruce S. Cooper, and Roberta Trachtman, *Taking Charge: State Action on School Reform in the 1980s* (Hudson Institute, 1991).

46. On the nineteenth century, see Nathan Rosenberg, ed., *The American System of Manufactures* (Edinburgh: University Press, 1969), pp. 28, 203–04.

47. The seminal study stressing the dominance of family background factors (including "structural integrity of the home") remains James S. Coleman and others, *Equality of Educational*

Opportunity (U.S. Department of Health, Education and Welfare, 1966), pp. 290–325, especially pp. 324–25.

48. On the most promising proposal for institutional reorganization, see John E. Chubb and Terry M. Moe, *Politics, Markets and America's Schools* (Brookings, 1990), chap. 6. On the parenting deficit, see William Mattox, Jr., "The Parent Trap: So Many Bills, So Little Time," *Policy Review*, The Heritage Foundation, no. 55 (Winter 1991), pp. 6–13; and Elaine Ciulla Kamarck and William A. Galston, *Putting Children First: A Progressive Family Policy for the 1990s* (Washington: Progressive Policy Institute, September 27, 1990), pp. 2–3. Currently, of every one hundred children born in the United States, twenty-five will be out of wedlock, and only forty-one will reach the age of eighteen living continuously with both parents. Japanese divorce rates are about one-fourth of those in the United States. Ninety-five percent of Japanese children live in married, two-parent households. Only 1 percent of Japanese births are illegitimate. Under traditional Japanese child-rearing, children are rarely left alone, and they spend five times as many hours per week studying as American children in the equivalent of seventh through twelfth grades. See Karl Zinsmeister, "Raising Hiroko: The Child-Centered Culture of Japan," *American Enterprise*, vol. 1 (March/April 1990), pp. 53–54; and Susan Chira, "The Big Test: How to Translate the Talk About School Reform into Action," *New York Times*, March 24, 1991, p. E1.

49. Many cases of escape-clause relief have been temporary or sporadic, although some major industries have acquired institutionalized protection. See Vinod K. Aggarwal, Robert O. Keohane, and David B. Yoffie, "The Dynamics of Negotiated Protection," *American Political Science Review*, vol. 81 (June 1987), p. 354.

50. This is not to say that section 201 has remained unchanged since its inception. See Richard L. O'Meara, "United States Trade Laws: Reexamining the Escape Clause," *Virginia Journal of International Law*, vol. 26 (Fall 1985), especially p. 270.

51. For a proposal along these lines, see Robert Z. Lawrence and Robert E. Litan, *Saving Free Trade: A Pragmatic Approach* (Brookings, 1986), pp. 105–12.

52. Murray G. Smith, "Negotiating Trade Laws: Possible Approaches," Murray G. Smith with C. Michael Aho and Gary N. Horlick, *Bridging the Gap: Trade Laws in the Canadian-U.S. Negotiations* (Washington: Canadian-American Committee, January 1987), p. 17. Logically, the principle of equal national treatment implies that antidumping regulation be limited to clear cases of predatory price discrimination (as under current U.S. antitrust doctrine). See Sylvia Ostry, *Governments and Corporations in a Shrinking World* (New York: Council on Foreign Relations, 1990), p. 91.

53. Richard Boltuck and Robert E. Litan, "America's 'Unfair' Trade Laws," in Richard Boltuck and Robert E. Litan, eds., *Down in the Dumps: Administration of the Unfair Trade Laws* (Brookings, 1991), p. 14. Commerce has only compared weighted averages of normal values with weighted averages of U.S. sales in a small group of cases involving perishable products and large numbers of transactions. Gary N. Horlick, "The United States Antidumping System," in John H. Jackson and Edwin A. Vermulst, eds., *Antidumping Law and Practice in the United States and the European Communities: A Comparative Analysis* (University of Michigan Press, 1989), p. 147.

54. See Tyson, "Managed Trade," pp. 173–76, and Lawrence and Schultze, "Evaluating the Options," in *An American Trade Strategy: Options for the 1990s*, pp. 34, 39.

55. P.L. 87–794, approved October 11, 1962, 19 U.S.C. sec. 1351.

56. This consideration still seems inadequately understood in Japan. The more open the Japanese market and the greater the stake of U.S. companies there, the less stomach these companies are likely to have for disruptive trade confrontations. See Robert Z. Lawrence, "The Reluctant Giant," *Brookings Review*, vol. 9 (Summer 1991), p. 39.

57. Several of the most successful bilateral settlements with Japan followed decisions by the United States to take the disputes to the GATT. Conflicts involving Japanese quotas on a dozen categories of agricultural products, leather goods, and, in 1988, beef and citrus were resolved with the aid of these proceedings. In all these cases, writes Edward Lincoln, "adverse decisions by GATT panels or even initiation of GATT procedures was enough to obtain action by Japan." The reason for this, Lincoln observes, is that the "GATT is a formal international structure for which the Japanese have great respect. To lose a decision represents an international humiliation for the Japanese, especially given the importance of international economic and trade issues in Japan." Lincoln, *Japan's Unequal Trade*, p. 160. For an excellent analysis of how the new section 301 can fit within the GATT's parameters, see Robert E. Hudec, "Thinking about the New Section 301: Beyond Good and Evil," in Jagdish Bhagwati and Hugh T. Patrick, eds., *Aggressive Unilateralism: America's 301 Trade Policy and the World Trading System* (University of Michigan Press, 1990), pp. 113–59.

58. The polls are quite clear on this point. A Council on Competitiveness survey taken in September 1991 posed the question this way: "In your opinion, which *one* of the following reasons best explains why America may have problems competing economically in the world and dealing with foreign economic competition?" Responses to the menu of answers broke down as follows: A. "The world has changed to become a global marketplace, and the U.S. hasn't done enough to adjust to the new challenges of economic competition." (41 percent); B. "The American work ethic and commitment to quality have declined, and other countries are trying harder." (31 percent); C. "Countries like Japan are out to be number one economically and they ignore the principles of free trade in order to get ahead." (19 percent); D. "All" of the above. (5 percent); and E. "Not sure." (3 percent). Peter D. Hart, Research Associates, Inc., *American Viewpoint* (Bossier City, La., September 1991), p. 9. Immediately following President Bush's trade mission to Tokyo in January 1992, a *USA Today* survey of public reaction asked, "Which comes closest to the way you feel?" Fifty-two percent subscribed to the statement "U.S. blames Japan for its own economic problems." Thirty-seven percent affirmed that "Japanese companies compete unfairly." Eleven percent answered "Don't know." Jessica Lee and James R. Healey, "Trade: 'Much More' to Do," *USA Today*, January 10–12, 1992, p. 1A.

59. Dan Balz, "Kerrey Wants U.S. to Get Tough on Trade with Japan," *Washington Post*, December 12, 1991, p. A16.

60. Despite the hype about how Japanese trade concessions, extracted during a presidential trip to Japan in 1992, would create "jobs," only 28 percent of the public seemed to agree. Jessica Lee and James R. Healey, "Trade: 'Much More' to Do," *USA Today*, January 10–12, 1992, p. 1A. By contrast, public attitudes toward extensive open-trade agreements, such as the proposed North American Free Trade Agreement, may be quite different. In the long term, NAFTA represents an impressive job-creating venture—a prospect the public may recognize.

61. Julie Johnson, "Reagan Is Optimistic on Trade Bill," *New York Times*, March 12, 1988, p. A37.

62. *Economic Report of the President, January 1989*, pp. 169–71, 182–83.

63. Senator John C. Danforth (R-Missouri) quoted in Jeffry E. Garten, "America's Retreat from Protectionism," *New York Times*, June 16, 1985, p. F3.

64. For a more general treatment of this point, see R. Douglas Arnold, *The Logic of Congressional Action* (Yale University Press, 1990), pp. 274–76.

65. See, for instance, section 1322, *Omnibus Trade and Competitiveness Act of 1988*, H. Rept. 100–576, 100 Cong. 2 sess. (GPO 1988), p. 95.

66. Fear of seeming "protectionist" was, of course, hardly the only reason for the lopsided affirmative vote. Senator Lloyd Bentsen, chairman of the Finance Committee, summed up congressional sentiment: "The minor things [problems in the FTA] were just overwhelmed by

what this agreement will do to strengthen the economies of both countries." Quoted in Clyde H. Farnsworth, "Protectionism Takes a Break: How Congress Came to Love the Canada Free-Trade Bill," *New York Times*, June 5, 1988, p. E4.

67. On the politics of GATT and NAFTA fast-track approval, see Bill Frenzel, "A Close Call for Free Trade," *Brookings Review*, vol. 9 (Fall 1991), pp. 44–47.

68. Representative Byron L. Dorgan (D-North Dakota), quoted in Keith Bradsher, "Senate and House Panels Back Free-Trade Talks with Mexico," *New York Times*, May 15, 1991, p. A1.

Index